CW00730723

Praise for
The Wholeness Work Esse

"…when I encounter fresh and enlightening practices, such as those Connirae Andreas reveals in her Wholeness Work, I feel like I've struck gold!"

~Tara Brach PhD, from foreword to
The Wholeness Work Essential Guide

"I've long admired Connirae Andreas's work. In this new book, she takes us into the most profound territory yet. We learn to access states of being that mystics extol in poetry. We discover that the gateways to that awareness are our difficulties. When we dissolve our shame and our longing for what's missing in our lives, peace, and open heartedness naturally arise. Her method, Wholeness Work, is straightforward and direct. It works!"

~Jack Canfield, co-author of the *Chicken Soup for the Soul* series and *The Success Principles*

"As I read this book, I began to feel a big "joy." I have practiced eight forms of psychotherapy, 10 different forms of Eastern meditation, and have spent seven years in monasteries and seminaries.

Core Transformation and the Wholeness Work being developed by Connirae Andreas are the most effective self-actualization tools I have seen in my 60 years of personal and professional practice. I believe they will compare, when seriously researched, as two to three times as effective (bringing, persons to moderate to high, self-actualized psychological states), as all of the popular mindfulness and meditation formats in current use."

~Frank Bourke PhD, Clinical Psychologist,
Research Scientist and Cornell Lecturer

"Dr. Andreas provides here practical, step-by-step formulas that anyone can apply for reducing suffering at its root. The techniques she lays out move us closer to the timeless spiritual ambition of dissolving the ego and coming back in contact with the preciousness of Life."

~Dr. Yoni K. Ashar, Assistant Professor, University of Colorado School of Medicine, Director of the Pain and Emotion Research Laboratory

"As the research and writings of Dr. Jung have shown us, the deep aim and problem of the maturing psyche today is to recover wholeness. So when pathways emerge that support this journey of the soul then my heart leaps with joy. When we bring our human presence and touch to those spaces in us and the world that are in a way held captive, we heal and we grow. Thank you, Connirae, for your contribution. I am so proud to walk the path with you."

~Judith Delozier, international trainer, co-developer, and designer of training programs in the field of Neuro-Linguistic Programming since 1975

"Connirae Andreas's Wholeness Work goes beyond a transformation technique. Her approach gives us a new map and explanation of the structures of the unconscious—and provides a precise path to freedom by dissolving those structures that hold problems and pain in place. This pioneering work in personal evolution through non-dual awareness is a truly breakthrough contribution that deserves an acknowledged place among the best personality theories, psychotherapies, and spiritual paths."

~Stephen Josephs, EdD, co-author of *Leadership Agility*, executive coach, with six decades of daily mind-body practices

"Connirae's Wholeness Work is different! How many millions of people have tried following a healing or spiritual practice without success? Well, if they had the gentle and complete guide from Connirae, they would actually find awareness, and internal peace. A great read that flows in a way that you can follow and transform your deepest issues into strengths. I highly recommend this book for everyone who is on a path of personal development."

~Shelle Rose Charvet, author of *Words That Change Minds*

"I felt my heart expand many times when reading this book. Connirae succeeds at bringing deep concepts to life in a way that feels so accessible. Healing, transformation, and liberation feels so possible. Wholeness Work is literally a roadmap to evolutionary expansion of consciousness. My own Wholeness Work practice was instantly deepened and I am already sleeping better at night. If I could enter a soundbite for big applause for the entire book, I would."

~Erica Newman, Core Transformation Coach

"I am delighted that Connirae Andreas's new book on Wholeness Work captures the same magical combination of precision and heart that I've have experienced in her workshops. Her unparalleled ability to make complex ideas easy to understand enables readers to successfully use the processes and reference additional, deeper content when they're ready. I am grateful for the privilege of being an early reader and helping her edit this book. I am especially excited to work with the new Authority Format… an important missing piece in the personal changework I've explored over 25 years."

~Susan Sanders, co-author *NLP: The Essential Guide to Neuro-Linguistic Programming*

THE
WHOLENESS
WORK

Essential Guide

— LEVEL I —

healing &
awakening

by

Connirae Andreas

Published by Real People Press
Boulder, CO USA

Copyright © 2024 Connirae Andreas

All rights reserved. No part of this publication may be reproduced, transmitted, or sold in whole or in part in any form, without the prior written consent of the author, except in the case of brief quotations embodied in articles or reviews, with proper citations or hyper-links. For information contact the publisher, Real People Press, at info@realpeoplepress.com. This work utilizes source material © 2007 – 2024 Connirae Andreas

Print book ISBN: 978-0-911226-78-2
E-book ISBN: 978-0-911226-79-9

The Wholeness Work® is a registered trademark of Connirae Andreas and Andreas NLP.

Cover design by SuperStories

Names appearing in this book for demonstrations and sharing examples have been changed to protect the privacy of the individual.

Disclaimer:
The methods described in this book have been found to be consistently gentle and transformational when tested with myself and many hundreds of clients and workshop participants from 2007 on. As with any personal growth book, readers are advised to use their own best judgment in using the methods provided. For those working with significant life issues such as abuse or trauma, or in the event of any concern about whether or how to use these methods for yourself, we recommend contacting a skilled professional who is thoroughly trained in these methods for guidance. The information presented in this book is offered to you as a service. By reading this book you agree that you are responsible for any results of your decisions and actions relating to your use of the information presented.

The information presented in this book is the author's opinion and does not constitute any health or medical advice. The content of this book is for informational purposes only and is not intended to diagnose, treat, cure, or prevent any condition or disease, related to physical or mental health.

This book is dedicated to
love—to the essential nature that is each of us.

CONTENTS

FOREWORD

The Wholeness Work Essential Guide invites us into the key inquiries in spiritual life: What serves awakening? What helps us realize who we are beyond the imprisoning sense of a separate self? What frees us to inhabit the loving awareness that is who we are? These questions guide my own life, and the practices that explore them are the heart of what I teach. So when I encounter fresh and enlightening practices, such as those Connirae Andreas reveals in her Wholeness Work, I feel like I've struck gold!

I first experienced the power of this work in a private session with Connirae. I had been grappling for years with tenacious feelings of blame and irritation that were keeping me from full openheartedness with a member of my extended family. I tried in various ways to work with my reactivity. Forgiveness practice had loosened some of the grip, but feelings of being tight and defended continued to arise when we were together. Afterwards, I'd notice the background of disappointment in myself for still being hooked. When a mutual friend told me about the spiritual depth of Connirae's work and suggested having a session, I was curious and game for trying it out.

During our time together, Connirae guided me through a process that felt entirely natural, allowing, and gentle—quite a shift from my efforts to vanquish reactivity! The key element was becoming aware of the felt sense of the 'I' who experienced resentment—and inviting that self to relax in and as the fullness of awareness. By the end of the session, my feelings of blame had transformed. Rather than a painful tightness in my heart, those feelings had become a slight sense of pressure floating in a vast and tender sea of awareness.

Soon after that session, I read and then subsequently re-read Connirae's book, *Coming to Wholeness*. Not only has the freedom I felt from that resentment endured, but I've found the process Connirae teaches has become a natural pathway in releasing the constricting identification that comes from a wide range of emotions, including self-judgment, anxiety, craving, and anger.

Like great masters through the centuries, Connirae offers a path for realizing and inhabiting awake and loving awareness in all circumstances of our lives. Though this might seem to us to be beyond reach, her lucid step-by-step instructions guide us in recognizing the unconscious clench of self-identity that keeps us feeling separate and deficient. And as we are introduced to the embodied and boundless presence of awareness, that sense of a separate self dissolves.

The beauty of this process is its naturalness. With repetition, we become increasingly familiar with the boundless luminous awareness that is our home, and discover a growing access to wisdom and love. This allows us to move through life with the blessings of trust, ease, and wellbeing—and to bring a healing presence into our world.

Friends, may you discover the gold in these teachings and practices, and may they liberate you into the fullness of who you truly are.

~ Tara Brach PhD, Author of *Radical Acceptance, Radical Compassion and Trusting the Gold*; psychologist, meditation teacher, and co-founder (with Jack Kornfield) of the Mindfulness Teacher Certification Program www.mmtcp.soundstrue.com

THE LONG AND WINDING ROAD

My Journey to Healing through
Wholeness Work
and How This Work Can Help You

When All Hell Seemed to Break Loose

It was the spring of 1997. I was a respected international trainer and developer in Neuro-Linguistic Programming (NLP) with a background of professional training in clinical psychology.[1] I'd authored books translated into over 15 languages and developed many change methods that were benefitting people. I'd developed a process called Core Transformation[2] that was consistently getting positive, even profound results. Emails and letters were coming in from people around the world thanking me and saying, "This helped me when I thought nothing could."

But now I was experiencing my own major life crisis. It seemed like *everything* was falling apart. My husband Steve and I were going through a difficult time. My health was deteriorating rapidly and it seemed like my body was shutting down. I was experiencing such bizarre symptoms that my best guess was that I was dying.

---

[1] To learn more about my background in Clinical Psychology and Neuro-Linguistic Programming, refer to AndreasNLP.com

[2] The book, *Core Transformation: Reaching the Wellspring Within* (Andreas & Andreas) teaches this method. Research documenting its effectiveness has been published in a peer-reviewed journal. You'll find the details here: www.coretransformation.org/core-transformation-research/.

The most troubling of these symptoms was the constant sensation of a strong surge of what felt like electricity going through my spinal column and out the top of my head. It was extremely intense—as if I were wired for 110 volts of current, but was plugged into a 220-volt outlet. It felt so real that when I looked in the mirror I almost expected to see a fountain of sparks shooting out of the top of my head.

Because this "electric" flow was non-stop, 24/7, it was almost impossible to do anything else. Thinking, reading, writing, sleeping, interacting with others—doing any normal activities—were all an extreme challenge. I didn't see how my body could physically survive it.

Given the vulnerable state I was in, it seemed unlikely I would live much longer; but I did think, *"If I'm going to survive, perhaps I need to do everything differently. If I let go of everything I think I know, maybe I'll have a chance."*

I'd been learning and teaching personal transformation methods for over 20 years, so there was a lot to let go of. However, it didn't seem like a question. I just did it. And my search for something—*anything* that could help me—began.

After a lot of searching that included seeing medical doctors, alternative health practitioners, and more, I finally discovered a gentle system of inner transformation that's helped me in ways far beyond what I could have expected. I experienced many positive mental and emotional changes, and even experienced changes at a physical level. Some time after I began using this method in earnest, I went in for my annual physical. At the end, my doctor turned to me, and said with uncharacteristic enthusiasm,

"Last time I saw you, you arrived in a wheelchair. I'm really glad to see you're doing so well!... You look completely different now," he said. *"Frankly, most people who have the kind of symptoms you had don't get better. But you—you look healthy and vital."* He paused and looked pensive. *"I'm curious what you attribute the change to."*

My doctor was in the middle of a busy day, so I offered the shortest answer I could. "I think what's made the biggest difference is a new kind of inner work that I'm doing. I call it '*the Wholeness Work.*'"

And now, after a decade-plus period of "hibernation" or "sabbatical," I'm grateful to have the energy and clarity to do the work I love.

Before, I hadn't been able to teach or do any client work, and I couldn't travel at all—not even for a short car ride. Now I can do all those things. I still have some unusual physical symptoms, but I'm able to cope with them and embrace my life. I'm writing, teaching, and discovering new ways to help people heal, awaken, and transform themselves.

a new "way"
that changed my life

In this book I will share with you the transformation system that's been so helpful to me. Wholeness Work has helped me in every area of my life. It helped me with emotional hot buttons that caused trouble in my relationship with my husband. It helped me with my perfectionism, my feelings of embarrassment and shame for being anything less than some idea of perfect. It helped me get over anxieties and fears. It helped me deal with the troubling events happening in the world; so that instead of being fearful, or reacting with anger, I felt a calm and loving presence. I had more capacity to accept what I can't change—it was as if I could experience a natural state that's deeper than the outer disturbances, that's intrinsically kind. I could go on and on with the ways it's helped me. Some of these I'll share later in this book.

After experiencing how it made my life better, I wondered if others would find it as useful as I was finding it. Now, after teaching it to thousands of other people, the answer is clear. Yes. I've seen thousands of others benefit. The results people share in each training and coaching session are deep and touching.

Here are some of the most common experiences people share:

- ✿ Stress dissolves easily and feelings of wellbeing increase
- ✿ Problems fall away
- ✿ Emotional wounds are healed and transformed—including problems that haven't responded to other methods
- ✿ Deep relaxation and resetting of the nervous system
- ✿ Better sleep
- ✿ Improved relationships: reduced reactivity, more connection and intimacy
- ✿ Greater access to creativity, to solutions—and a ready sense of humor

And I'd like you to have these same benefits—if you want them. That's what this book is about.

Before I give you a preview of what Wholeness Work is and the surprisingly wide-ranging benefits, I want you to know two things.

First, that if you try out the methods in this book, your story will be different than mine. However, if you actually do the exercises, there's a strong likelihood that you'll experience your own version of positive life changes and transformation. As I've taught Wholeness Work to others, I've learned that these methods appear to be universally useful. Your life might be going really well… or not so well. You might be experiencing a lot of stress, or not. Either way, there are so many potential benefits from Wholeness Work—for *you*. This is because with Wholeness Work we have a way to reach the universal structures of the unconscious that hold problems in place, and keep us from living life to its fullest. And with this ground-breaking approach, we have a specific way to kindly invite these structures to heal and transform.

Second, I want you to know that whatever your life context, you can use Wholeness Work as a part of what is already meaningful to you. If you're part of a religious group, have a spiritual teacher, or a spiritual path, *you can use Wholeness Work within your chosen life context*. I think you'll find it aligns with the deep purpose of almost every spiritual path and can even deepen and enrich your experience of your chosen path.

Some pastors and spiritual teachers are beginning to teach Wholeness Work explicitly to their community because they recognize this alignment.[3] If you already have a meditation practice, you can use it as part of that practice, or as something you explore at a separate time, whichever fits best for you. Wholeness Work is not intended as a replacement for your chosen spiritual beliefs or community.

And of course you don't need to have a spiritual path or spiritual beliefs for these practices to be profoundly useful.

The Search and Spirituality

During that dark time I told you about earlier, my search for deeper change quickly led me to explore the world of spirituality. I'd already explored what was available in Psychology[4], personal growth systems, and NLP. After decades of study, I recognized that for my own change, I needed something more—something deeper. Perhaps the answers I was looking for were in the spiritual domain.

Many Eastern spiritual teachers talk about experiences they call Awakening that result in a shift of consciousness. The shift they describe is clearly something that goes further than any therapy method or NLP method could bring about. They describe a fundamental shift in consciousness that results in a profound sense of wellbeing. But it's more than that. They report that when one makes this shift, the ordinary "suffering" and stresses of life fall away. *And I wanted that.*

---

[3] If you are a spiritual leader and want to offer Wholeness Work to your community, I encourage you to begin by going through the full Wholeness Work trainings, Levels I – IV. This will give you a depth of experience with this work. Please see recommendations for Wholeness Work trainers at TheWholenessWork.org. You can also refer your people to our classes if you prefer.

[4] In this book, when I refer to "psychology" I am speaking in terms of general knowledge and/or personal insights, and not providing professional advice. For professional advice, contact a licensed psychologist.

So I began. I read everything I could find about awakening, trying various forms of meditation, and sitting in many spiritual circles. I sensed something important was happening here and I surely benefitted. I liked immersing myself in what felt like circles of loving presence, and being around the sincere striving of so many seekers and teachers.

Exploring spirituality was bringing me to this deeper level. Yet after quite a few years sitting in spiritual circles and following the meditation advice given, I began to have a sense of déjà vu. *"Something's missing here, too."* We were listening to ideas about an awakening of consciousness. It sounded good and most of us could experience at least a *beginning* of what was talked about. But there didn't seem to be any reliable path to get there.

That's when my background in NLP came in handy. I'd worked both on my own and in partnerships, to create "models" or protocols for making specific positive changes. We used NLP patterning tools to map out what someone with a skill or capability did, often unconsciously, that resulted in their ability. As one example, my husband and I mapped out an effective mental strategy for recovering from grief and loss.[5] I'd already participated in developing many protocols or guides for doing something people usually assume "just takes time." So I felt an almost automatic impulse to find a precise and reliable path, to experience what the spiritual teachers talked about. I wondered, *What if Awakening can also be mapped out?*

Then, I began a series of inner explorations. These explorations felt different than my previous NLP modeling. I wasn't figuring things out in a logical way. This time I was letting the change process emerge in a more organic way from within. Using myself as the guinea pig, I began noticing what was needed for me to experience deeper change.

My First Experiment... And the Beginning of Wholeness Work

As I investigated spiritual teachings, one premise stood out: most Eastern spiritual paths teach that the key to Awakening is to let go of

---

[5] This method is described in the book, *Heart of the Mind,* Andreas & Andreas (1989) Chapter 11; and a video demonstration is available at AndreasNLP.com (store).

the ego. However, most paths didn't seem to have a set of instructions for *how* to do that. Some paths even said, "It's not possible to have any instructions" or "It just happens through grace."

I thought, *"What if it would be possible to have a set of instructions—a clear roadmap—to this state of consciousness called Awakening?"*

What I'm sharing with you in this book is, I believe, exactly that: A clear roadmap to the transformation of consciousness we could call Awakening. And just as the spiritual teachings predicted, I found that stress, emotional difficulties, and "suffering" of all sorts began to fall away too.

When I did the first explorations within myself, the change I noticed was subtle. No bells or fireworks announced, "This is Awakening!" I wasn't even sure I was on the right track.

But as I continued experimenting, it became clear that the initial subtle results were beginning to add up to something quite profound. What began as subtle shifts became stronger and stronger. These experiments began making permanent positive changes in my consciousness. I gradually felt a greater sense of wellbeing. I was emotionally triggered less frequently. I enjoyed easier and better sleep. And so much more. The whole thing felt effortless. The more I practiced in this way, the more it felt like an ultimate kindness to my system. And it was bringing me to a place of greater ease in life.

At last, I could meet, heal, and transform anything that emerged in my experience. Using this process even calmed and transformed the bizarre and disconcerting physical symptoms that I'd been experiencing. The super-charge in my nervous system would settle and calm when I took a few moments to meditate in the way you'll learn in Chapter 4. My heightened sensitivity to any kind of stimulation settled as well. I gradually felt comfortable with a wider range of sensory stimulation—I was comfortable in more environments without a negative impact. Then, after doing a format you'll learn in Chapter 5, I experienced a substantial increase in energy level, giving me the stamina to teach again.

Increasingly I sensed, "This is on the right track"—It's the same thing spiritual teachers described. The processes that have become the Wholeness Work method are the first ways I found that I could reliably soothe, relax, and reset my mind-body system. And, I am not alone—these processes have helped thousands of people.

In this book, I'll share these methods with you. It's not just one thing. You'll find Wholeness Work to be a sequence of methods, each building on the last, that together guide you in a journey of evolving consciousness. And the result is that we experience more peace as stress falls away. Emotional and behavioral issues, even ones that have been difficult to change, begin healing at a deeper level.

The reason we're able to get a deeper level of healing at the emotional level is because Wholeness Work maps out the structures of the psyche that hold "suffering," or ordinary limitations in place. These structures are universal, but haven't been clearly mapped out before. Once we understand what these structures are, and how to find them, significant change becomes much easier.

The Psychology Side and the Spiritual Side

As I began using Wholeness Work as a daily practice and teaching it to others, it became increasingly clear that this method was offering surprisingly deep psychological healing—deeper than anything I'd encountered before. And it may also offer a more dependable, and possibly more complete, way to spiritual growth.

Here's why.

On the psychology side, Wholeness Work offers a breakthrough in the way we understand the structure of the unconscious. In this book I'll guide you in how to discover these universal unconscious structures that hold emotional issues and stress in place. Wholeness Work has a unique, carefully-worded set of questions to ask ourselves inside, that lead us to easily find and transform these structures. When you go to this deeper level of experience, change becomes kinder, gentler, and easier.

On the spiritual side, you'll also discover in these methods, a precise path to what we might call Awakening—the type of awakening that spiritual teachers talk about and embody. The specific questions to ask inside will help you release what we can call the "limited self" or "small self" that spiritual teachings describe as the source of suffering. *And,* they will also give you gentle way to shine the light of Awareness through every nook and cranny of the unconscious.

For both the psychology side and the spiritual side, Wholeness Work takes us to a level of experience that's deeper than content. Often therapy methods and spiritual development paths focus on *content*—the story of our life and the meanings we make about it. With Wholeness Work we go to a level of experience that's deeper than the story, making healing and transformation kinder, gentler, and more complete.

what's in this book
more than dissolving the 'I's

In this book I'm sharing with you the same methods that have already benefitted many training participants and clients. Wholeness Work meets you where you are—gently and kindly guiding you in deep healing and transformation. And I'd like to give you a preview of what this is.

First Step: Dissolving and Integrating the Ego or Limited Self
In Chapters 2-4 you'll learn a simple and direct method for dissolving the experience of "limited self" or "small self." It feels amazingly gentle and kind—like nourishment. This is what spiritual teachings describe as the key to awakening. These "limited self" structures have been out of our conscious awareness, but they're what's responsible for holding limitations and suffering in place. You'll learn an easy way to find them, and through using these processes, you're likely to experience a kind of freedom and release from many challenging life issues.

The methods for dissolving the ego came to me first, and it's important to learn and use these *first*.

Next Step: The "Not-Self" Structures—Inner Authority and Self-Nurturing

After benefitting from these first Wholeness Work methods for some time, I discovered there's more to an authentic and complete Awakening—an awakening that fully penetrates our entire being (including mind, body and emotions)—than just dissolving the ego. So in the second half of the book, I'll share with you the next part: Finding and healing the "not-self" structures. The methods you'll learn in Chapters 5 and 6 will take you to even deeper healing and transformation. In Chapter 5 you'll learn a Wholeness Work method that can help us completely shift our relationship to authority, rules, and judgment. This method is key to transforming many life issues, such as perfectionism and self-criticism. Then, Chapter 6 provides a blueprint for deep healing of emptiness and loss, as well as for recovery from deficiencies in nurturing many of us experienced in childhood.

And sleep. Almost everyone who uses Wholeness Work tells me their sleep improves—often significantly. They sleep more deeply and wake up with more energy than before. Chapter 7 will tell you how to gain these benefits.

At the end of the book I'll share more about Wholeness Work as a comprehensive system of transformation, and about the changes from Wholeness Work that go deeper than fixing our problems.

The Ripple Effect

Using Wholeness Work to attend to an issue or feeling can have unexpected and positive ripple effects. Here's an example: A woman came to me wanting to learn how to use Wholeness Work as a meditative practice. We met once a week, and in between she practiced the Wholeness Meditation briefly each day. After three or four meetings, I asked her, "How is it going?" And she said, "Well it's going pretty well, but you know the weirdest thing is happening."

"What's that?" I asked.

"Well, my life is changing too." And I was thinking, "Whoa, I wonder what she *thought* would happen?" I had no idea she wasn't aware that this was a part of the intention. But she must have been thinking this was just for relaxing—it's "just a meditation." So I asked, "How is your life different?"

She said, "There's less drama. Well, actually there is still plenty of drama; it's just that I don't get caught in it now. It's happening both at home and at work. At home, my kids still have plenty of their own mini-dramas, but ... I have this knowing that things will be fine and I can just deal with it. And at work it's the same thing. Things still happen that would have caused me a lot of stress before, but I'm not getting caught up in them now. I feel calm and have more energy to just do my job."

That's just one example. I wonder what positive changes and ripple effects *you* might experience from doing Wholeness Work.

My First Glimpse of Awakening—An Experience with Dr. Milton H. Erickson

A pivotal experience in my 20's laid the groundwork for me to develop Wholeness Work many years later. It was a profound experience that I only later recognized as my first glimpse of Awakening.

Let me tell you about it…

> *…About an hour or more into the session, as I sat there, all of a sudden I became a different person—that's the only way I know how to describe it. Within a matter of seconds, I suddenly felt like I had never felt before. The experience was more than I could put into words, but I felt a sense of complete and profound wellbeing. Plus I had a kind of wordless knowing that whatever happened, I would be OK—things would be fine no matter what. I had never felt that way before, in such a complete way.*

> *I assumed the man sitting on the other side of the circle in the purple suit had something to do with this, but I sure didn't have any idea how.*

The man in the purple suit was none other than Dr. Milton Erickson, renowned American psychiatrist who specialized in medical hypnosis and family therapy. This transformative experience occurred during a week-long workshop that I had the privilege to attend with a small group of therapists at Dr. Erickson's residence in Phoenix, AZ in 1979, the last year of Erickson's life. I've described the experience in detail here:

www.thewholenesswork.org/articles/origin/

In the weeks after this experience, I was in touch with a deep kind of wellbeing that felt independent of circumstances. Whatever happened—whatever could happen—I felt a knowing that at some deep level everything is completely OK—more than OK. It felt like finally *knowing* something that had always been true, but somehow I hadn't recognized it. During this time I came to clarity about a difficult life decision I'd been agonizing over. Things just fell into place. I knew what I needed to do and did it from a place of love and without attachment to how others might respond. I'd never been able to do that before.

Unfortunately, this feeling of wellbeing didn't last. It soon began to unravel, and I was back to feeling my old insecurities and at times, my old reactive emotional responses. Wanting to get back to that feeling of wellbeing, I signed up for another week-long seminar with Dr. Erickson. Unfortunately, shortly before this seminar was to take place, Dr. Erickson passed away.

I was devastated. My hoped-for doorway back to deep wellbeing was gone. Yet through this I recognized that perhaps now it was my job to find the way to the profound wellbeing I'd briefly enjoyed. *I now knew this deep wellbeing was possible—and possible for me.* Searching for a way to get back to the profound wellbeing I'd experienced through Dr. Erickson led me to develop a new method that goes beyond classic NLP. I called it Core Transformation,[6] because it resulted in a deeper and more complete change than anything I'd learned in NLP thus far.

---

[6] The complete Core Transformation process came together in the summer of 1989, and since then it has helped thousands of people across many countries and cultures to bring about profound changes in their lives. Many of them had tried everything on their biggest life issues without success and discovered Core Transformation provided a way to resolve those issues. A randomized controlled trial showing the effectiveness of Core Transformation was published in *The Journal of Counseling and Development,* by Dinesh J. Braganza, Richard M. Gray, et al. (July 2019).

For a while, I thought I'd finally found everything I'd been seeking. With Core Transformation, I was able to reliably guide my clients to much deeper and more satisfying changes than I'd been able to before. And it was even working for me. I was experiencing reliable change for myself for the first time. I used it as a daily practice that felt kind and gentle.

Then, in 1997, I experienced a life crisis that led me to question everything. It was the health crisis I described for you at the beginning of this introduction. At the time I was anything but happy. But now, looking back, I'm grateful for the way life nudged me and revealed it was time for me to go still farther, and explore deeper. It was through letting go of everything I thought I knew, that I became open to experience a greater ease in life than I'd ever known before.

And *this* time, unlike the experience with Dr. Erickson, the gains with Wholeness Work have been permanent. They last.

I think this is no accident. When a profound—even spiritual—experience is delivered from the outside, as happened for me with Dr. Erickson, I've come to think that it's not likely to last. I've come to believe that true spiritual progress happens when it's not something done *to* us, but when we actively participate in the process. That's what we can do with Wholeness Work.

CHAPTER 1

THE ONLY DECISION
THAT MATTERS

Years ago, when I was exploring with different spiritual teachers, I attended a meeting where a participant asked the teacher about a major life decision she was facing. She was feeling very anxious about making the right decision, and asked the spiritual teacher what to do.

The teacher paused, and then surprised us all by saying, "It really doesn't matter…." The teacher continued, "You know, there are only a few decisions each of us make in our entire lifetime that actually matter." I confess that my jaw sort of dropped when he said that—so this statement stood out for me. Somehow it rang true, even though I didn't know exactly what this teacher meant. And I wondered, "What are the decisions that matter for me?"

Was it whom I decided to marry? That seemed important.
Was it what I decided to do for a living?
Was it where to live?
Or how many children to have?

If there were only two or three important decisions, which ones were they?

Well, I believe I've finally come to understand what that teacher meant. And actually there's only one decision that matters. Not even two or three. What seems true to me (now seven decades into my life) is that only one decision really matters. And it's the decision to *consciously participate in my own unfolding—in my own "awakening."*

Life offers each of us challenges, whether or not we choose them. And the result is that we can't help but grow, each in our own way. And this is good—we can't really avoid it. But to step forward and *consciously choose* to participate in our own unfolding, our own Awakening, this takes things to a different level. There is a certain level of personal development that can only happen when we choose to participate in the process. We choose growth.

And when we do this, none of the other decisions have that same degree of consequence. No matter which person we decide to marry, which job we take, where we live, how we support our children or community, etc. Whatever the decision, it's going to go better if we are consciously choosing to use whatever happens each day as part of our development, when we're consciously participating in our own unfolding.

But *how* do we consciously participate? Wholeness Work gives us a simple, precise, and gentle way to do that. With Wholeness Work, we can kindly notice and include *all* of our intentions, *all* of our emotions, thoughts, and reactions. With ongoing practice, each intention, emotion, or thought becomes a doorway to greater wellbeing and wholeness. Each life experience becomes a doorway to being more of who we are, and who we can be. To more resilience, more peaceful presence, more social and emotional intelligence, more creativity. To more love and more humor.

If you find this intriguing, I'm excited to work together.

CHAPTER 2

YOUR FIRST WHOLENESS WORK EXPLORATION

Finding the 'I' Inside

"Your task is not to seek for love,
but merely to seek and find all the barriers
within yourself that you have built against it."

I've always loved this quote from Rumi, the Sufi poet. To me, it perfectly describes the spirit of Wholeness Work. With Wholeness Work we'll be finding and melting away the inner barriers we've built within ourselves against love. The more I've learned to do this work, the more the practices feel like full-on self love, and the more I experience love within—and even that I *am* love.

If you read the introduction, you have a sense of where this book is going and the potential benefits for you. Wholeness Work can give you a way to kindly transform and heal almost any kind of emotional difficulty or troublesome thoughts, and more. This is because, for the first time, *we have a reliable way to find and transform the structures of the unconscious that hold problems in place.*

I discovered the first of these structures because of what I learned from Eastern spirituality about Awakening and the ego. Awakening sounded like something quite wonderful in itself, but I was also drawn to this because the spiritual teachers said that when one truly awakens, ordinary life problems fall away.

But let's start at the beginning…. Here are a few background ideas; then, I'll guide you in the first exploration in Wholeness Work.

The Key Spiritual Teaching

As I participated in spiritual circles, perhaps the most universal teaching I encountered is that if we want to experience "awakening" or "enlightenment," we need to let go of our ego. Enlightenment = loss of ego. What *wasn't* clear was how to do that.

Some of my teachers were saying, "There can't be steps to this—it just happens" or even "If someone claims to have steps, it's not the real deal." So I attempted to make myself available for this "just happening." I definitely wanted to experience this.

But as I turned inward and meditated, occasionally I felt curious and wondered, "What if there *is* a precise way to do this? What if there's essentially a "science" to this—so that if we understand what actually shifts in our psyche when someone "awakens," we can all do it. What if it's as "knowable" as the science behind starting a fire with a match? This seems magical to someone who doesn't understand. But matches can now be created so that anybody can easily light a fire.

Maybe there's a similarly reliable path to this shift in consciousness that's so significant people call it "awakening." I decided to attempt to find this path, this procedure, this "science."

What is the Ego?

I realized, if we want to be able to dissolve the ego, the first question to answer, was "What is the ego in experience?" There are lots of *definitions* for the word "ego." It's possible to discuss these endlessly—and I'd been part of groups that did just that. But the discussions didn't bring us any closer to the experience.

So I came back to this question, "What is the ego, *in experience?*"

The simplest answer to this question is "the ego is the 'I'." We all use the word "I" many times each day. "I'm reading this book." "I'm going to talk to my friend." "I want to solve this problem."

But what is the 'I' in experience? That's what we're going to explore next.

Before I guide you, I want to share a key idea that's foundational to Wholeness Work and will help you understand your first exploration.

Every experience has a location.

It's obvious that everything that exists in the world around us has a location. I have a cup of tea on my desk, and the cup is in a particular location. There's a tree outside my window, and it's in a particular location.

It turns out the same thing is true of experiences in our inner world. Let's do a simple thought experiment about this. Please think of a really ripe banana.

Now notice where your inner image of the banana is located. If you're not sure, you can just guess. Does it seem to be right in front of you? Or is it a little to the left, or to the right? Is it close to you or farther out? Perhaps it's above your line of sight or below.

Even if you're not consciously seeing anything, usually it's possible to "guess" where the representation of the banana is located within your inner landscape.

Why location matters...

If I want to interact with or change something in my outer world, it's obvious that I need to know where it's located. I can't give someone a hug unless I know where they are and move toward them. And if I want to drink that cup of tea, I need to know where it is, to pick it up.

The same thing is true in our inner world. If we want to change something within, we need to start by noticing where it's located—to literally find it.

This understanding can help us find the ego, or the "small self" that each of us has within.

You'll see how it's easy, when you know what questions to ask.

So, let's get started. If we're going to dissolve what might be called our "ego," the first step is to actually find it in our experience. The exploration in this chapter lays the groundwork for what's to come. Wholeness Work isn't about mentally understanding something. That won't help you at all. It's through actively experiencing the work that something remarkable begins to happen. So I invite you to join in this beginning experience. It's deceptively simple. Actually doing the steps is what will prepare you to benefit from everything else to follow.

discovering elements of our inner world
exploring together

Okay, are you ready to explore?

First take a moment to get comfortable. If you're sitting down, let your body find a comfortable position.

Next, read each step of this exploration. Then pause to experience it yourself. If you'd like, you can close your eyes to fully experience each step.

Step 1: Find a body sensation.
Turn your attention inward and notice any sensation happening in your body in this moment. It can be anything at all. There's no right or wrong answer.

You might notice a sensation in your torso somewhere, or in your neck or head, arms, legs … anywhere. Just notice whatever sensation comes into your awareness. (If you notice more than one sensation, just pick one for this exploration.)

For example, when I do this now, I immediately feel a slight tingling in my belly.

Examples of what others have noticed...

Ari: *There's a sensation in the back of my neck—it's warm.*

Twana: *I notice a sensation in my ribcage—kind of a wooziness.*

Davis: *I notice something behind my naval.*

Mari: *There's a sensation on the top of both of my forearms.*

What do *you* notice? It doesn't matter if the sensation that you become aware of is pleasant, unpleasant, or neutral. Just notice the sensation itself, and notice where the sensation is located.

Step 2: Notice the size & shape.
Now as you notice this sensation somewhere in your body, the next step is to notice how much space it takes up. What is its "size and shape?" This might seem like a strange question, but it's usually easy to answer.

For me, this tingling in my belly is about the size of a grapefruit, but oval-shaped and without any distinct edges.

Take a moment to notice the size and shape of the sensation you're exploring. It might be large; it might be small. It might be round, square, oval-shaped, or it might have a shape that's difficult to describe. Just take a moment to notice how much space this sensation takes up, and its approximate size and shape.

Step 3: Notice the "sensation quality."
And now, pause to notice what I call the "sensation quality" of this experience. For example, when I sense in and through that area I notice in my abdomen, it's tingly and also a bit warm.

If you sense in and through the area of the sensation you're aware of now, there might be a sense of warmth or coolness, heaviness or lightness. It might be still, or there may be a sense of movement. It might be tingly or fizzy, prickly, or smooth. There could be a sense of electricity or bubbliness or vibratiness. Or something else. It might be something difficult to describe in words, and that's fine. You can just notice the sensation itself even if you can't find a word to describe it.

Examples of what others have noticed...

Rob: *The sensation at the top of my forearms is oval-shaped and about an inch thick. Sensing in and through, it's tingly and feels like it's expanding.*

Sue: *The sensation I noticed is in the back of my neck. It's small, about plum-sized, but has an irregular shape. Sensing in and through, there's a darkness and heaviness.*

Amira: *I noticed a sensation in the middle of my head. It's about the size of an orange, and round. Sensing in and through, it's almost transparent, but has a quality of light.*

Luis: *The sensation is in my ribcage and it's fairly large. It's mostly inside my body, but almost as if it extends out in front of my body an inch or so also. Sensing in and through, it's warm and there's a smooth stickiness about it.*

Ale: *The sensation behind my naval is shaped like the rings of Saturn. And sensing in and through, it's moving— swirling around. And sort of airy.*

Now that you've noticed the location, size and shape, and sensation quality of a body sensation, you're ready for the next step.

Step 4: Find the 'I'.
We begin this next step by simply saying to ourselves what we've noticed so far. For me, I say, "*I* am *aware* of this tingly sensation in my belly."

As you notice the body sensation you discovered, you can say: "*I … am aware … of this* [_fill in the sensation quality you noticed_], *in* [_fill in the location_]."

When you think that thought to yourself, this is a true thought, right? You *are* aware of this sensation. So just experience this: "*I am aware of this sensation here.*" You might even emphasize the word "*I*" a little bit. "*I am aware of this sensation.*"

Next, ask the question inside: "*And where is the 'I' located?*"… This might seem like a strange question too, and it's okay if it doesn't make any sense. Just notice what location comes to mind…. "*I am aware of this sensation….*" And where is this 'I' that's aware? *Where* is the 'I' located?"… And just notice what location immediately comes into awareness.

You might immediately notice a location … or you might not be sure … Either way, just go with the first location that comes to mind.

If you're *really* not sure, try it again. Go back to noticing the body sensation again. And as you're noticing this body sensation, this time think to yourself very slowly and softly: "*I … am aware … of this sensation….*" And now notice: "*Where is the 'I' located? Where's the 'I' that notices?*" … Just go with the first location that comes to mind. It's okay to guess.

The location that emerges for you might be inside your body somewhere. Or it could be located outside of the body. If it's outside the body, it might be close or it might be far away. It might even be partly in the body and partly outside the body.

Examples of what others have noticed...

Leah: *The original sensation was in my forehead. Small and round. When I asked: "Where is the 'I' that notices?" I immediately became aware of this place in the back of my head. It's round-shaped, and maybe five centimeters in diameter.*

> Rob: *When I asked "Where's the 'I'?" I immediately noticed this space about two feet in front of me and to the left. It's cloud-shaped, and kind of fuzzy and damp.*
>
> Jerad: *The answer that came to me is right in the middle of my chest. It's glowing and radiant.*
>
> Rachel: *This seems strange but it's two locations at once. The original sensation was in my chest. And when I asked "Where's the 'I' that notices?" I became aware of two oval-shaped areas, one on each shoulder. It's mostly outside my body—above my shoulders, but a little bit inside my body, too.*

When we ask, "*Where's the 'I' that notices?*" each person finds something different. And if you do this experiment again, it may be completely different next time. And each answer we get is beautiful in its own way—though it may or may not seem beautiful at first. We'll discover more about that as we go along.

 If you'd like to listen to my voice guiding you through this exploration, you can use the QR code on the left or find a free version of this demonstration at: www.andreasnlp.com/resources/free-wholeness-intro-video/.

Step 5: Notice the size & shape of the 'I'.
You've already noticed where the 'I' is located. Now you can notice the size and shape of this 'I'. It might be small; it might be large. It might be shaped like a ball, or like an oval, a column, a dome, a square, or anything really. Just notice the size and shape of the 'I' that emerged. If you're not sure, it's ok to notice the approximate size and shape. It might be something nondescript, or it might not have a definite border.

Step 6: Notice the sensation quality of the 'I'.

Now gently sense in and through the space of this [the 'I'] to notice the sensation quality in and through the area.... By "sensation quality" I mean it might be dense or it might be airy. It could be warm or cool, light or heavy. There might be a sense of movement, or stillness. It could be foggy, transparent, or vibrate-y ... or anything else. Just notice the sensation itself.

Examples of what others have noticed...

Anna: *My 'I' is in front of my face, about a foot out, and it's shaped like a cloud. And sensing in and through, it's fairly airy and cool.*

Ron: *The 'I' is behind me, and above. It seems round, but it doesn't have a definite edge. It's as if it's just an invisible empty space.*

Joy: *When I asked "Where is the 'I' that notices?" I immediately became aware of something above and behind me. It's shaped like a dome, about an inch thick. And sensing in and through the space of this, it's kind of dense and prickly.*

George: *The body sensation I started with was in my lower back. An achy sensation. The 'I' that notices is in the middle of my head. It surprised me. There's a vibrating or pulsing, yet it feels peaceful at the same time.*

Step 7: Experience "What is Awareness."

Now we're going to notice something else. Let's go back to that sentence: "*I am aware of this sensation.*" We've already explored the 'I', and the "sensation." We know what each of these means in experience. We know their location, size and shape, and sensation quality.

Now let's explore that middle word—"aware." Let's discover what "awareness" is in our experience.

After teaching this to many people, I've noticed that different people have completely different experiences for "awareness"—even people who've meditated a lot.

However, there is a particular way of experiencing Awareness[1] that works well for this process. So that's what I'm going to guide you in this right now.

A few moments ago I invited you to notice a body sensation. You could probably do this easily, and that's because Awareness is already present throughout your physical body. And right now if something were to lightly bump you on the knee, you would automatically be aware of this.... If something were to touch you on the shoulder, you would notice this.... And this is because Awareness, or the capacity to experience, is already present in and throughout the physical body. You wouldn't need to "send" your awareness there—"Oh let me send awareness to my knee"—you would just automatically be aware of it.

So right now you can pause to experience the Awareness that's already present in and through your entire body. It's the *capacity to experience* that's present, even before anything happens.

And the same is true for the space all around us. We can easily experience the space all around us. This capacity to be aware is already present in and through the space that's all around. So if someone were to snap their fingers on your left side, or call your name, there would be an automatic receiving of the sound.... And if a sound happens on the right, there's an automatic receiving of the sound.... And the same thing is true if there's a sound in front, or behind, or above, or in any direction....

And the same is true visually. With your eyes open or closed, it's easy to be aware of the space that's all around, in every direction.... If your eyes are open, you can easily see in front of you and to the sides. And even without eyes in the back of your head, you know

---

[1] Starting now, when you see "Awareness" with a capital "A," this means this word is being used with the specific/specialized meaning I'm explaining here.

the space is there, too. There's a visual sense of space behind you as well as to the sides and front. And if your eyes are closed, you're still aware that this space didn't go away just because you're not looking at it right now. Even with eyes closed there's this sense of space extending in every direction simultaneously.

And you can pause to experience this right now in this moment....

And this space that's everywhere at once ... in our subjective experience, we can't really find an edge or border to this. We might mentally know that if a sound were 10,000 miles away, or on the other side of the world, we probably wouldn't hear it, right? We can mentally know that. And yet, in our experience, this sense of space all around, it doesn't have an edge or border. We can't find a line anywhere where we could say, "Oh, if a sound happens on this side of the line I'll hear it, but if it happens on the other side of that line, I know I wouldn't be able to hear it."

So this experience of the space that's in and through the body, that's all around us—in our subjective experience, there's no edge or border.

PAUSE NOW

Please take a moment to experience this now.... Pause to experience this "capacity to be aware" that is present in and through the physical body ... and in and through the space all around in every direction....

And it might feel pleasant just to experience this. It's like "Ah…" this sense of space that's through the body, that's all around, this capacity to experience that's in every direction simultaneously.

Step 8: Try an experiment.

So now we're going to return to the 'I' that we found a moment ago.

Wherever you found the 'I'… attend there again. And notice again the size and shape of the 'I' that you found.

Take a moment to sense in and through this area, again noticing the sensation quality in and through the space….

Now I'm going to invite you to ask a question inside that might seem a little strange. There's no need to understand it—you can just notice what happens.

First gently sense in and through the space of the 'I', experiencing the sensation quality…. Now read the next sentence to yourself in a slow and soft voice, and allow whatever happens to happen….

> *Notice what happens, when the sensation of the 'I'… is invited to open and relax … in and as the full field of Awareness … that's all around and throughout….*

Now just allow whatever happens to happen. And whatever happens is fine. There may be a subtle shifting, or a big shift … or it may be that nothing at all happens….

If something is already happening, you can allow it to continue however it does until things settle. Just pause, allowing it to take whatever time it takes until things settle.

If nothing is happening yet, you can try it again. Repeat the invitation to yourself, perhaps a little more slowly this time, allowing whatever happens to happen.

So again notice the sensation of the 'I'. Whether it's tingly, warm, cool, dense, airy, or something else, attend to the sensation of the I and now (reading very slowly and with a soft voice)….

> *Notice what happens when the sensation here is invited to open and relax in and as the full field of Awareness that's all around and throughout.*

And then you can just allow whatever happens to happen, without effort.[2]

What did you experience?

You may have experienced a shift that's very subtle—almost imperceptible. Or you might have experienced something more substantial. Or perhaps nothing happened. There isn't a right or wrong way to experience this. Whatever you experienced, even if nothing, is the right experience for you in this moment.

If you did experience something, then you have a beginning experience of what Wholeness Work is all about. If you experienced nothing so far, just know that there's always a good reason for this. Sometimes it just means that you need a partner to guide you so that you can just relax into the experience. But usually it means that the experience you were exploring needs some additional Wholeness Work "keys" for a meaningful shift to happen. With Wholeness Work, there's never a need to push or force anything to happen. (Any attempt to "make" something happen is actually counter-productive.)

It's always about finding the easy way. Whether or not you experienced a shift from this first exercise, what you just did will lay the groundwork for the next exercise.

Whether you experienced something subtle, something more dramatic, or whether you experienced nothing at all, is fine. With Wholeness Work we're always honoring whatever our real experience is; there's no need to push or force it to be any different than it actually is.

---

[2] Listening to my voice guiding you can make it easier to do this exploration. You can experience this in my free video introduction to Wholeness Work, use this QR code or the link. www.andreasnlp.com/resources/free-wholeness-intro-video/watch/. You can just close your eyes and follow my voice, which may make it easier for you to have the full experience.

Examples of what others have noticed...

Raul: *The 'I' was a cloud in front of me. It was small and a bit dense and dark. When I invited the sensation of the 'I' to open and relax, I don't know what happened but something relaxed. I realize now that I'd been having a mild headache, and it's gone now.*

Ruby: *My 'I' was in my heart area. Actually half inside my chest and half outside. And the sensation quality is hard to describe, but it was sort of a glowy mist. Light, but there was also a sadness to it. When I invited it to open and relax, I felt myself taking a deep breath. It was like this glowy mist turned into a fluid that then started flowing through my whole body and then I guess it disappeared. Anyway, there wasn't anything separate any longer. While this happened my body first started feeling more heavy, and it was like something deep was crying. Then it released and I just felt more grounded without the weight. I don't know what that was about, but I was surprised. That's a lot that happened just from this simple exercise!*

Annie: *My 'I' was just to the right of my right ear. It was small and almost invisible. It was as if it had invisible sparkles to it. When I invited it to open and relax as Awareness, it's like it turned into a smile. Literally. I felt myself smiling. The change happened mostly in my upper body. It was like throughout my head and the area around my head, the space seemed more clear and open and peaceful.*

Greg: *The 'I' was above my head and behind me a little. It was dark and dense. And when I invited it to open and relax, nothing happened. It just stayed the same.*

Whenever I guide a group in this exercise, I'm always amazed at the variety of experiences that people have just from this simple experiment.

** A Visual Representation of Finding the 'I' **

Here are three examples of finding the 'I'. The 'I' you find might be located inside your body or outside; it can be anywhere.

a new way
of being present
about this exploration

So what is this all about? What did we just do with this experiment?

I've guided thousands of people in this exercise, and each person's response is unique. So your experience is the perfect beginning to exploring Wholeness Work—even if for you nothing happened, as was the case with Greg.

If something did shift already, what did you notice? The most common theme is that many people experience some kind of relaxation. It might be just a little bit of relaxation, or it might be a deep relaxation or sense of peace. It might even feel "deeper" than muscle relaxation. Sometimes there's a sense of expansiveness or vastness. And I'd like to offer you a way to begin understanding this.

Baby Consciousness

Each of us starts our experience on this planet as a newborn. You probably don't remember what it was like to be a newborn, but you've seen babies—perhaps a little niece or nephew, or your own child, or the child of a friend. It can feel special to be around a newborn because they look out at us with a wide-eyed open expression that feels peaceful. This is because newborns don't yet have a separate sense of self—they don't have these small 'I's that we were just finding. They are experiencing life as "wide-open awareness."

Developmental psychologists will tell you this same thing. They tell us that newborns don't have a sense of an 'I' or a sense of separate self. For a newborn, life is just experience happening. Being alive is a flow of color, movement, sights, sounds, sensations—it's experience happening. And the newborn can't tell the difference between themselves and their mother's breast, or themselves and the carpet. It's just experience happening, without any sense of a separate self.

At some point in time, we start to realize that "*I am separate from the carpet.*" And "*I'm separate from the sandwich sitting over there on the table.*" And that recognition is useful; it helps us function in the world. If I didn't know that my body is different from the sandwich on the table, then if I start feeling hungry, I wouldn't know what to do. But if I know the sandwich is separate from me, I'm able to take appropriate action. To satisfy my hunger, I know to get the sandwich and put it in my mouth.

So recognizing that our physical body is separate from the environment is an important understanding. It's necessary for us to function on this planet.

This sense of self, however, develops in a way that's a little surprising. Who would have guessed that when we think 'I', at the unconscious level we're accessing a small place in space.... That when we think: "*I want to talk to my friend*"—or "*I anything,*"—that at the unconscious level we experience something like what you just found in doing this exploration.

Each person's experience of the 'I' is different. No two are exactly the same. And yet what they all have in common is that the 'I' is smaller than the full field of Awareness.

Who are we really?

When we ask, "*Where is the 'I' located?*" each of us finds some place in space. It's as if at the unconscious level, *that's who we think we are.*

And that is very interesting. Because when we go to solve a problem, we think: "Oh, *I* want to solve this problem," or "*I* really need to talk with my partner about something," or "*I* want to accomplish this task." And if we're taking a vacation, we might think, "*I* want to go have fun."

And who is this 'I' that's doing these things?

Each person's experience of the 'I' is different. No two are exactly the same. And yet what they all have in common is that usually the 'I' is a fairly small place in space. So at the unconscious level, it's as if we're attempting to live our life from this fairly small place in space. Literally, when we think, *'I* am going to solve this problem," what is this 'I' that's going to solve it? Well, it's similar to the 'I' you just found. It's a place in space—probably a fairly small one.

Now, that's really, really interesting. Because if *'I'* want to solve a problem, hopefully, I would bring my entire neurology, my entire nervous system to solve the problem—not just a limited place in space, right? And yet what we're all doing—what we've all learned to do unconsciously—is we're living our lives as if we're this small place in space—which we're not.

So who are we really?

I don't pretend to have an ultimate answer to that question. But I think that certainly, *who I am really* is going to include this full field of Awareness that I can easily access when I just pause and check in. Surely "who I am" is not more limited than that. Surely it includes all of that.

This is what we begin to access through the Wholeness Work. We begin to access who we really are—this full field of Awareness that we really are. With the exercise you just did, you invited the

'I' to literally relax back into this full field of Awareness. When this happens we regain direct access to our full nervous system and to our full consciousness which may even be something beyond the nervous system. And we don't even need to talk about if and what that might be.

The Fist Metaphor

Each 'I' we find inside is like a hand in a fist. If you make your hand into a fist right now, that's a contraction of muscles on the physical level, right? And it takes effort to do that.

The 'I' is a contraction of *consciousness*. It's similar to making a fist, but on a different level. Somehow from this whole that we are, this contraction forms. I'm not going to go into how the I's are formed right now. It's not important to understand that at this point. But it might be useful to know that each of us has many 'I's, not just one. You'll discover this as you continue with the exercises in this book. We each have many of these contractions of consciousness. We're not aware of them consciously, but—as you'll soon find out—it's easy to discover them using Wholeness Work.

So we are all going around living our lives as an 'I'. In the next chapter you'll do an exercise where you discover more of these 'I's. And the different 'I's become engaged in different contexts. But we'll get to that later.

Right now let's just explore this fist metaphor a little more.

What happens on the physical level if I tighten my hand into a fist? And let's say I'm not aware that I'm doing it. What's going to happen if I keep living my life like this, with this fist tightened all day and even all night?

I might begin to feel a little tired, right? I might feel stressed out. I might think: "*Gosh, I'm feeling tired and stressed, and I just don't have the energy I used to have.*" So I might decide to go to a therapist or life coach to see if they can help me with this.

My therapist or coach might offer me a lot of strategies for dealing with stress. Perhaps my coach suggests I take a hot shower, or try relaxing in a hot tub each evening, or get some exercise, or a weekly massage. My coach might teach me some ways to deal with difficult people in my life. And these all might be useful strategies.

But if the 'I' remains—if this "inner fist," this contraction of consciousness remains—there's going to be a subtle stress on the system that continues to use up my energy and wear me out.

So that's what we're finding with the Wholeness Work. These 'I's are literally contractions of consciousness, just like a fist is a contraction on the physical level. The Wholeness Work gives us an easy way of discovering this extra work we're doing at the unconscious level without realizing it. It helps us get very quickly to this subtle effort that we're putting in.

When we invite the 'I' to "open and relax as Awareness," we're inviting a contraction of our consciousness to literally relax. It's like allowing our muscles to relax on the physical level—but this relaxation is at a deeper level. Then we can experience ourselves increasingly as this whole of Awareness so that we can move through life as that. In a nutshell this is what the initial phase of Wholeness Work allows us to do.[3]

Wholeness Work taps into universal structures of our consciousness. This means it can be effective for anyone—including *you*. They key is using this work in a way that both engages these universal structures, *and* matches how your personality is uniquely organized. I'll be teaching you more about what this means as we go along.

In the next chapter, you'll explore "The Heart of Wholeness Work." You'll learn a more complete Wholeness Work format that makes it possible for most people to experience positive shifts in their daily life—including transforming stress, relationship hot buttons, and more. Ready?

---

[3] My first book on Wholeness Work, *Coming to Wholeness: How to Awaken and Live with Ease*, includes another version of this beginning exploration and more details on the "fist" metaphor.

CHAPTER 3

THE HEART OF WHOLENESS WORK—THE BASIC PROCESS

Transforming a Life Issue

Most people coming to the Wholeness Work have issues in their life they'd like to transform. Perhaps you do too. The good news is that you can use the Wholeness Work to successfully transform a wide range of life issues. Often people find healing or relief from issues they've struggled with for years. This is because with Wholeness Work, we're going right to the source—we're transforming the deeper cause that has held problems in place. Spiritual teachers might call this "awakening," but it's also easy to see that this makes a difference on a practical level, including in our emotional life.

You can use Wholeness Work to transform…

- ❀ Relationship issues
- ❀ Stress
- ❀ Difficult emotions
- ❀ Unwanted habits
- ❀ and much more

In this chapter you'll learn the Wholeness Work Basic Process. This is the "heart" of Wholeness Work. This format includes several essential keys that you'll utilize in all the additional Wholeness Work formats.

This format builds on your experience from the last chapter. We start with similar steps, but you'll notice that very soon I add something new. This new element is important—it makes the work even more *powerful* and more *complete*. Many people find it also makes the process a gentle match for their system.

Want a glimpse of what this new element is? It's about…

finding the layers of ego or 'i'

When you did the exploration in the previous chapter, you found an 'I', right? It turns out that each of us actually has many 'I's. And these 'I's are organized in layers. It's almost as if the ego is more like a set of nested dolls—or perhaps several sets.

Sound intriguing? Or maybe puzzling? You'll find out what I mean by this in the following demonstration. Finding these "layers of 'I's" is essential for deeper, more complete work. I'll show you how to do it in a way that's easy and immediate.

How This Chapter is Organized

The Wholeness Work Basic Process offers you many potential benefits. To make it easy for you to experience these benefits (not just mentally understand them), I'm including…

- ❀ A demonstration of the Basic Process.
- ❀ An "Overview Flowchart" so you can see the process in one simple picture.
- ❀ A step-by-step script you can use to guide yourself through the process and experience your own results.
- ❀ Notes and teaching points that will help you understand what we're doing; why it's significant; and how to make adaptations when needed.

Choosing An Issue to Work with for the Basic Process

Wholeness Work is often effective even with life's major issues. In fact, it gives people deeper transformation than anything I know, except perhaps Core Transformation.[1] Many people have told me, "I've tried so many things and I couldn't find anything to fully address this issue of mine until I found Wholeness Work." Even though this method is effective with the "big" issues, it's important to start with an issue that's medium to mild in intensity when you're learning. So when you do this exercise yourself, be sure to start with an issue that's mild to medium in intensity for you.

The Demonstration—and How to Learn from It

As you read the following demonstration, you may enjoy allowing the words on this page to become a movie of the interactions between Eva and me unfolding in front of you. Or, if you choose, you can step into Eva's shoes and go through the experience as if you're her, having the same experience she's describing. Either way, you don't need to work at it. You don't even need to understand it. Simply reading through the demonstration in an easy and relaxed way will lay the groundwork for your own experience of this method to be fuller and richer when you try it out.

These are the two main options I recommend the first time you go through this chapter. However, a third option is to pick an issue of your own, and follow the instructions I give to Eva. If you do this, be sure to pick something that's medium to mild in intensity. I suggest picking something that pushes your buttons, but you know it doesn't cause any real harm. For example when a car cuts in front of you on the freeway, or somebody bumps you in the grocery store line, or your husband, wife, partner, or friend does something a little irritating

---

[1] Core Transformation is another "deep transformation" method I developed earlier, that's closely aligned with the Wholeness Work. Core Transformation has different benefits, yet the two methods support each other. To explore this methodology, go to www.coretransformation.org/.

the heart of wholeness work

demonstration of the basic process[2]

Sneak Preview: The Results for Eva

EVA: *My upper body up to here is covered in light.*

ME: *What is it like now when you think of this person doing this thing (that used to be irritating)?*

EVA: [She bursts into laughter.] *I will be happy about it[3].*

Finding a Beginning

I've asked Eva to pick something to work with that's medium to mild in intensity: "Something that pushes your buttons, but you know it doesn't cause any real harm." Eva has picked an experience of someone doing something she finds irritating. I don't know anything more about the content.

Accessing the Response

ME: OK, so can you think of a time when this happened recently?

EVA: Mm hmm. It happens all the time. [She nods and chuckles.]

ME: Okay, you picked a good one. [I smile.] So, if you put yourself into the situation just enough so that you can notice your feeling response—

EVA: [She sighs and turns inward, closing her eyes.]

ME: ...where is the feeling response located?

EVA: In the chest. [She taps her chest a few times.]

---

[2] This demonstration is edited for clarity and ease of understanding. Redundant or unnecessary comments have been removed.

[3] This demonstration is from a training in Germany. Eva's responses are usually in German and have been translated into English.

ME: In the chest. [Eva nods.] Okay. Great.... And notice the size and shape.... Notice how much space this takes up.

EVA: It's like a blob…filling the whole chest. [Eva touches her chest again, showing the width of this area.]

ME: Excellent.... So, this seems to be filling the whole chest. But it might be a little bigger; it might be a little smaller. It might be moved out a little bit in the front, or to the back, or on one side or another.

So notice the subjective experience of the feeling, where it's located.... The size and shape.... And can you tell me if it's a little bigger or smaller? How is it different than the chest?

To You/Reader: Eva said "filling the whole chest." When someone says it's the same as a part of the body, I usually ask for a little more information. Because the feeling responses we have are never going to be an *exact match* for a part of the body, and it's helpful to notice the difference.

EVA: It's smaller.

ME: Okay, excellent. And sensing in and through this area in the chest, what's the sensation quality in and through this "blob" place in the chest? .... It might be warm or cool. It could be heavy. It could be light, smooth, rough, vibrate-y....

EVA: Heavy and soft.

ME: Heavy and soft. Okay, excellent.

Session Notes: The Beginning Experience	
Location	*In the chest (filling but smaller than the chest)*
Size & Shape	*Like a blob*
Sensation Quality	*Heavy, soft*

Finding the 'I'

ME: Okay, now you could say—and it would be true: *"I am aware of this heavy and soft sensation here in the chest,"* right? [I speak slowly as I guide her in attending inward.]

EVA: [She nods a few times, eyes closed.]

ME: So, as you think this thought: *"I am aware of this sensation..."* [I speak slowly, with emphasis.]... Where is the 'I' that's noticing?

EVA: ...It's in my head behind the eyes. [Her body is very still.]

ME: Okay, and what is the size and shape?

EVA: [She sighs.] ... It's like a cloud....

ME: Like a cloud.... And so now sensing in and through the space of "this that's like a cloud," what's the sensation quality? ... And again, it might be heavy, it might be light, it might be airy. It could be dense, it could be vibrate-y. It could be sparkly.

EVA: It's unrest—unrest-like movement. And it's dense. [She moves her fingers with some agitation to express the movement quality.]

ME: Moving, and dense.... Okay, excellent.

Session Notes for the 'I'	
Location	*In the head (behind the eyes)*
Size & Shape	*Like a cloud*
Sensation Quality	*Moving, dense*

Noticing The Layers of 'I'

To You/Reader: So far I've guided Eva through what we did in Chapter 2, in the guided exploration, so it probably seems familiar, right? Now I'm going to add several steps that are important. These extra steps will make the process more complete and more effective.

As it turns out, people don't have just one 'I', they have a series of 'I's. We could call it a "Chain of 'I's." Later in this chapter I'll explain why it's really, really important to find this Chain of 'I's. I'll also share why doing this makes the process more powerful—plus a lot easier!

Now let's go on to discover a simple way to find this Chain of 'I's.

Finding the Second 'I'

ME: So, Eva, we've found one 'I'. But it turns out that we all have more than one 'I', and it helps a lot to find them and include them. Here's how we do it...

So, this here in the head behind the eyes, that's like a cloud, moving and dense... [I'm guiding Eva's attention to the first 'I'. Eva opens her eyes and nods.] ... sensing in and through this ... you can also think, *"I am aware of this,"* right? *"I am aware of this that's moving and dense."*

EVA: Mm hmm. [She smiles and nods.]

ME: Yeah. And where is the 'I' that notices? Where is the 'I' that's aware of this?

EVA: It's in my head, in the back ... this projection screen. [She gestures with her right hand to the back of her head.]

ME: Okay. And this in the back of the head, that's kind of like this projection screen. What's its thickness?

EVA: Very, very thin.

ME: Very thin. Okay, And about what are its dimensions?

EVA: [Her hand curves behind her head, gesturing to show the dimensions.] ... Like the whole head.

ME: So it curves around, in the back of the head, and it's very thin.

EVA: Mm hmm. [She nods, eyes still closed.]

ME: Okay. Now in the outer world we live in, things can be really thin, like this piece of paper is thin. [I hold up a single sheet of paper from my note pad.] But everything in the outer world we live in has three dimensions. So even this paper has its own thickness to it.

And the same is true with our inner world. So, this here that curves in the back of your head... here... it's thin, but it has its own thickness. [Eva is looking at me with pursed lips and open eyes, nodding as she listens.]

So sensing in and through the space of this... that's very thin... what is the sensation quality in and through? [Eva's eyes close again, as she checks inwardly.] It could be dense, it could be airy.... It could be smooth; it could be rough.

Eva: It's transparent.... Almost transparent. [Her voice softens and lowers.]

Me: Okay, so it's almost transparent. Excellent—

Eva: —Flat, like a....

Me: And flat. Yeah. Now what is the sensation quality in and through, this that's transparent? Sometimes it's difficult to put these things into words, and that's okay. But notice the experience itself....

Eva: Mm hmm.

Me: Yeah. And there could be smoothness, roughness, even like stickiness or...

Eva: It's like glass.

Me: Like glass. So, ... Is it like glass all the way through? Is there a hardness to it?

Eva: No, it's just like you go over it. [She gestures in front of her chest, as if running her hand over a smooth and flat object.]

Me: Okay.

To the Group: So far, she's giving us surface qualities... And this is a really good start. I'm just going to give her time to also begin sensing *in and through* the space, because sometimes we're quite surprised. It can be very different from what we expect. Or, it might be what we expect. Who knows?!

Me: So, taking a moment to gently sense in and through... it's very thin. You have to kind of catch it before you're sensing gets out the other side.

Eva: [Eva is sitting very still.] Mm hmm, mm hmm. [She chuckles.]

ME: Yeah. Sensing in and through, what's the sensation quality? It could be a sense of... even a vibrational quality.

EVA: Mm hmm. It's something like that. [She nods.] It's sparkling.

ME: It's sparkling. [Eva sighs, her body relaxing a little more as she checks.] ...
Okay, good.

Session Notes: The 2ⁿᵈ 'I'	
Location	*Back of head (like a projection screen)*
Size & Shape	*Very thin (wrapping around the head)*
Sensation Quality	*Almost transparent, flat, like glass, sparkling*

Finding the Third 'I'

ME: So now we go even farther. You're aware of *this* too, right? This that's sparkly back here. [I direct Eva's attention to the second 'I' we just found.]

EVA: [She nods and smiles as she attends to the second 'I'.]

ME: So, you could say, *"I am aware of this sensation, also."*

EVA: Mm hmm. [Eva exhales.]

ME: So, where's the 'I' that's aware of this?

EVA: ... Above the head. [Her right hand gestures above her head.]

ME: Okay, great. And what's the size and shape?

EVA: [She smiles.] It's like a soccer ball—a half soccer ball.

ME: A half soccer ball. Okay, great. And sensing in and through the space of this, the half soccer ball... What's the sensation quality in and through the space? ... [I hold my arms up around my head mirroring her gestures for the location of the third 'I'.]

EVA: Soft and warm.

ME: Soft and warm. Okay, thank you.

Session Notes: The 3rd 'I'	
Location	*Above the head*
Size & Shape	*Like a half soccer ball*
Sensation Quality	*Soft, warm*

To You/Reader: Now we've found three 'I's. This is usually enough for the Basic Process to work. Nonetheless, I decided to guide Eva in finding one more 'I'. This is because she can find them easily, and finding one more 'I' is likely to make the process get more complete results for her. You'll see how this plays out….

Finding the Fourth 'I'

ME: So, you're aware of this that's a half soccer ball, that's soft and warm, right? … aware of this also… [I'm inviting Eva to attend to the third 'I' now.]

     So, *where's the 'I' that notices this?*… And another way to ask the same question is, *"Where is the perceiving of this happening from?"* [I'm speaking in a soft, gentle tone.]

EVA: [Her body is remarkably still.] … It's in the middle of the head, but it's radiating outside…. Mm hmm. Mm hmm. [Eva gently raises her right arm, bringing the fingers of her right hand together to show the location, and then gracefully opens both arms outward, showing the radiating movement.]

ME: Middle of the head, radiating out.

EVA: Mm hmm. Mm hmm.

ME: Ok, great. And this—in the middle of the head, radiating out—sensing in and through, what is the sensation quality in and through the space of this?

EVA: Light…. It's moving. Very soft, gentle movement. [She speaks slowly and softly, making a slow and elegant figure-eight with her hand.]

ME: Soft, gentle.

EVA: And it's expanding. [Her arms open outward in a flowing movement.]

ME: Okay. Soft, gentle movement, expanding.

To the Group:
And the gentle expanding Eva is experiencing may already be anticipating the next step.

Session Notes: The 4th 'I'	
Location	*Middle of the head*
Size & Shape	*Radiating outward*
Sensation Quality	*Light, soft, gentle movement, expanding*

To You/Reader: Now we've elicited four 'I's. The next phase of this process is to do what I call "integration."

— A Key Concept —

You might have heard the word "integration" used in other kinds of therapy or coaching. In Wholeness Work, "integration" means something a little different. Actually it's quite different. It means something that has been separate, becomes one with the whole. So next we're going to invite each 'I' (which has been a separate structure inside), to dissolve back into the whole field of Awareness. Then the 'I' is no longer a separate structure, but is merged with the Whole. We do this with each 'I', one at a time, as I'll demonstrate now with Eva.

Inviting the Fourth 'I' to Integrate

ME: Now we're going to begin the integration phase. So, *this* ... from the middle of the head, that is light with the soft moving. [I'm drawing Eva's attention to the fourth 'I'.] Check... does the sensation here welcome being invited to open and relax in and as the full field of Awareness? [I begin speaking more slowly and softly to make it easier for the inner processing to happen.]

EVA: … Yes, it's done it already. [A peaceful smile appears as she nods. There is a palpable stillness.]

ME: Okay. Great. Yeah, it's as if it's going, "Can you keep up with me here?" [Eva smiles.]

… Okay, lovely, beautiful…. And so that's already settled? That's complete? [Eva softly nods 'yes.']

To You/Reader: Notice that when I invited Eva's 'I' to integrate, I used a different wording than in the exploration from Chapter 2.

In Chapter 1, on the step inviting integration, I asked you to "Notice what happens <u>when</u> the sensation of the 'I' is invited to open and relax…." Here I'm asking, "<u>Does</u> the sensation of the 'I' <u>welcome</u> being invited…."

This wording change is important. I want to make sure the 'I' doesn't feel pushed to do anything—even slightly. So instead of telling, or inviting, the 'I' to do something, I'm asking if the 'I' *wants* to be invited to do something. There is no imposition, no force. It's a yes/no question, and if the 'I' doesn't *welcome* being invited to integrate, we don't even invite it. Later in this chapter I'll explain what to do if the answer is "no."

— A Key Concept —

Wholeness Work is based on inviting, and not pushing for any change if it's not fully welcome. This is to make sure that this process happens in a gentle way that her system welcomes. This gentle and "absolutely no force" approach is essential for changes at the deep level we're working with. This is what allows the changes to become both deep and lasting.

Inviting the Third 'I' to Integrate

ME: Okay. So now we go back the way we came. The fourth 'I' has integrated, so now we go to the third 'I'. The one that before was in the location above the head.

EVA: Mm hmm. [Her eyes are closed and body is still. She appears deeply engaged in the process.]

ME: What is there now? Is it the same, or a little different?

EVA: [She pauses to check.] … It already dissolved.

ME: Okay. It already dissolved…. So just in case anything is remaining, even at the unconscious level, I'd like to invite your Being to sense in and through the area… and if anything is remaining … this is also invited to open, relax, dissolve, melt … as the full field of Awareness….

… And what's the experience of that?

EVA: Hmm… I am… my upper body up to here is covered in light. [She gestures showing the area covered in light.]

Inviting the Second 'I' to Integrate

ME: Okay… So now we go to the one before that which was inside the head—this film on the back of the head. Checking there now, what's there now? Is it the same or is it different?

EVA: [Eva sighs, then pauses to check.] … I can sense it a little bit, but it has partly dissolved.

ME: Yes. Okay… And this is very interesting, because sometimes when the last 'I' dissolves, the 'I's before it also change quite a bit. They begin integrating on their own.

So, let's make sure that everything is included. Anything remaining … the sensation of whatever is there now can also be kindly invited to also open, relax, dissolve, melt….

EVA: [Smiles peacefully.]

ME: … Because it's just like when the physical hand is in a fist, and the Awareness comes through, the relaxing just wants to happen. And that's what's occurring here. These 'I's were totally unconscious … but as they come into consciousness, and Awareness comes into the location, there's this natural inclination to dissolve. [I speak slowly and softly to support the integrating that's happening, as Eva looks increasingly more relaxed.]

Inviting the First 'I' to Integrate

ME: So now we go to the place that was in the head behind the eyes. And what's there now? Is it the same or is it a little different?

EVA: … It's all one.

ME: It's gone?

EVA: Mm hmm…. It's all one.

ME: We can just invite the system, in case there are any remnants of anything, even at the unconscious level … it can be invited to also open, relax, dissolve, melt.

EVA: [Eva sighs, her body relaxing even more.]

ME: … Yeah. And you can just take your time with that, and when things settle you can let me know….

EVA: [Eyes closed, body very relaxed and still, Eva nods.]

Inviting the Original Feeling Response to Integrate

ME: Okay, so now we go to the place we started—that chest area—and notice, what's there now? Is it the same? Is it a little different?

EVA: It's changed, but there's still some pressure left.

ME: Okay. So, it's changed but definitely something still there.

EVA: [Nods, eyes closed.]

ME: So kindly sense what remains. It's almost as if the field of Awareness is sensing … and let's invite the sensation here—how it is now—this is also invited to open and relax, in and as the fullness of Awareness.

EVA: [Breathes deeply, then smiles.]

ME: Yeah.

EVA: [Her body releases more with another exhale, and a soft smile appears.]

ME: And really letting that go how it goes. And when these releases happen, we can just … it's sort of a bowing to it … just letting it happen in its own way. It's not something we need to do anything about. It just happens … Yeah.

EVA: … Good. [Eyes closed, nodding and smiling warmly. Her expression shows the beautiful change that has taken place in her through this session.]

Checking in the Original Situation

ME: Okay. And so now we just do a check … Being this way, with these 'I's integrated, and the original feeling integrated … Being this way … what is it like now when you think of this person doing this thing?

EVA: [She looks relaxed, and bursts out in laughter.] I will be happy about it!

ME: Okay. [I'm smiling.] Maybe you can tell him to do it a little more so you can have a good time. [I laugh along with Eva, playfully suggesting she encourage him to do more of what used to irritate her.] Isn't that interesting?

EVA: Yeah … Yeah. That's great.

ME: And if you would like, you can imagine him doing this thing again, and just notice how it is now, in a few situations.

EVA: [She laughs and seems amused.] I will have many moments to experience this. [Eva means that since she worked with something that happens frequently, she'll experience her new response frequently.]

ME: Yes, lots of opportunities to have fun with this.

EVA: Yeah.

ME: **To the Group:**
So, this is quite lovely, how she is demonstrating this exercise for us.
[To Eva] Thank you so very much.

EVA: Thank you. [She dips her head showing her appreciation.]

Full Session Notes: Wholeness Work Basic Process Demo	
Beginning Experience	
Location	*In the chest (filling but smaller than the chest)*
Size & Shape	*Like a blob*
Sensation Quality	*Heavy, soft*

First 'I'	
Location	*In the head (behind the eyes)*
Size & Shape	*Like a cloud*
Sensation Quality	*Heavy, soft*

Second 'I'	
Location	*Back of head (like a projection screen)*
Size & Shape	*Very thin (wrapping around the head)*
Sensation Quality	*Almost transparent, flat, like glass, sparkling*

Third 'I'	
Location	*Above the head*
Size & Shape	*Like a half soccer ball*
Sensation Quality	*Soft, warm*

Fourth 'I'	
Location	*Middle of the head*
Size & Shape	*Radiating outward*
Sensation Quality	*Light, soft, gentle movement, expanding*

The Results for Eva—and What it Might Mean for You

Watching Eva's nonverbal expressions, I could see she'd experienced a change, and her words confirmed this. Something irritating has become a non-issue, and even a source of humor—in Eva's words, "fun."

This might seem surprising, but I've experienced something similar many times doing the Wholeness Work. I used this process regularly in the relationship that mattered most to me: my relationship with my husband. Any time I felt irritated or hurt by something, I guided myself through this process and it gradually made a huge change in our relationship.

Instead of always taking things "seriously," or feeling like I was being "put upon," or that I needed to take a stand and set boundaries, often I ended up finding the whole thing funny. I found myself teasing him about things that used to bother me. And he started teasing me back. We could playfully deal with these issues which we now recognized were really rather minor.

I want to be clear… If you choose to use the Wholeness Work with your relationship issues—and I hope you do—your experience might be quite different. What you can count on is a positive shifting of some kind—some way of coming into a better balance for *you*. We become clearer about what really matters to us. Some things we realize we DO need to speak up about. I had some of those, too. And after using Wholeness Work with my emotional hot buttons, it became easier to set boundaries and speak for myself from a place of kindness and clarity, rather than judgment or outrage. This made it easier for my husband to hear me and take me seriously, without feeling criticized or judged.

Other times what seemed "charged" before no longer pushes our buttons. We might even find it funny. It's a special kind of humor. We're not laughing *at* anyone—we're laughing *with* them. It's as if we're all in on the cosmic joke now. We get our human frailties; we get the universality of it. We get that it's not serious in the way we thought it was, and it's kind of funny how we each can get caught in it.

Understanding the Endpoint

I'd like to talk about the "endpoint" of this process—if we can even call it that.

When you get to the end of this process, your response might be quite different from Eva's, and that's fine. With Wholeness Work, whatever your experience is each step of the way—and at the end— is fine. In fact it's just perfect.

If I start with an irritation, at the end I might discover, "Oh...I'm not irritated anymore; now I'm feeling more resourceful." But what if I discover, "I'm not irritated anymore, but now I'm feeling sad."— or some other emotion. This is also totally fine. This lets me know the work with the irritation is complete. And it reveals that my next piece to work with is the sadness. I would then cycle through the same process, with the sadness as the beginning point.

In this example, we could say that initially the irritation was covering up the sadness, so I wasn't even aware of it. Integrating the irritation lets me notice the sadness, which was there all along. And now that I can notice it, I can include this feeling also in my work, so that I reach a full resolution.

So whatever feeling or thought response you work with initially, that might be all there is to it in the situation. If there's more, the Wholeness Work makes this easy for us to notice.

Sharing Experiences

When I listen to other people sharing what happened for them when they did a Wholeness exercise, it activates something within me and makes it easier for me to discover and allow the experience that's right for me in the moment. Maybe that will happen for you, too.

Here are a few examples of what participants in my trainings have shared. These are typical experiences, yet I admit I did pick some of the strongest ones. If you don't notice much the first time (or first few times) you try this, it's fine. You're not alone. For me personally, the results at first were really, really subtle—almost imperceptible. Then, the more I did this process, the more they began adding up. It took a while for me, but it was worth it.

Examples of what others have noticed...

Evan: *The situation I picked was someone cutting in front of me in line. When this happens I (used to) sort of lose it—You know, "How could they!" After doing this I feel pretty neutral. It's not a big deal.*

Claire: *It was a wonderful experience. It's incredible that looking back at that situation, it really has no charge. It's amazing how relaxing doing this can make you feel—just so much lighter.*

Taylor: *What surprised me most is how the original feeling completely changed. I was feeling tense and plugged in. And after doing this I felt how much fun it is in that situation. So I could react completely differently.*

Lena: *I've always found it irritating when my husband speaks to me in a certain tone of voice. It's like he's looking down on me or judging me or something. So I worked with that. Now when I think about it, it just seems kind of amusing. I could almost call it "sweet." He's just being him, I guess, and it doesn't offend me.*

Wilson: *I've been doing this over the last couple of days. I'm finding it's very easy with fear. Anything I'm afraid of, it seems to just fall apart and dissolve.*

Rhonda: *It was an extraordinary experience. The third 'I' was hesitating about integrating, so we found the fourth one. And it was a very interesting because it was a gigantic space. And then we did the relaxation, and it was incredibly beautiful. It was like melting and expansive. And it's just really a very profound mystical experience. It was really special.*

Lee: *It was pretty profound. A testament to the process, because my partner for this exercise and I were both pretty inexperienced, but it ended up going quite smoothly. I had one 'I' that was light, and fluffy. And one that was really dense, and I didn't think it was going to dissolve. And I feel like giving the time and maybe repeating it back once or twice, slowly, [helped].... I listened to you [Connirae]. And you said, "speak slowly." And it didn't feel like it was going to dissolve, but it did, actually.*

flowchart
the basic process

Here's a simple illustration that shows you the steps and flow of the Basic Format in one picture.

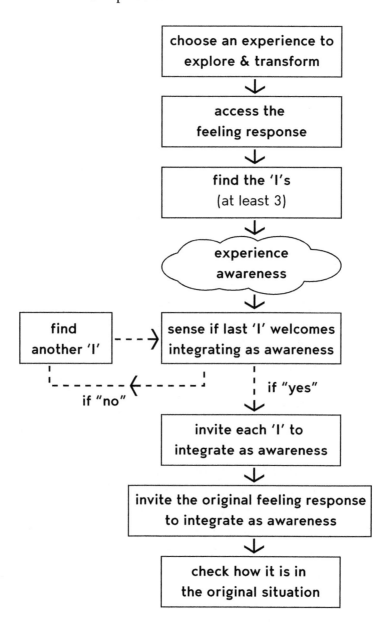

step-by-step guide
the basic process

Are you ready to try it yourself?[4] Simply read each step below, and pause after each instruction in italics; then, close your eyes and experience that step.

Then notice whatever answer comes to you.

 Do you want to jot down brief notes for each answer you get as I did when guiding Eva? Use this QR code to print a worksheet for *this* process or go to www. thewholenesswork.org/BookResources.

Step 1. Choose an experience to explore.
Pick an issue or difficult experience that's medium to mild in intensity. Choose something that pushes your buttons a little, but you know it doesn't really hurt anyone or cause harm. [It's important to pick something minor your first time through!]

Step 2. Step in and access the feeling response.
Imagine it's happening now, and notice how you feel in response.... [For example: "I feel irritated," or "I feel hurt," or "… sad," etc.]

- *Notice where this feeling response is located. [It might be in your belly somewhere. It could be in your chest. It could even be partly inside your body and partly outside. It could be anywhere.]*
- *Notice the size & shape.*
- *Now sense in and through this area, and notice the sensation quality.*

There might be a sense of heaviness, pressure, vibration, fizziness, or bubbling. It might be warm or cool. [It may be something you can't put into words, and that's fine. Just notice the sensation that's there....]
And what sensation do you notice?

---

[4] If you want to watch a demonstration before you try it yourself, you can find a short demo at the very end of this free video training: [www.andreasnlp.com/resources/free-wholeness-intro-video/. Go right to time code 46:39.]

Step 3. Find the 'I'.

Now you could say, "I am aware of this sensation." [The sensation you noticed in Step 2.]

- *And "Where is the 'I' that is aware of this sensation?" Where is this 'I' located?...* [Notice whatever location comes to mind. It might be somewhere in your head or body, or outside your head or body somewhere....]
- *And what is the size & shape of this 'I'?*
- *Sensing in and through this area [of the 'I'], what is the sensation quality in and through this area?*

    [It might be foggy, clear, dense, or empty; heavy, light, vibrate-y, still, and so on. If no words quite describe it, that's OK. You can just notice the sensation itself.]

Step 4. Find the Second and Third 'I's (the 'I' Chain).

Now, you could say... "I am aware of this [_sensation quality of previous 'I'_] sensation, here in [_location of previous 'I'_]," right?

- *So "Where is the 'I' that notices this?" Another way of asking the question is "Where is the perceiving happening from?"*
- *And what's the size & shape of this 'I'?*
- *And sensing into this area that's [_location of the 'I'_], what is the sensation quality in and through this area?*

Repeat Step 4 to find a Third 'I'.

Now check the sensation quality of the third 'I':

If it's fairly airy or diffuse and insubstantial, go to Step Five.

If it's still quite dense and substantial, then repeat Step Four to find another 'I' until you get to an 'I' that's less dense or substantial. Then go to Step Five.

Step 5. Experience Awareness.

Now take a moment to experience Awareness.... Right now, you can easily sense in and through your body, so Awareness is present throughout your body.... And if a sound happened on one side of you, you would hear it automatically, without effort.... If a sound happened on the other side, you'd also be aware of it without effort.... And even if your eyes are closed, it's easy to have a sense of the space that's all around.... Awareness is this effortless capacity to notice, which is throughout the body, and all around ... and there isn't really any edge or end to it.

And you can experience this all, simultaneously, right now....

Step 6. Sense if the last 'I' welcomes integrating with Awareness.
Now return your attention to the last 'I' that you found.

Sensing again the sensation quality in and through this 'I', check: "Does the sensation of this 'I' welcome the invitation to open and relax, in and as the fullness of Awareness?" [It doesn't matter if the answer is "yes" or "no." This just lets you know what to do next.]

If "Yes": Go on to Step 7.

If "No": This means you need to find another 'I'. Here's how:

You just noticed that the sensation [of the last 'I'] doesn't want to open and relax, right?

- *So "Where is the 'I' that notices this?" ... Where is the perceiving of this happening from?*
- *And what is the size & shape?*
- *And what is the sensation quality in and through this area?*

Now you've found the next 'I', so next you check if this 'I' welcomes integrating.

- *Check inside... Does the sensation here [_in the location of this 'I'_], welcome the invitation to open and relax, in and as the fullness of Awareness that's all around and throughout?*

You can continue finding another 'I', until you get to an 'I' that welcomes being invited to integrate with Awareness. Then go on to Step 7.

Step 7. Invite each 'I' to integrate with Awareness.
With this 'I' that welcomes integrating ... Notice what happens when the sensation of the 'I' is invited to open and relax ... in and as the fullness of Awareness, that's all around and throughout.... There can

be a gentle sensing into the sensation in this location, and an allowing the opening and relaxing to happen in its own way. You aren't really doing anything—just sensing how it occurs on its own, without effort. (If you are experiencing a relaxing, melting, or dissolving, just stay with it until things settle. Enjoy the sense of relaxation, peace or flow as long as you like.)

Next, invite each previous 'I' to integrate. You'll do this one at a time, in reverse order. So you start with the last 'I' elicited, then the next-to-last, and so on.

Here are the steps:

- *Check in the location of the previous 'I' you found. Notice what's present in this location now. Is it the same as it was before or a little bit different? Either is fine. Just notice however it is now.* [It might be the same as before, or it might have changed in some way. For example, it might be more airy now, less dense, or a bit expanded.]
- *Now notice what happens when the sensation quality present now is invited to open and relax ... in and as the fullness of Awareness, that's all around and throughout ... There can be an allowing of it to happen in its own way.* [Allow all the time you need for things to settle.]

Now repeat the previous two bullet points with each 'I' in the chain, until all the 'I's have been invited to integrate.

Step 8. Invite the original feeling response to integrate with Awareness.

- *Now gently return your attention to the location of the original feeling response (from Step 2). Is the sensation here the same as it was before? Or is it a little bit different? (It's fine if it's the same or different, just notice how it is now.)*
- *Notice what happens when the sensation here now is invited to open and relax ... in and as the fullness of Awareness ... that's throughout the body and all around.*

- *Now there can be an allowing of whatever happens. You can enjoy this experience as long as happens.*

Step 9. Check how it is now in the original situation.
Being this way, with the 'I's dissolved, and the original feeling dissolved, what is it like now, when you imagine being in whatever situation you were working with?

** A Visual Representation of the Basic Process **

Here are two examples of finding the 'I's. Each 'I' can be located inside the body, or outside; it can be anywhere.

three ways
your experience
might change

Here are the three most common ways your experience might change from doing this exercise...

You might feel neutral. When you think of the person doing "that thing," your response is just "ho hum" now—hardly worth noticing.

Your initial feeling is resolved, but now you're aware of a different emotion. For example, if you initially felt irritated, perhaps you now feel sad. This is a step forward. It means the first feeling is fully transformed, and this makes it possible for you to notice if there's another emotional response related to this same trigger. Now you can easily "get to" this response as well, so it can also be transformed and healed. If a second emotion is present, you can just cycle through the Basic Process again, starting with the new emotional response.

You might feel more compassion toward the other person. You might experience a felt sense of understanding them more—or spontaneously accepting, even loving them a little more fully, including their foibles, rather than being annoyed by them. When it happens through Wholeness Work, it's not something we have to try to do or to "practice." It just happens naturally.

— A Key Concept —

You don't need to *try* to have any particular response. Just notice the response you have. The Wholeness Work helps us become ever more whole and kind and compassionate, starting with ourselves, then often flowing (naturally) outward to others, too. But it begins with kindness to ourselves. This mean we "get" that our responses are just fine; we can acknowledge, include, and love whatever our real responses are, each step of the way.

tips

Finding the 'I'
If it doesn't feel easy to find the 'I', here are several tips that might help…

It's okay to guess. I've noticed that if I "just guess," often I can go forward more easily. And often something useful and relaxing happens, even if I was "only guessing."

Realize that the 'I' you find might be "invisible"—it might be just a sense of space, rather than something you can see, like we see objects in the outside world. If we're expecting to find something "visible" or "tangible," we might miss the fact that our attention does go to a certain location in space, when we ask, "Where's the 'I'?" So if the answer you get is just a sense of space, that's totally fine.

You'll find more tips for "finding the 'I' in the book, *Coming to Wholeness: How to Awaken and Live with Ease.*

Language and Pace

In a recent training, several people shared these insights after doing this first exercise. I'm offering them here in case you find them useful.

"The language in the script was very helpful. Especially the reminder of allowing the opening and relaxing to happen in its own way, that you're not really doing anything, just sensing how it occurs on its own without effort. I can see I've had the habit of *trying* to do it. And hearing that language each time allowed me to let go more and to see how it happened."

"I found it extremely helpful to go slowly, and just let each 'I' be felt in a gentle way, sensing the 'I's, connecting with the texture. I've never done this before, and that helps a lot. My partner and I probably spent a couple of minutes sensing and describing the 'I', and it made all the difference. And hearing my partner repeat it back to me helped to fully connect with it. I really enjoyed it…."

integrating
the limited self
understanding what we're doing

Now that you've experienced the Wholeness Work Basic Process at least once, you might be curious to understand more about this process. How does it work and why is it effective? Here are some of additional insights you might find helpful.

The Fist upon Fist Metaphor

In Chapter 2, I talked about how the 'I's we find inside are like a hand contracted into a fist. They're a contraction of consciousness.

In this chapter you've learned how to find a Chain of 'I's. Often the first 'I' we find isn't actually in a position to integrate. You can get a picture of what's happening inside by making your right hand into a fist in front of you. Then use your left hand to grasp firmly around your right fist. Now you have two fists, the second one surrounding the first. In this position, the first fist can't open and relax, even if it wants to.

This is similar to the Chain of 'I's we find inside. It's functionally like this, not physically. The next 'I' isn't usually physically surrounding the first 'I'. It could be located anywhere. However the next layer of 'I' *functions* to hold the first one in place. The first one can't release until the "outer layer" goes first, and has opened and dissolved into Awareness.

This is why this process is more powerful and easier to use. We don't try to convince an 'I' to open and relax into Awareness. If it can't or won't easily do this on its own, we simply find another 'I'.

The Value of Finding the Chain of 'I's

It was an important discovery to recognize that most people have Chains of 'I's inside—not just one 'I'. As I mentioned a moment ago, the "outer layers" of 'I' often hold the first 'I' we find in place. So finding the Chain of 'I's is what makes this significant transformation possible—and easy.

Even if the first 'I' *IS* able to integrate, there's usually value in finding the Chain of 'I's, because…

The first 'I' usually integrates more completely when our "outer layers" of 'I' have already dissolved into Awareness.

When more 'I's integrate, more of us relaxes. More constrictions of consciousness are able to release back into the whole of our consciousness. And this matters! Often these "outer layers" of 'I' releasing really makes a difference in our fully accessing "just being present as Awareness." Each 'I' that we find inside, is a source of unconscious stress/effort. So each 'I' that releases back into the whole means we have a deeper inner calm that's just present.

Why do we ask for three layers of 'I'?

In this Basic Process, I ask you to find three layers of 'I' because...

Sometimes an earlier layer will say "yes" it's willing to integrate even if it's a bit reluctant.

By getting the Chain of 'I's, we are including some more pervasive and significant layers of inner contraction. We could describe this as a "higher" level of generalization, but that doesn't fully describe it. You can discover this for yourself by noticing what it's like when you find a few "layers of 'I'" instead of just one. Does this make the change feel stronger for you?

If you find more layers, the change will most likely be more profound and/or significant.

How do you know how many 'I's to get?

After doing this with many people, I noticed that if the 'I' is open, airy, and not dense, it will usually welcome integrating. So I'm having you begin by asking for three 'I's. If the third 'I' is "open and airy," i.e., "not dense," then you can go to the Integration Phase and find out if it welcomes integrating.

If the third 'I' is fairly dense, then ask for another 'I' until you come to one that is less dense/more open and airy. Usually this means finding three to five 'I's.

On rare occasion someone can't find any more 'I's after the first one or two. If this happens, you can go to the Integration Step.

Here's an exception to be aware of: once in a while—even though someone has already found six or seven layers of 'I's—the 'I's are still quite dense. If this happens, you can shift to asking if the sensation of that last 'I' found wants to try integrating even a little bit. Experimenting with a beginning experience of integration can sometimes work better than continuing to find more layers of 'I's.

answering your questions

If you have questions about this process or are curious about what people frequently ask in my trainings, read this segment now. Or, you can return to these Q &A's later to explore a specific question or to deepen your understanding of Wholeness Work.

Emotions vs. Sensation Quality

Q When I sensed into the 'I', it was angry. Is that the sensation quality?

A Sometimes when people check for the sensation quality, they first notice an emotional quality, like "angry" or "sad" or "hurt." If an emotional quality is present, then it's important to begin by acknowledging whatever emotional quality you notice. This feels kind to the system. Then the next step is to let go of this word, for example "angry," and allow a sensing of the sensation itself. When you let go of the word "angry," then the sensation is easier to notice. Perhaps there's a roughness or smoothness. Is it dense, or sort of airy? Is there a warmth or coolness to it? This is the sensation quality. And it's important to shift from the emotional quality to noticing the sensation quality. This is what makes it possible to do the next step of integrating with Awareness.

Emotion words such as "angry," sad," or "afraid," are actually interpretations of our experience. With Wholeness Work, we shift from the emotional label, to noticing the sensation itself. In the Resources Section of this book, you'll find a chart with examples of "Sensation Quality" words vs. "Meaning/Interpretation" words. See my previous book, *Coming to Wholeness,* Chapter 11, for a full chapter on recognizing the difference between "meaning/interpretation" words, and "sensation quality" words, and how to shift to sensation quality.

Flat vs. 3-D

Q The 'I' I found is flat. It's like a flat sheet of paper. So there isn't really anything to sense in and through for the sensation quality. Should I just notice the sensation of the surface? The surface is kind of smooth.

A I understand that it appears flat. However, in Wholeness Work everything is actually 3-D. In the outer world we live in, everything is three-dimensional. A sheet of paper is thin, but we're living in a 3-D world, so it does have a certain thickness to it. When we do Wholeness Work, we discover that everything in our inner world is also three-dimensional. This 'I' that looks like a sheet of paper appears to be quite thin, yet it does have a certain thickness to it. So if you pause and gently sense into this that's thin yet still has a thickness—it's possible to begin sensing something more. It can be useful to start by sensing the smoothness of the surface as you already have... And then you can go beyond this, and sense in and through this very thin structure ... to begin sensing this space ... And if it's not easy to do this consciously, then there can just be the intention of sensing in and through this very thin space ... the intention to register, to notice the sensation quality that's in and through the space.

Organs of the Body

Q What if the 'I' is my eyes, or my brain, or my heart?

A The 'I' is never going to be exactly the same size and shape as an organ of the physical body. So if it seems to be your "eyes," your "brain," your "heart," or some other physical organ, check inside again and notice how it might be a little different. If it seems to be "my brain," you can check: might the experience of this 'I' actually be a little larger or smaller than the physical brain? Might it be a little farther forward or a little farther back? Or a little to the right or the left? If you check in this way, this will help you attend to what we want to attend to for this process. It isn't about a physical organ.

We might call this a more "energetic" experience, one that happens to be located with some overlap to a part of the body.

The same is true for a beginning feeling. We are exploring our subjective experience, and this is very unlikely to be exactly the same as the size and shape of a physical organ.

A Memory or Feeling Comes Up

Q When my 'I' dissolved, a memory from my childhood came up. Is this OK? Do I need to do anything?

A Sometimes when an 'I' dissolves, a memory or a feeling emerges. That's fine— even good. The memory or emotional response is likely related to the 'I' that just released. So as the 'I' releases, the memory and emotional response are also emerging to dissolve and integrate. You don't need to understand it. It doesn't need to make sense. Just welcome it and let this, as sensation, also dissolve into the field of Awareness that is you. All of it can be kindly included.

And, with any kind of inner work, sometimes people remember something that they aren't sure if actually happened. Fortunately, when we do this process, we don't need to know whether a memory happened or if it's more like a dream, that our unconscious presents that may have symbolic meaning. Either way, it can be included in the process.

Starting Feeling Doesn't Integrate

Q At the end, what if the starting feeling doesn't integrate?

A Once the 'I's are merged with Awareness, usually the original feeling you were working with welcomes integrating. Sometimes it even starts happening on its own. However, if it feels difficult or unwanted, it's important to pause. This means something else needs to happen first. Here are two things you can do…

You can find a second Chain of 'I's. Sometimes there's another Chain of 'I's related to the starting feeling and holding it in place. So you can explore what happens if you just cycle through the same process again and notice what chain of 'I's emerges this time.

You can check if there's a reaction happening. (See the section in the Wholeness Meditation Chapter called "What about distracting thoughts and feelings?")

With Wholeness Work, we never try to make something happen. This process is all about gentleness and relaxing of force, not adding force. In the trainings we teach how to respond to each situation so that:

Using this process feels kind and gentle.

You can find the place in your inner world where change is welcome.

"Nothing much happened," or "It was intense!"

Q What if I don't feel anything happening?

Sometimes the experience of integrating is quite subtle—almost imperceptible. Other times the experience feels strong and powerful. Both are totally fine. You can trust that your system will do what's the best fit for you—and your inner structure— in the moment. There are reasons why some integrations are almost imperceptible and others strong. But that doesn't matter for the moment. What matters is to know that even when the integrating is almost imperceptible, something useful is shifting in your mind/body system.

Q What if the integrating is intense? Is this OK?

Most people experience some integrations as "mild" and others as "strong" or intense. If you do the Wholeness Work as a daily practice, you're likely to experience some of each. A more intense integration might feel like a burst of heat, or vibrating, or waves of energy or light flowing through the body. When an integration feels strong, be sure to give your system plenty of time to allow the release happening to flow through and settle. Of course, it can be helpful to check in with a trained guide if you have any questions or concerns.

— A Key Concept —

As a reminder, if we're using the Wholeness Work in the gentle and kind way intended, always allowing what "wants to happen," and never forcing, we learn to increasingly trust our body/mind system to integrate naturally so that our overall body/mind system becomes more relaxed, unconstructed, and whole.

An 'I' is already integrated

Q After inviting the last 'I' to integrate, I checked with the next-to-last 'I' and it was gone. What do I do?

A This happened in the demonstration with Eva. After Eva's fourth 'I' had integrated, when she checked the third 'I' it was gone. Nothing was there. Sometimes this happens. It's as if that final 'I' was the only thing holding one or more of the remaining 'I's in place.

 If that happens I like to still invite *"anything that may be remaining"* to also dissolve and melt into the whole of Awareness. You may remember I did that when I guided Eva in the demonstration. (See "Inviting the third 'I' to integrate.")

Should the "integration" always go through the space all around?

Q When I invited the beginning feeling to integrate, it seemed to flow through my body, but not through the space around me. Is that OK?

A Yes, that's fine. It's good to allow it to go however it goes. Each time you do a Wholeness Work exercise, your experience of integration is likely to be a little different. Sometimes you might experience the integration primarily through the body; other times the dissolving might happen mostly outside the physical body. Sometimes it might flow through the body and the space close around the body; other times there might be a dissolving and flowing that spreads through the wider space all around. An emotional feeling is more likely to integrate through the body, and possibly beyond the body. There's no need to push it to be anything more or different than it is.

Do you always need to do Step 5, experience Awareness?

Q In the demonstration with Eva, you skipped Step 5, "Experience Awareness." Why?

A The reason for Step 5 is that pausing to experience Awareness can make it easier for the 'I' to dissolve into this spacious presence that's all around in every direction. When I guided Eva, she had already just experienced a detailed exploration of Awareness in class with me and the group. So I knew that the experience of Awareness was already fresh for her, and it would likely be easy for her to experience it again.

When you guide yourself in this method, I encourage you to pause to experience Awareness, at least the first few times. After that you can just notice if doing Step 5 continues to add something for you.

What Are Your Questions?

If you encounter something different and you're not sure what to do, here are some suggestions...

First, know that there is always an "easy way" to work with whatever you find. Learning Wholeness Work is like learning to walk. There may be challenges at first, but each one of us learns to walk easily and effortlessly. This will happen for you with Wholeness Work as well if you stay with it.

You may find the answer to your situation in one of the next chapters in this book. The Wholeness Work is simple—yet there's a lot of subtlety to it. My goal is to pack this book with as much useful information as I can. I'm offering it to you in the sequence that most of my clients and workshop participants have found effective. However, each of us is unique, and you might need something *now* that's in a later chapter.

You can also join a Wholeness Work training. In the live trainings I can answer your questions as they arise, and trained coaches help you adapt the process to your needs. You can also contact a Wholeness Coach to help you one-on-one.

important distinctions

Occasionally people tell me, "I really like Wholeness Work… and it reminds me so much of Carl Rogers', or Virginia Satir's, or so-and-so's work." I consider this a big compliment because I admire both Carl Rogers and Virginia Satir. Having had the opportunity to meet them both and watch them work, I respect that their work came from a place of deep kindness and respect for each person. Both Carl Rogers and Virginia Satir beautifully embodied this kindness, and many spiritual teachers do as well.

Because adults often learn by connecting new information to what they already know, noticing similarities in philosophies or methodologies is natural. And, yet I think you'll get the most benefit from Wholeness Work if you come to it with a completely open mind. I'm going to encourage you, as much as possible, to start fresh.

So I invite you to consider how Wholeness Work as a system and practice is different—how it's unique from the methods that have come before. Wholeness Work includes several breakthroughs, which if you use them to their fullest, can help you get deeper, more complete, kinder, and gentler change. The more you understand the full Wholeness Work system, the more you can get this benefit in ways that deeply honor you, and help you experience your natural essence, which is and always was, beautiful. Here are the main breakthroughs we've covered so far.

Wholeness Work actually locates the ego or small "self."
Spiritual teachings from many traditions tell us that human suffering is the result of the "ego." Many philosophies refer to the ego as the "small self," because when we experience ourselves as our ego, we aren't experiencing the fullness of who we really are. These traditions also tell us that when the ego dissolves, our human suffering also melts away.

Wholeness Work gives you a precise way to actually do this:

You can actually *find* the 'I' or the ego in your experience.

We have a specific way to invite it to dissolve, so that you can begin experiencing the fullness of your being—experience yourself as the full field of Awareness that you are.

And going beyond this is the discovery that there are actually multiple small selves within each of us. You can find the entire Chain of 'I's.

Including this Chain of 'I's is also a breakthrough in being able to transform and heal inner division in an easy and kind way. When the first 'I' doesn't easily dissolve, we can just find the next one. Each transformation of a small "self" within feels nourishing, relaxing, and freeing, and brings us to ever-greater wellbeing.

These are not small discoveries. As I've been preparing this book for you, more than ever I have a deep appreciation of and respect for the method itself. And, I feel a sense of awe for what these methods lead us to discover within each of us.

We really are zeroing in on the "science" of a very special and significant kind of shift in consciousness. There is a precision behind each step in the processes you'll learn in this book. Learning the science behind the "magic" can make it possible for Awakening to become accessible to us all.

Each component of this work adds something valuable. Taken altogether it's quite a complete roadmap to your own blossoming, to your own wellbeing, to your own happiness.

Wholeness Work is gentle—we don't need force.
Essential to the Wholeness Work is the principle of "no force." This means it's something that each of us needs to intentionally choose to do. Only you can decide if you want to take on the practice and enjoy the benefits.

Wholeness Work is a deep way to transform limiting beliefs.
People recognize that beliefs are important. Limiting beliefs can… well, keep us limited. What might not be obvious is that Wholeness Work—by its nature—transforms our limiting beliefs. This is because the 'I's inside always contain limiting beliefs about ourselves,

and/or the world around us. So every time we find an 'I' inside and invite it to dissolve, limiting beliefs are dissolving along with the 'I'.

An added benefit is that we don't even need to consciously identify what our limiting beliefs are. When we notice something that troubles us and find the related 'I' Chain, we will also automatically be finding the 'I's containing the limiting beliefs that have an impact on the quality of our life.

Here's another interesting thing to understand about beliefs: Even "positive beliefs" involve some inner rigidity. They involve forming a fixed view of things—and in some sense imposing this fixed view on "reality." With Wholeness Work there's no need to replace a limiting belief with a positive belief. When the 'I's dissolve, we have greater capacity to experience "life as it is." We have less need to define ourselves and others around us. We become increasingly flexible and able to be present, and respond from this presence and kindness to whatever situation we are in.

And the beauty is that we never have to talk ourselves into changing. It's a natural and easy process—the feeling is of me being more of who I already am.

Wholeness Work dissolves distortions—the unconscious filters that color our experience.

As we grow up, dealing with our unique life challenges, we unconsciously create filters on life. It's almost as if our early life experiences lead us to look at life through clouded lenses or glasses, that we didn't realize we were wearing. Our current experience can literally become tinted by things that happened in our earlier years, or distorted in other ways. This is natural and perhaps was even useful for us to do at the time.

However, now as adults, it's also extremely useful to be able to release these distortions, and filters. And it's the 'I's we find inside that maintain these distortions. So when the 'I's relax, our distorted views of life naturally fall away. Some clients and workshop participants tell me, "It's as if the air is clearer now." You may experience your own unique shifts. Doing Wholeness Work allows us to more easily "see things as they are."

And the good news is that it's a relief. It's so much better than looking through those clouded glasses. We begin to know at a visceral level that we are already completely ok, and our true essence is something that can never be damaged. We gradually begin to experience that "we are love." We come to the kind of insights people sometimes gain from deep meditation experiences, or from psychedelic drug trips when those go well. We gain a feeling of being at peace, and a knowing that everything is fine. A wellbeing that just *is*.

the spiritual side
& psychology side

Wholeness Work brings psychological healing and spiritual development.
In almost every class I teach, someone comes to me and says, "I'm a long-time spiritual seeker, and I love this! You're providing a way to actually do what spiritual teachers talk about. You're offering a reliable path."

There are ways Wholeness Work offers us something valuable both from the psychology side and from the spiritual side. Here's a quick recap.

From the Spiritual Side, we discover...

The 'I' actually exists. It's something we can locate in our psyche. And we need to, otherwise we "bypass" our actual experience.

There are multiple 'I's. What's called the ego is not one thing. We need to know this to actually dissolve the ego and experience "awakening."

It's not about ignoring or bypassing these 'I's by telling ourselves, "Those aren't 'real' anyway." It's about reclaiming the energy that's currently being used to form and maintain these 'I's. This energy is part of our aliveness. It's good. It's positive. True spiritual development happens when we reclaim this energy, not get rid of it.

From the Psychology Side...

Instead of trying to change our troublesome feelings, we dissolve the experience of separate self that has been holding the feeling response in place. When we find the 'I's related to our emotional issues, the change process is easier, kinder, and more complete. The 'I's are what have been holding our stress and our problem issues in place.

We are integrating the 'I's with the full field of Awareness, rather than leaving parts remaining as separate structures inside, or just merging two "parts" with each other. This results in a more profound and complete change.

If you did the exercise in this chapter, you may already have begun to experience how the Wholeness Work's Basic Process can lead to a dissolving of tension and stress.

This method offers a breakthrough in our ability to dissolve stress and release ourselves from a lot of drama and suffering in our lives.

Now let's go farther ... Are you ready to take the next step? Join me in the next chapter to explore how to use the Wholeness Work Meditation Format as a daily practice or a quick, in-the-moment method to "refresh and reset."

CHAPTER 4

THE MEDITATION FORMAT

Resetting Your Mind-Body System

In this chapter you'll learn the Wholeness Work Meditation Format. We can also call this the Present Moment Practice. You'll discover how your present moment experience—whatever is happening for you right now—can become a doorway to deep relaxation and a gentle resetting of your nervous system.

Thousands of people have used this practice to transform any daily stress and have come to an experience of peaceful presence and resilience. And I continue to use it for my own wellbeing. This simple practice can be surprisingly effective, even in the midst of significant turmoil in the outer world. I hope you will try it and discover for yourself how it's possible to find "peace within," even when we have challenging life circumstances—even when there isn't "peace without."

You don't need a life issue to get results.
If you've been in personal growth for a long time, continually finding another issue to work with can start to feel like "work." With the Meditation Format, you don't even need to think of an issue to work with. Yet this simple life practice offers more than relaxation—it helps us grow, evolve, and change for the better.

A Restorative Process that Fits into Your Life

The Meditation Format gives you a relaxing and restorative process that you can benefit from even if you only have five minutes. Maybe you're waiting in a checkout line at a grocery store or in another context where you have just a short amount of time. And of course, if you choose to use the process for a longer time, maybe 20 minutes or half an hour, then it becomes richer. So, it's up to you when and how you do this life practice. Do it for a few minutes or a longer time depending on your mood, and you'll receive cumulative benefits.

A Practice That Makes Meditation Easy

You might be someone who already meditates, or you might have zero interest in meditation. Both types of people have told me they love Wholeness Work.

Many people who've found meditation a struggle, tell me this is the first practice they've been able to do—and enjoy doing. With Wholeness Work there's no struggle. You'll see why in this chapter.

Experienced meditators often say that this format brings them to a deep state more quickly and easily than they've experienced before.

If you have no interest in meditation, you might be surprised at how this simple format can be a nourishing life practice. Once you know the steps, doing it feels like a reward—like a day-trip to the spa—rather than something you have to do.

Dissolving the Ego with New Choice Points

The Meditation Format is actually similar to the Basic Process you learned in Chapter 3. However, learning this format is important because:

You can start with where you are in the moment. You don't need an issue.

You will learn two new "choice points." Knowing these can make it easier to "meet" your experience in a simple and kind way.

You will get more practice finding and dissolving the 'I's, so you're ready for what's coming up next. In Chapters 5 and 6, we will go on to completely different territory. You'll learn two powerful processes that are NOT primarily about dissolving the ego. These are "Reclaiming Authority," and "Integrating What's Missing." You'll be ready for these processes after doing the exercise in this chapter.

Experiencing Awareness—Valuable But Not the "Whole Deal"

At the beginning and ending of the Meditation Format, we experience Awareness. To really experience Awareness can be such a luxurious thing. While that's nice, it's not the reason this method is so effective. This process is uniquely effective because of what's sandwiched in between. In fact, it's these "in between" steps that bring us to a richer and more complete experience of Awareness.

Let's get to that now...

meditation format
demonstration

Sneak Preview: The Results for Rana

"... something radiating all around...

"... more peaceful...

"... I'm just being in the moment... Just being here.

"... It is beautiful..."

How to Learn from this Demonstration

You have a choice in how to experience this demonstration. As you read, you can imagine you're watching and listening to Rana and to me. Let the movie unfold in front of you. Or, you can pretend you're Rana and go through as if you're her, and enjoying her experience. A third option is to do the process yourself. If you choose, each time I ask Rana a question, you can pause and notice what answer emerges for you.

And you don't need to consciously decide in advance. As you read you may find that something is transforming for you as well even without your tracking it. This demonstration builds on what you learned in Chapters 2 and 3. To fully benefit, please read those chapters first.

Experiencing Awareness

ME: So, Rana, as you're sitting here now, you can just close your eyes, and find a comfortable position. And you can move a little bit to get really comfortable.

RANA: [Shifts position and smiles.]

ME: Yeah… and then take a deep breath and relax, and just allow yourself to experience the field of Awareness that's all around. So, take a moment to just notice that there's this capacity to experience… that's already in and through the body.... And we can each sense this ourselves … and then we can become aware that this capacity to experience is also all around us in space, all around in every direction.... There may be a sense of spaciousness.... There may be a sense of presence ... or just be a sense of space.... Or sometimes people experience it as a *field* of Awareness because it extends in all directions— it's everywhere at once. You can start with where you are in the moment. You don't need an issue. Just this capacity to notice, even before there are any experiences....

And can you do this easily and comfortably, in this moment?

RANA: Yes. [Nodding.]

ME: Lovely, beautiful.

Finding a Beginning

ME: Okay, so now, allow yourself to notice whatever you notice…. This might be a sensation in the body. It could be a thought, it could be an image, it could be an inner voice. It could be a tension, or a constriction. It could be anything at all. Just allow yourself to notice whatever you notice … whatever experience emerges … and gets your attention right now. And whenever you notice something, you can let me know what that is.

RANA: … A slight tension in my neck. [She tilts her head and gestures to the back of her neck.]

ME: Okay, tension in the neck…. And as there's a noticing of this "tension" here in the neck, notice the area that it takes up…. Is it a large area? A small area? … And what is its shape and size?

RANA: … It seems to be there on the back of the neck … the entire neck. [She moves her right hand up and down the back of her neck.]

ME: Uh huh … Good, [so we have approximately the size (from Rana's gesture)]. And what's the shape?

RANA: … It's like a block of wood. [With her right hand she outlines a block shape in the space in front of her.]

ME: Okay, great, "like a block of wood."

To You/Reader: Rana is describing her experience metaphorically: "It's *like a block of wood.*" When someone uses a metaphor, I guide them in shifting their attention to notice the sensation quality. Here's how…

ME: So now, Rana, it looks like a block of wood…. And letting go of this image, if there's a sensing in and through the area, through the space of this, what's the sensation quality that's actually present there?

RANA: … [Pausing, lifting her right hand and moving her fingers gently back and forth, as if sensing into the area with her fingers.]

ME: And it might be a tingly-ness, there might be a roughness, there might be a sense of hardness or denseness … or, there might be airiness…. We can't really predict or know until we sense there.

RANA: There's a pressure…. It seems dense … not very dense, but dense.

ME: Okay, great, it seems dense and there's a pressure…. Now, when somebody says "pressure," that means something is pressing on something. So, Rana, is it that something is pressing on this [that's dense/shaped like a block of wood]? Or is it that this [this dense area], is pressing on something else?

RANA: It looks like the top of my head is kind of pressing down on my neck. That's what it feels like.

ME: So, is this area that's kind of dense, like a block of wood … is it under pressure then? From above?

RANA: Yes. [Her eyes remain closed, she pauses, eyebrows slightly furrowed.]

ME: There's a sense of denseness there?

RANA: Yes.

ME: Okay, beautiful.

To You/Reader: I asked Rana a few questions about her experience of "pressure." This isn't part of the usual process, and you won't usually need to do this.[1]

Session Notes: The Beginning Experience, "Tension"	
Location	*The back of neck*
Size & Shape	*The entire neck area, shaped like a block of wood*
Sensation Quality	*Dense (not very)*

[1] In the Wholeness Work Levels II – IV trainings, we learn more options for working with "pressure." It's best to start in the simple way I'm demonstrating here. Sometimes that's all that's needed.

Finding the 'I'

ME: So now we find the 'I' [like we did in Chapter 3]. So, Rana, you could say and it would be true, *"I am aware of this dense place in my neck."*

RANA: I am aware of this dense place in my neck....

ME: Yes. And even just thinking it on the inside,... *"I am aware of this."* ... Where is the 'I' that notices?

RANA: It's on the top my head, here. [She smoothly lifts her left hand above her head.]

ME: Okay, lovely. On the top of your head.... And is that above your head?

RANA: Yes, above my head. [Again, raising her hand, eyes closed.]

ME: Yeah. And what's the approximate size and shape?

RANA: Looks like a cap. Like a bottle cap. [Her left hand makes the shape of a bottle cap.]

ME: Like a bottle cap.
Okay, and about how big is it? Can you show us with your gestures?

RANA: Yeah. [She indicates a small size with her pointer and thumb.]

ME: Yes, interesting.

RANA: [Smiles, looking ready.]

To You/Reader: Rana again offers a metaphor for her experience: "Like a bottle cap." So next I invite her to shift attention to notice the sensation quality.

ME: So, Rana, first notice the metaphor ... *"It looks like a bottle cap,"* ... and now what we do is sense in and through the space to find the sensation quality. So, sensing in and through this area that looks like a bottle cap ... what's the sensation quality here? [I match her hand gestures to indicate location.]

RANA: It's warm. [Her left hand is still raised above her head, palm close to her hair, bobbing slightly as she senses.]

ME: It's warm.

RANA: Yeah.

ME: And anything else, like light—

RANA: —Quite light, actually. [Rana interrupts me to affirm this quality, before I have time to offer a menu of options.]

ME: Warm and quite light. Okay. Lovely. [Rana lowers her left hand and raises her right hand briefly, appearing absorbed in the experience.]

Session Notes: The 1st 'I'	
Location	*Top of head*
Size & Shape	*Like a bottle cap*
Sensation Quality	*Warm, quite light*

Finding the Second 'I"

ME: Now ... I'm going to do something I don't need to do in the Meditation Format, but there might be benefit. And that is to find the second 'I'.

So, Rana ... there's a noticing of this (the first 'I') ... that is warm and light, that's above your head.... *"Where is the perceiving of this happening from? Or where's the 'I' that notices this?"*

RANA: About a meter on top. [She extends her left arm above her head, pointing upward.]

ME: Okay, one meter up. And what's the approximate size and shape?

RANA: Again, I'm seeing a metaphor, like a fountain of water. [She giggles, again lifting her left hand above her head.]

ME: Like a fountain of water.

RANA: Yeah, and maybe this is the size of it. [She gestures to show the size.]

ME: Great. And this is lovely, that you're noticing the metaphor and that you're just reporting it, just how it comes to you. Some of us will have a metaphoric experience. Many of us won't. And however we experience it is the perfect thing. Our system is just revealing to us in its own natural way. And it's useful for us to just go with however our system presents these things to us.

       So, noticing this fountain of water ... and sensing in and through the space of this—of what looks like a fountain of water—just sensing in and through the space ... What's the sensation quality here?

RANA: ... It's cooler. [Her eyelids press lightly together, quivering, as she senses inwardly.] ... Pretty light.

ME: Cool.

RANA: Yeah.... Pretty light.

ME: And pretty light. Okay. Great, and that's plenty. That's lovely.

Session Notes: The 2nd 'I'	
Location	*A meter above the head*
Size & Shape	*Fountain of water*
Sensation Quality	*Cool, pretty light*

Sensing If the 'I' Welcomes Integrating with Awareness

ME: Now we're going to do something differently than we did with the Wholeness Work Basic Format you learned in Chapter 3. Instead of getting three layers of 'I', we're going to check with the 'I' we have, and find out if it already welcomes dissolving, integrating as the field of Awareness.

       So, this is what I'd like you to do now, Rana.... Sensing in and through this space here, that's cool, and kind of light [I'm asking Rana to attend to the second 'I' she just found.] ... check: "Does the sensation of this welcome ... being invited to open and relax and dissolve, in and as the full field of Awareness ... that's all around and throughout?

[As I ask this question, Rana's face and body start relaxing.] ... Yeah, and I can see that's already happening. Yeah, and so you can just allow that to continue however it does.... Yeah ... and you can let me know when things have settled.

RANA: ... Yes.

Inviting the First 'I' to Integrate

ME: Okay. Great. So now let's go to the one before that, which was at the top of the head. And how is that now? Is it the same or is it a little different?

RANA: ... A little different.

ME: Okay ... So, sensing how it is now, notice what happens when the sensation here now is invited to also open, relax, dissolve, melt in and as the full field of Awareness that's all around and throughout. [She inhales and exhales softly.]

That's right ... And you can just let that happen however it happens.

... Yes. And relaxing into the happening of that ... That's right. And you can let me know when everything is settled.

... Yeah. [Eyes closed, Rana's body is very still. Then she nods.]

Inviting the Beginning Sensation to Integrate

ME: Okay, lovely. And now we check back with the original place, in the neck area. [I gesture towards my neck with both hands behind.] And is that the same? Or is it a little different?

RANA: ... It's different.

ME: Okay, and how is it now?

RANA: The block has kind of disappeared now.

ME: The block has kind of disappeared.... And what is there now? Is there anything of it remaining? Or is it just space?

RANA: No, I think it's not there actually.

ME: It's not there at all? Okay, all right. So perhaps it's already completely integrated and dissolved into Awareness. Just in case there's anything at all remaining, let's invite whatever may be there, if anything, to also open, relax, to dissolve and melt in and through the whole field of Awareness.... That's right ... [I can see it's already happening.] ... and you can just let go to whatever happens.

RANA: [Sighs as her body goes into a visibly deeper relaxation.]

ME: And it may be that what wants to happen is all of Awareness can relax and open, in and as the area here, in the neck. Or perhaps the Awareness already present in this location can wake up to itself....

And some of those words may have meaning, some of them might not. You can just allow anything that happens to happen, including if nothing happens, that's fine, too....

To You/Reader: Did you notice that I offered Rana three different possible ways this integration might happen? I call these "the three directions of integration." This is a new "choice point," and I'll explain more about it later in this chapter. Rana probably didn't need these "three directions" this time. But sometimes the second or third "direction" is needed for the integration to happen easily.

ME: You can let me know whenever things settle. If they've already settled, that's fine. If it wants more time that can be allowed.

RANA: ... It's settled. [She speaks softly and slowly, from a deep state of stillness. She is relaxed and motionless, as it appears to be a deep release.]

ME: It's settled. Okay, great. So now, how was that? Did you notice anything additional? [The beginning sensation was already "gone," so I'm asking if Rana experienced any additional shifts from me inviting "anything remaining" to integrate anyway.]

RANA: You're talking about at the end? [Rana opens her eyes.]

ME: Yes.

RANA: Yeah, I just saw myself floating and something radiating all around. [She moves her left hand up, hovering it momentarily, then opening both arms up and out wide to show her experience.]

ME: Okay, something floating and something radiating all around.

RANA: Yeah, more peaceful....

ME: And more peaceful. Okay. Lovely. Beautiful.

To You/Reader: Even though the beginning sensation was mostly gone already, inviting "anything that may be remaining" to integrate often feels good and produces additional integration.

Resting as Awareness

ME: Okay, that is the full Meditation Process. That's one round. And we can do a second round. Or we can just we can just rest as Awareness for as long as we enjoy it, because this is a pleasant space to be in, right?

RANA: Yeah. Thank you so much. [She says warmly and prepares to leave.]

ME: And stay here just a little bit longer ... because I want to emphasize how this—both the integrating phase and just resting as Awareness—is the part that's healing and restorative on all levels. Doing this feels restorative on the physical level as well as on the level of thought, the level of our psyche ... to just let ourselves rest in this space of open Awareness. And we can do that for as long as happens.

And then, our system may give us something else to attend to. We're in this space of Awareness and then "Oh, there's another thought, sensation." Something else happened.

So, Rana, as you turn inward again now, is it just open Awareness? Or is there a next thing to notice?

RANA: ... [She closes her eyes and turns inward quietly.] ... I'm just being in the moment, I think right now, nothing else is there.... Just being here.

ME: And it's nice to just be in this beautiful, lovely space. Okay, so then we are finished. This is the Meditation Format. Thank you, Rana.

RANA: Thank you so much. It is beautiful. [She is gently swaying and has a glowing smile.]

Full Session Notes: Wholeness Work Meditation Format Demo	
Beginning Experience:	*"Tension"*
Location	*The back of the neck*
Size & Shape	*The entire neck area, shaped like a block of wood*
Sensation Quality	*Dense (not very)*

1ˢᵗ 'I'	
Location	*Top of head*
Size & Shape	*Like a bottle cap*
Sensation Quality	*Warm, quite light*

2ⁿᵈ 'I'	
Location	*A meter above the head*
Size & Shape	*Fountain of water*
Sensation Quality	*Cool, pretty light*

two new choice points

This Meditation Format demonstration shows you two new choice points you can use any time you do Wholeness Work. The wording for these new choice points is in the Step-by-Step Guide. You'll start learning them in an easy way when you follow the script as you do the exercise. The two choice points are *when* we invite integrating—and *how*.

When We Invite Integrating

In the Basic Process, we found a Chain of 'I's, and then started integrating. Perhaps you experienced how doing this often makes the experience more powerful and complete.

However, sometimes the very first 'I' we encounter welcomes integrating. If so, it's simpler and more direct just to invite it to do so. In the Meditation Format I'm giving you an easy script for doing that. We just ask the first 'I' that emerges if it welcomes integrating. If it does, then we invite it to go ahead.

Often when people begin practicing Wholeness Work, there's a lot of benefit to asking for a Chain of 'I's. (This is why in the demonstration I guided Rana in finding a second 'I', even though I was teaching the Meditation Format.) But once you've been practicing Wholeness Work for a while, you may discover that sometimes it's easier to just invite the first 'I' to integrate. With Wholeness Work we're always sensing for what our system wants to do—for what feels natural.

How We Invite Integrating

There are three different ways to invite integrating. I encourage you to play with these options.

In the explorations you did in Chapters 2 and 3, the wording I gave you to invite integrating is what I call the first "Direction of Integration." The script guides you in inviting integration in the way that works for most people, especially when beginning Wholeness Work.

However, sometimes an 'I' or a starting sensation needs to integrate in a different way. This is when it can make all the difference to offer the other two Directions of Integration. Here's a brief description for each of the three Directions of Integration.

The First Direction: the 'I' Relaxes into Awareness

You've already experienced this in Chapters 2 and 3. The sensation of the 'I' has been contracted into a relatively small space. So we invite the 'I' to dissolve and melt back into the whole of Awareness. You might experience this as the sensation of the 'I' going from a concentrated central position to opening or dissolving or flowing outward. It may feel like a dispersal outward in all directions. It's similar to what you can observe happening when you put a drop of food coloring in a bowl of water. The color gradually disperses in all directions.

The experience of the 'I' relaxing into Awareness might be something like this…

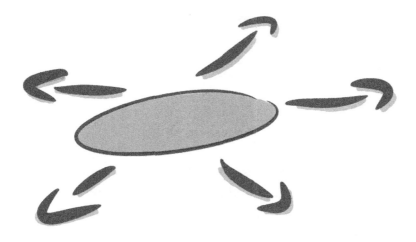

'I' → Awareness

The Second Direction: Awareness Relaxes/Opens into the 'I'

Instead of inviting the 'I' to open into Awareness, we invite all of Awareness to flow into and as the sensation of the 'I'. This can seem impossible. How can something so vast go into a smaller area of space? Yet if you don't try to understand it, sometimes this is what the 'I' wants to experience. When it's the right kind of integration for the 'I', it will feel natural and it will feel like a welcome release. It might feel like all of Awareness kindly opening into and as the sensation of the 'I', and then this can lead to a natural melting or dissolving of whatever was being held there in a rigid form.

The experience of Awareness opening into the 'I' might be like this…

Awareness → *'I'*

If this doesn't make sense to you, that's fine. It usually means this isn't the kind of integration that fits for you right now.

The Third Direction: No Movement

With this direction of integrating, we invite "the Awareness already present in and through the space of the 'I', to 'wake up to itself.'" It can feel literally like something "waking up" without any sense of movement needed. What is already present "wakes up."

The experience of the 'I' waking up to the Awareness that's already present might be like this…

'I' = Awareness

Again, if this direction doesn't make sense, it usually means this isn't the best fit for your system right now.

The Importance of Three Directions

You might wonder why we need three Directions of Integrating. Isn't one enough?

The short answer is "no." Most people need the first direction when they begin Wholeness Work. But for almost everyone—maybe everyone—there will come a time when that direction won't work. This is because the kind of integrating required needs to match the kind of constriction. If you close your hand into a fist, there is really only one way your fingers can open and relax again. Each finger opens outward from where it's attached to your palm. But what if you tried to open the fingers from the other end. If you tried to open your fingers from that place of connection to your palm, it just wouldn't work.

Each 'I' inside is literally a contraction of our consciousness. So the integrating happens when the effort of this contraction is allowed to relax. The integrating needs to reverse what happened when the contraction formed. By offering all three directions, we make it easy for your system to respond to whatever fits.[2]

If this doesn't make sense to you on a mental level, it really is fine. You can just read the script in the Step-by-Step Guide, and let the process happen for you in whatever is the easiest way.

---

[2] If you want to know more about the three directions of integration, there's a full chapter on this in my earlier book, *Coming to Wholeness: How to Awaken and Live with Ease.* (Chapter 13).

flowchart
meditation format

In the following flowchart, you can see the main steps of the Meditation Format in one image.

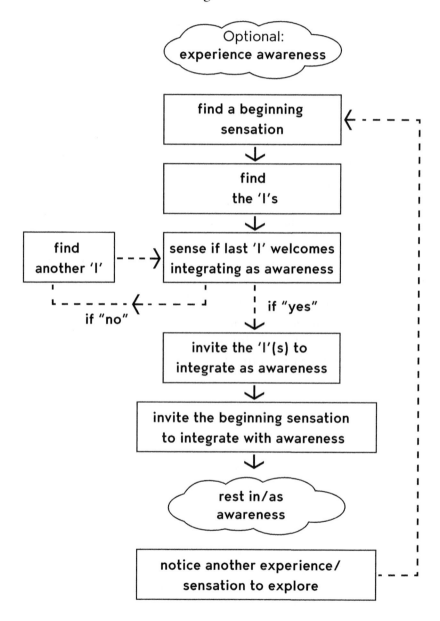

step-by-step guide
meditation format

Now try it out yourself. You can do this meditation sitting in a comfortable chair or lying down. I recommend finding a place where your back and entire spinal column are supported so that when your body releases, you have support.

Getting Ready: Experience Awareness
With eyes either open or closed, allow your body to find a comfortable position....

You can take a moment to experience Awareness. ... The capacity to experience ... that's throughout the body ... and all around. It may be experienced as a sense of spaciousness ... of presence ... that's everywhere at once. ...

Step 1: Find a beginning.
Now do a mind-body scan and notice whatever you notice. Allow whatever relaxes easily to relax ... and notice what remains. ... This could be a tension, a sense of constriction or heaviness, an emotion, an image that comes to mind, an inner voice, anything at all. It may be something that doesn't quite fit into any of these categories. ... Just notice whatever you notice.

- *And where is this experience located?*
- *And what is the size & shape?*
- *Sensing in and through this area, what is the sensation quality? ...*
- *There might be a sense of heaviness, pressure, vibration, fizziness, or bubbling. It might be warm or cool. It may be something you can't put into words, and that's fine. Just notice the sensation that's there.*

Step 2: Find the 'I'.
You can recognize, "I am aware of this [_sensation quality from Step 1_] sensation," right?

- *So where is the 'I' that's aware of this sensation? ... Where is the perceiving happening from? Just notice whatever location comes to mind.*
- *And, what is the size & shape? [of this 'I']*
- *Now notice the sensation quality in and through this area.*
- *[It might be foggy, clear, dense, or empty, heavy, light, vibrating, still, and so forth. If no words quite describe it, that's OK. There can be a noticing of the sensation itself....]*

Step 3: Sense if the 'I' welcomes integrating with Awareness.
Now gently sense for what is welcome: "Does the sensation of this 'I' welcome the invitation to open and relax as the fullness of Awareness?"

If "Yes": Go to Step Four.

If "No": This lets you know to find another 'I'. Here's how:

You just noticed that the sensation here [_in the location of the 'I'_] doesn't welcome the invitation to open and relax, right?

- *So where is the 'I' that notices this? ... Where is the perceiving of this happening from?*
- *And what is the size & shape, and the sensation quality of this new 'I'?*
- *Now check: "Does the sensation of this 'I' welcome the invitation to open and relax as the fullness of Awareness?"*

Do this until you find an 'I' that welcomes integrating with Awareness. Then go on to Step 4.

Step 4: Invite the 'I' to integrate.
Notice what happens when the sensation of this 'I' is invited to open and relax ... as the fullness of Awareness. ... And this can happen in its own way, however feels natural.

Here are some additional ways to invite integrating, if useful.

…Or perhaps what wants to happen is for all of Awareness to open and relax into and as the sensation here…. Or it may be that the Awareness already present in and throughout the sensation here wakes up to itself…. There can be a sensing of what wants to happen—what begins to happen naturally on its own … without effort.

If there are more 'I's: Invite each previous 'I' to integrate, going from last to first.

Now let's check in [_the location of the 'I' before the one that just integrated_]. … First notice: Is it the same as it was before, or is it a little bit different? Either is fine.

Now notice what happens, when the sensation quality here now … is invited to open and relax … as the fullness of Awareness…. There can be an allowing of this to happen in its own way.

Optional Wordings: *Or it may be that what wants to happen is for all of Awareness to open and relax in and as the sensation here … Or the sensation here may begin waking up to itself.*

Step 5: Invite the beginning sensation to integrate.
Now let's return to the location you started with. What is the sensation here now? Whatever sensation is there now, gently feel for which way the integration wants to happen. It may be that this sensation wants to open and relax into and as all of Awareness. It may be that the sensation here wants all of Awareness to flow into it. Or it may feel like the Awareness that's already present in this location wakes up to itself…

Now there can be an experiencing of whatever happens. And if/ when a relaxing and melting is happening, there can be an enjoying of this for as long as you like.

Step 6: Rest as Awareness.
There can be a "resting in and as Awareness" for as long as you like.

Optional: Cycle through the process again.
You can continue using the Meditation Format for as much or as little time as you like. If another sensation, or feeling, or response

emerges, there can be a gentle noticing of the location and sensation quality and you can cycle through the process again.

You can go through these steps once, or multiple times, in a single session.

Sharing Experiences

Here are a few experiences that people in Wholeness Work training sessions shared about doing this exercise.

"I felt amazingly peaceful, really quickly."

"I started yawning on the integrating step. It was like my body was releasing tension I didn't even know was there."

"I've tried meditating before and it felt like a struggle because I'd have these distracting thoughts and couldn't stay focused. But this was easy because I can just notice and include the distracting thoughts." (See the upcoming section: "What About Distracting Thoughts and Feelings?" for how to do this.)

"I started with a chronic pain and was surprised that it was almost completely gone at the end."

"My body just let go and I was enjoying being relaxed."

"I'm a long-time meditator and doing this I went into a deep meditation state really quickly. Usually it would take more time. I also noticed that with my previous mediation practice, it felt really wonderful but the blissful state I went into felt separate from real life. With [the Wholeness Meditation], I don't separate from anything. It feels like part of my life."

---

change
without struggle
why wholeness meditation works

Wholeness Meditation offers a kind and direct way to include and actually integrate *everything* in our present moment experience. We start with present moment experience. That's the obvious part. Then we go on to include some important but often overlooked aspects of our experience…

The 'I's—the "perceiving self" that is usually activated in each moment.

Interfering thoughts, emotions, or distractions. We don't need to bypass them either.

I'd like to explain why including each of these additional aspects of our experience is important—and makes Wholeness Meditation feel so easy and effortless—without struggle. When we include these things, it becomes possible and easy to "rest as Awareness" in a more complete and full way. In fact the field of Awareness itself becomes more rich and complete when we get there this way.

Even people who find meditation difficult often find Wholeness Work Meditation easy and natural. And if you don't resonate with the word "Meditation," it's fine to think of this as being a simple nourishing practice.

Finding and Relaxing the 'I'
Quite a few forms of meditation instruct people to "*rest as Awareness,*" or "*be Awareness,*" or something like this. If we try to do this without finding, welcoming, and integrating the 'I's, it usually becomes effortful because it bypasses an important aspect of our unconscious experience. The 'I' does exist at the unconscious level: it's an inner contraction of consciousness that—if not released—continues to stress our system. This is a kind of "spiritual bypass" that is often not recognized. When we find and integrate the 'I's, the experience is easier, more relaxing.

In addition, when the 'I's release into Awareness, the field of Awareness that we experience actually becomes richer and fuller. All of this makes the experience more nourishing and more relaxing.

All in all, the experience is more complete, and totally unforced.

As far as I know, Wholeness Work is the first form of meditation that offers an explicit way to find and relax the 'I's that exist on the unconscious level. Prior to Wholeness Work Meditation, spiritual teachings focused on how "the 'I' is an illusion; it doesn't really exist." With Wholeness Work we recognize that "yes, the 'I' isn't real" in the sense that my body, or a car, or the food in front of me exists. It's something we've made up; BUT it does exist as a structure in our unconscious. So it's important not to bypass this. It's important to include this "bit of consciousness that is me" and give it the opportunity to finally release itself into the fullness of Awareness. Otherwise, this 'I' remains inside as a contraction of consciousness that continues to generate stress.

embracing distracting thoughts & feelings

The demonstration with Rana flowed quite easily, but you might wonder: "*What do I do if a distracting thought comes in?!*"

If you do Wholeness Work Meditation over time, this is likely to happen. It does for almost everyone—possibly everyone. And with Wholeness Meditation this actually becomes a useful part of the process.

With many forms of meditation the instruction for dealing with distracting thoughts is something like, "*just return your attention to your breath*" (or to a mantra, or a point on a wall, or a candle, etc.). However, most people find it takes a bit of effort to "bring the attention back." It's another way to bypass our actual experience. With Wholeness Work we don't need to do that. Instead, if our attention goes somewhere else, we just follow our experience. This makes Wholeness Meditation easy and simple.

How do we do it? Here are several examples to show you.

Examples of Following Your Experience

With Wholeness Work you don't need to "resist" any interfering thoughts. You don't need to bring your attention back to your breath, or even to the steps of this process!

We always follow our experience. We include whatever happens in our thought or feeling life. We notice the thought, and then shift out of content to noticing where it's located, and of course then we notice the size and shape, and the sensation quality.

You can use the Meditation Format to follow your experience no matter what it is. With the Wholeness Work Meditation you can easily include any experience that emerges.

Here's one example...

IDA: You asked me to notice a beginning sensation, but already I'm wondering if I'm doing it right.

ME: Ok, good. Thank you for letting me know. That's exactly what I need for you to do—to let me know what your experience is.
So you said, "I'm wondering if I'm doing it right."

IDA: [Ida nods.]

ME: And where's the 'I' that's wondering if I'm doing it right.

IDA: [Ida smiles and immediately gestures to a place to the right of her head.] It's here.

ME: OK, great. And what's the size and shape of this here.

To You/Reader: And now we can just use the Meditation Format with whatever Ida answers. We notice the location, size and shape, and sensation quality. We invite it to integrate and if it doesn't welcome integrating we find another 'I'.

Here's another example...

RON: When I turn inward and start doing this, first I notice a body sensation, but then my mind wanders. I start thinking of other things.

ME: Ok, good ... And do you want to play with this a little right now? [Ron nods.] Ok, You can turn inward ... and check for a body sensation. [Ron closes his eyes and nods as he follows along.]... and let me know when the mind starts wandering....

RON: Ok, it's already happening. I'm already thinking of other things and losing focus.

ME: So ... where's the 'I' that's thinking of other things?

RON: —I'm not sure. Your question caught me by surprise.

ME: OK, great. So right now, where's the 'I' that's not sure? ... or maybe ... where's the "one who" is caught by surprise? [Notice that again I'm just following Ron's experience. We shift attention to his most recent experience and just follow that.]

RON: Ok, I think it's here. [He gestures behind and above his head.]

When we shift to attending to whatever distracting thought or feeling is emerging and ask, "Where's *this* 'I'?" usually it's easy for the person to notice. Most of us can notice the 'I' that's actually activated in the moment, if we're asked about it.

You can learn more about how to include reactions and any other experience that emerges...

See Chapter 7, "Better Rest and Sleep."

There's a full chapter on reactions in my earlier book, *Coming to Wholeness: How to Awaken and Live with Ease.* (Chapter 20, "Reactions")

In the Wholeness Work training sessions, our support staff assists you in learning to deal with these as they arise. We can help you "catch" the 'I' that's activated in the moment.

answering your questions

Meditation Posture

Q Do I need a special posture to meditate?

A Use a body position that's comfortable for you. I like to sit in a chair or lie down with my arms and legs uncrossed. These positions give my back and spinal column full support. During the integration many body tensions release spontaneously. This can happen most easily when your back is supported.

When the 'I' is Metaphoric

Q What if my 'I' looks like an object such as a block of wood, a fountain, or a sun?

A Most of the time the 'I's we find inside don't look like anything in particular. You might just notice a location in space that has a size, shape, and sensation quality.

However, for Rana, both the beginning sensation and each 'I' looked like something from the physical world: "a block of wood," "a bottle cap," "a fountain."

The 'I's you find inside might also appear like a familiar physical object (e.g. "It looks like a cloud," or "an umbrella"). If you find that an 'I' looks like something else, here's what to do.

First acknowledge: "Yes, it looks like a block of wood." Then you can let go of the image, and sense in and through the space the image takes up. There can be a noticing of the sensation quality in and through the space.

This way you are acknowledging your experience, and then gently attending to a different level of the experience. Shifting attention to the sensation quality (instead of what it looks like) is what will make it easy to integrate this small 'I' back into the whole. This demonstration with Rana gives you an example of how to do this.

When to Ask for a Second 'I'

Q In the demonstration, why did you ask Rana for a second 'I'?

A When doing the "pure" Meditation format, we just take the first 'I' we find and ask if it welcomes integrating. If yes, we invite it to do so. If not, we find a second 'I'. Rana's first 'I' was already "light." Most likely it would have been comfortable integrating.

However, when we first learn the Wholeness Work, most of us come with quite a few layers of 'I'. It can be beneficial to include more of these layers. This makes the work feel easier and kinder. So when you begin using the Meditation Format, you may want to ask for a second 'I' also.

Then, if you use the Wholeness Work over time, you may find that you encounter fewer layers of 'I' remaining. In this case the Meditation Format might flow most easily for you if you just invite the very first 'I' you encounter to integrate.

What if the 'I' only partially integrates?

Q What if an 'I' starts integrating, but doesn't finish? When I invited one of the 'I's to integrate it started expanding and got more transparent and a lot larger, but it was still there. Is this OK?

A Yes, that sounds just perfect. This is what I call a "partial integration." The 'I' Structure has begun to integrate; it's moving in the direction of complete integration. And we trust that the system knows how far it can go right now. When it integrates all the way, there won't be any separate structure in existence any longer. It will be one with the Whole. But if it stops after partially integrating, there's always a good reason.

When something integrates only partially, it might mean...

This is as much as it wants to integrate right now.

It needs a different "direction of integration" to fully integrate.

Another structure needs to be noticed and included before this one can integrate. For example, there could be another 'I', or another structure such as what I call an "Authority." You'll learn about that in the next chapter.

For now, just enjoy the partial integration. It already offers a beneficial release within. What's perfect is that you are allowing it to happen as it does, without pushing it to do anything beyond what's natural in this moment.

For some people most integrations happen in full. For others many integrations happen just a little bit at first. You don't ever need to push for more to happen than does. However, if you find yourself "pushing for more," this is an important reaction to include. Find the "one who" is pushing for more integration, and invite this to integrate. Doing this can be quite powerful. (In *Coming to Wholeness,* see Chapter 20, "Working with Reactions.")

Auditory and Visual Experiences

Q What if my starting experience is an inner voice or an image?

A You treat this exactly the same way as when you start with a body sensation or feeling.

If you have an inner voice, you notice where it's located. Maybe it's to the left of your head. It can be anywhere. Just notice where it's located, and notice the size and shape of this area where something is speaking. And notice the sensation quality.

Sometimes you might notice an image or picture is kind of stuck in your mind. So just notice where it's located. Maybe when you check it's actually located out in front of you. Notice the space it takes up—the approximate size and shape of this image. And then sense in and through this location, for the sensation quality.

With both voices and images, we let go of the content or meaning, and shift to noticing the location, the size and shape, and then the sensation quality. This shifts us to a different level of experience. And we can resolve stressful thoughts at a level that's "beyond the content." When we do this, we tend to discover a peaceful presence, from which it's easier to deal with whatever the situation is. And it's a lot easier. We don't have to figure it out with our conscious minds. Navigating life becomes easier. When we use this process, our emotional intelligence starts improving immediately—because solutions start coming to us from the whole.

Resting as Awareness vs. Cycling through Again

Q At the end, should I just "rest as Awareness," or cycle through the process again?

A At the end of this demonstration, I invited Rana to just rest as Awareness, and then notice if another body sensation or image, voice or thought emerges. For Rana, she found herself just enjoying the experience of Awareness.

Most of us will find that if we rest as Awareness for a while, another experience will emerge. If this happens, you can cycle through the Meditation Format again, using this new experience. You can continue for as long (or as short) a time as you like. Each experience that you "greet and process" in this way, leads to an increasingly deep relaxation and resetting of the mind-body system.

Interfering Thoughts

Q What if I have interfering thoughts that come up as soon as I turn inward?

A This is such an important question! Most people DO have interfering thoughts that seem to interrupt the process. But with Wholeness Work, NOTHING can actually interrupt or interfere with the process. Because each and every thought that emerges, we just include. Look back at the section in this chapter on "What about Distracting Thoughts and Feelings?" for several examples of how to do this.

"Dense" Sensation Quality and What It Might Indicate

Rana's starting experience was "dense" and it included something pressing on it. Denseness is an indicator that it may also be valuable to use the Authority Format with this same experience. You'll learn the Authority Format in the next chapter. (I recommend learning the Authority Format in the way that it's taught. Later, you can return to any dense structures from previous exercises, if they haven't already fully integrated.)

With Wholeness Work, you don't need to do everything at once. We begin with what's easy, and each little bit that we do nourishes our being. *And each little bit we do makes it easier to benefit from the next time you do Wholeness Work.*

Just the Meditation Format, with no add-ons, already resulted in many visibly useful shifts for Rana.

significant subtleties

As you know, Wholeness Work is about gentle transformations— big and small. To get the best results from your explorations using these formats, it helps to follow the steps *as they are described.*

Sensing In and Through vs. Experiencing from the Outside

When we do Wholeness Work, we begin by noticing the location of an experience. Then we notice the size and shape (or the area it takes up), and finally we "*sense in and through*" to notice the sensation quality. Taking the time to "sense in and through" is an important step. Doing this makes the integration easy and natural.

The Language: Use the Script

I encourage you to use the exact wording in the scripts, especially while you're learning the processes. The scripts are carefully written— each word is chosen with intention and designed to guide your inner experience in a specific way. These scripts have also been tested and improved over years of using them with clients and workshop participants.

When people change the wording, they're usually convinced that their alternate wording is just fine. Sometimes they add hypnotic language that they believe adds to the effect, but usually the changes they make actually dilute the impact. Often their alternate wordings contain subtle assumptions that get in the way of the method's full effect.

Some of the purposes of the wording go beyond what we can cover in this book. So I'm just going to suggest that you use the wording I'm providing—until the process becomes so familiar that you don't need words at all.

what happens over time
how your experience might change

Starting with the 'I'
Once this practice becomes more familiar, when you turn inward, instead of noticing a body sensation, sometimes the first thing you notice might be an 'I'. When that happens your practice might look like the following flowchart...

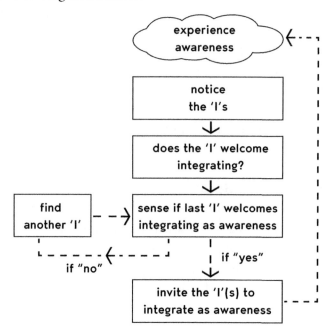

Just Resting as Awareness

After you've done the process quite a bit, there may be times when you find yourself spontaneously relaxing as Awareness when you begin meditating. You may not need to notice the 'I' who is aware because there may not be one. If it's easy to simply relax all perspectives in/as Awareness, you can just enjoy this experience. When a perspective, feeling, response, etc., emerges—just invite/allow it to melt or dissolve back into Awareness. You don't even need to notice if it is an 'I' or a "Response." Just notice the location and allow it to melt—or perhaps you as Awareness can just fall into it from everywhere at once.

Most important is doing whatever you do in an easy, gentle way. If the process seems difficult, you can simply enjoy relaxing as Awareness—without attempting to *do* anything. Notice what's already at peace. And *being* Awareness, there can be a natural allowing of whatever emerges to be present or to flow through and you don't need to do anything about it.

There are more ways your practice might change as you use the process over time. This is because the structure of your unconscious is actually changing the more you use these methods. The underlying principle is to always follow the natural flow of experience.

Using Wholeness Work as a daily practice leads to a natural resetting of the body-mind system at perhaps the most fundamental level.[3] Practicing on a daily basis results in an inevitable process of personal transformation and evolution that is likely to be subtle, but dependable. It is good for physical health, as well as mental and emotional wellbeing.[4]

---

[3] You can find more detail on the Wholeness Work methods presented in Chapters 2-4 in the book, *Coming to Wholeness: How to Awaken and Live with Ease.* I've included the basics again in this book; so you're prepared to learn the methods in Chapters 5 and beyond.

[4] This statement about benefits in physical health and emotional wellbeing is based on anecdotal reports from numerous people using this practice. We look forward to future research to test and potentially verify these personal experiences.

Whether you use the Meditation Format as a daily practice or just "in the moment," it can have powerful, lasting benefits. A friend of mine tells me her mom used to offer the following advice about keeping her living space pleasant, "If you clean up *as you go along*, it's much easier." She often thinks of her mom when she does a little "in the moment/on the go" body-mind system cleanup. And, she finds herself enjoying the benefits of applying her mom's philosophy to her Wholeness Work.

In the next chapters, you'll learn two formats that can take your journey of transformation to the next level. They go beyond "dissolving the ego" to the next step in emotional healing and awakening. Many people find these next formats to offer a significantly deeper transformation than just the ones we've already covered.

Are you ready to explore these game changers?

CHAPTER 5

THE RECLAIMING AUTHORITY FORMAT

Healing Perfectionism, Judgment, Shame and More

Have you ever struggled with self-criticism or feelings of unworthiness? Perhaps you have a critical inner voice that always seems to find something wrong with what you do. Most of us have experiences like this. At times, we might even feel like we have to do things perfectly, just to be OK.

The common theme in these experiences is that they all involve some kind of judging. For most of us this kind of inner judging is difficult—or even impossible—to just turn off. We might find ourselves arguing with the critical inner voice, but the voice doesn't just disappear. Or we might find that even when others show us kindness, somehow we feel undeserving, or we can't fully take it in.

The flipside of this is that we might also find ourselves judging other people. We might find ourselves frequently becoming irritated or annoyed by other people's behavior. Perhaps we even wish we could be more easy-going; but again the tendency to judge isn't something that we can just turn off at will.

These experiences can be challenging to change because there are hidden structures at the unconscious level holding them in place. You've already discovered the first hidden structure. It's the 'I's—or we could call it the limited self. In Chapters 2-4, you've learned how to find and integrate this.

However, to fully transform judgment—whether we're judging ourselves or others—there's a second important hidden structure that we need to notice and transform. In this chapter, you'll learn what this structure is, and how to find, transform, and heal it in a simple and kind way.

When we know how to do this, it becomes possible to have deep and lasting change in many persistent issues that many of us have spent years or even decades struggling with.

Beyond the 'I's
a second inner structure

So what is this second hidden structure of the psyche that can lead us to deeper healing? I call it the "inner authority." This universal structure of the unconscious holds many kinds of "suffering" and stress in place.

The 'I's (what we've been exploring so far) are our experience of *Self.* Spiritual teachings tell us that learning to dissolve the ego is important. Yet there's a freeing next step: finding and transforming what we unconsciously code as "not Self." The "authority" is the first of these that we need to find and transform, for deeper and kinder inner integration.

In this chapter I'm going to share a simple format for finding and transforming the "inner authority" so you can feel the results. In preparation, first I'll tell you:

How I discovered the Authority Structure within
The potential impact of Inner Authorities
How Inner Authorities are formed
A checklist of life issues where this method offers significant value
Why we'll start with embarrassment or shame

How I Discovered the "Inner Authority—Learning from Embarrassment and Shame

When I began my Wholeness Work practice, I focused on "dissolving the ego"—finding and integrating the 'I's within. Since many spiritual teachings describe this as the key, I thought, "Now that I have a way to do this, perhaps this is everything I need. Perhaps this will take me the whole distance." A lot of my stress was already falling away; emotional reactivity was often yielding to a feeling of peace inside.

Yet I noticed outer events could still sometimes trigger feelings of embarrassment, shame, or unworthiness. I became curious about the structure of these experiences, and wondered, "How is it possible to feel these things?"

The first thing I realized is that for me—or anyone—to feel embarrassment or shame, requires having the sense that we've violated some rule or standard. If there's no authority or rule-maker present, how could we feel ashamed? How would we get there? It wouldn't be possible. So it occurred to me that I must be carrying around some kind of "inner authority"—making it possible for me to feel embarrassment, shame, and other things as well [e.g., unworthiness].

This recognition led me to explore within myself, to actually *find* this unconscious "Authority" structure. After carefully testing and refining the method with myself, and then clients and workshop participants, I came to the reliably effective format you'll learn in this chapter. It's simple—as easy as finding the 'I's inside, but we need to ask different questions. I quickly realized that these inner Authority Structures are as universal as the 'I's. Everybody has them. And everybody I've encountered so far has benefitted—significantly— from finding and integrating them.

The Impact of these "Hidden Players" called Inner Authorities

Shame, embarrassment, and quite a few other problem experiences, *presuppose* an authority. In other words, it wouldn't be possible to experience these problems without an inner authority. We notice our unpleasant feeling, but we haven't been consciously aware of these internalized rule or standard setters whose presence actually *causes* the feeling. These Authority Structures within are powerful "hidden players." They have a strong impact on how we feel and what we do in many areas of life.

So how did these Inner Authorities get there? How did they become part of our unconscious inner structure?

How Authority Structures Form

When we're born, each of us arrives on this planet as a dependent infant who couldn't survive without caretakers. From our point of view as a young child, our caretakers are amazingly knowledgeable and powerful. They know how to make food appear, how to keep us warm, and provide shelter. They teach us a lot about how to survive, how to stay safe, and how to navigate life challenges—both simple and more complex.

These caretakers create the context in which we live. They set the rules and determine the consequences. These authorities in our outer world have an important role in our lives. So perhaps it's not surprising we might develop authorities in our inner world as well.

Forming an inner experience of authority gives us a way to have continuity—to carry around the rules our outer authorities have given us. But these Authority Structures are created from the understanding of a small child. This tends to be based on simple and rigid ideas with lots of judgment included. And just like the 'I's, the way the Authority Structures form is not what we might expect. They are unlike any way we might design them if we did it consciously, and they don't look or sound like what we might anticipate. In addition they haven't been adapted to fit with adult understandings, and they certainly haven't been updated to reflect the understandings of "the wisdom of the whole" of us.

Sometimes the most impactful rules are those that we were never explicitly taught, but that we learned through interacting with others. For example, what if a child spontaneously expresses his/her feelings about something, and their caretaker gets angry, or even tells the child to shut up? This child might conclude it's not okay to have or express feelings. The child might just begin to avoid expressing feelings—without consciously realizing they're doing it.

Does this make you start to wonder what authorities or rule-setters you might have internalized inside? And what present-day feelings and behaviors these hidden players may be contributing to?

Fortunately you won't need to figure this out. But by following the simple exercise in this chapter, you'll discover interesting answers unique to you.

And, when you find these Authorities inside, most likely what you find will be completely different than you might expect. You'll get an example of this when you read the demonstration in just a moment.

A Checklist: Issues that Transform with the Authority Format

Essentially everyone benefits from the Wholeness Work Authority Format. We'll start by transforming and healing experiences of embarrassment and shame. Transforming these is a big deal. And, the Authority Format will also help you heal and transform many other experiences of stress or difficulty. Here's a partial list of the issues where this method can be significant in your healing...

Self-criticism
Feeling unworthy
Perfectionism (holding one's self up to impossible standards—trying to avoid feeling deficient)
Needing to please others
Stage fright or performance anxiety
Anxiety (in general)
PTSD
Guilt
Needing to prove "I'm right."
Feeling like "I don't belong."
Expecting to be rejected—"They won't accept me."
Depression
Embarrassment
Shame

Operating in overdrive—trying to overcome a feeling of "I'm not worthy."

Lack of motivation—e.g. "There's no point in working hard because I'm not worthy anyway."

Procrastination

Feeling rigid about how things "should be"

Judgment of or contempt of others

Anger or frustration

The Wholeness Work Authority Format will give you a simple way to find the inner Authorities that unconsciously guide our lives. And then you'll learn how to transform and integrate them. You can discover for yourself how doing this often frees us in unexpected ways.

For most of us, living without judgment is a radical transformation. So it doesn't need to happen all at once. With this method, you can do this one step at a time. Each step has its own benefit because you feel increasingly relaxed in living your life. Many people tell me that *cumulatively* they find the results of using this format are nothing short of astounding.

Why We'll Start with Embarrassment or Shame

The first time you try out this format, I'm going to suggest you start with an experience of embarrassment or shame, just as I did. Why?

Embarrassment and shame are the easiest ways to start finding unconscious rule structures inside. Usually, this method either fully resolves, or makes a significant healing shift, with embarrassment or shame. And transforming such experiences is likely to be life changing.

I began by using this format with my own experiences of embarrassment. Before using this method, I got embarrassed super easily. Sometimes I would feel myself turning bright pink and I didn't even know what exactly I was embarrassed about. As I used this method, that happened less and less often. At this point I haven't felt embarrassed in a long time.

Not feeling embarrassed isn't in itself that big of a deal. I never considered feeling embarrassed a big problem. What does matter to me are the other changes that happened as a result of that shift. I began feeling free to just be myself, without needing to please others or having others approve. I feel more at ease in so many areas of my life. Here's one example: before I did Wholeness Work, I felt anxious each time I walked into the room to teach a new class. Now I feel at ease. I'm just present. It's SO much easier this way. Throughout my life I'm more comfortable with the possibility of making mistakes; I'm more OK that if I try something new I might blow it. I could go on.

I've also come to appreciate that Awakening is an ongoing evolution, a gradual unfolding—it's not about being "done." And I know that if I find myself feeling embarrassed again sometime, it just means I've been given another opportunity to heal and integrate. It's just another doorway "into the arms of the beloved," as Rumi would say.

The value of healing shame isn't a new idea. For decades, thought leaders in personal growth—such as John Bradshaw (author), Gabor Maté (Canadian physician), and Brené Brown (shame researcher)—have discussed how feelings of shame or embarrassment are important to recognize and heal. However, prior to Wholeness Work, when people have tried to heal shame, their approach has been to attempt to work with the *feeling* of shame. That's the hard way. With the Wholeness Work we have an easy way. We're going to use a simple line of questioning to discover the inner Authority that's responsible for feeling shame. You'll see how finding this leads to an easier, more direct, and much more complete healing and transformation.

I want you to know at the outset, that <u>this is a key format</u>. It's one worth doing over and over again. Many people even report positive shifts in health through using this method. It was definitely significant for me. After doing this process a few times, I gained the physical stamina to come out of a decade-long "hibernation" and start teaching again.

The Authority Format has helped free many people from experiences of shame, embarrassment, unworthiness, perfectionism, judgment, and much more—and it can free you, too. Later in this chapter, we'll explore more opportunities to apply this format.

Please read the following demonstration before trying it yourself as this will prepare you for a richer experience.

authority format in action
demonstration

Sneak Preview: The Results for Anne

"The horrible emotion that I had with it before is gone....

"I can't even think about it
[the experience that used to elicit shame.]
It's just gone.... [That incident] no longer has any relevance.

"It [this change] feels pretty big—freeing."

Picking Something to Work with and Stepping in

ME: So, Anne, you have an experience that you'd like to explore?

ANNE: Yeah. [She nods "yes."]

ME: Okay, and is it embarrassment, or shame, or something else?

ANNE: Shame, shame.

ME: Okay. Shame. And when you think about it right now—are you already experiencing it? [Anne looks neutral.] —and if not, you can just step into the last time you experienced it.... [Anne's expression and breathing change as she begins to imagine the experience happening.] ... Yeah ... just enough to begin to notice your feeling response....

And now notice the location—where is this experience you're calling "shame"?

ANNE: [Gestures to her chest.]

ME: Okay. In the chest area.

ANNE: Yeah. [She closes her eyes.]

ME: Okay. And now notice the size and shape.

ANNE: … So, it's like an oval. [Eyes closed, she draws an oval shape in front of her chest with her right hand.]

ME: Like an oval. Okay. And when you check, is this experience that's like an oval here in the chest area … is that all inside the body? Is some of it outside, some inside? What's the location?

ANNE: It's mainly inside, but there's a little bit outside. [Anne's expression becomes more neutral, as she attends to the exact location.]

ME: Okay. Inside, and a little outside.

To You/Reader: The feeling of embarrassment or shame might be somewhat unpleasant or intense. When we shift to noticing location, size and shape, and sensation quality, often there is an immediate shift out of reacting to the situation, to a more neutral sensing of our actual experience. This is a useful shift as we begin processing the experience.

ME: [To Anne:] Great. Okay, so Anne … now as you check in this area that's mostly inside the chest, but a little bit out in front … sensing in and through this area, what's the sensation quality?

ANNE: It feels like right in the center—it's as if it's solid, forming a line. And then around it, it's a bit less dense. [Eyes closed, she draws a line in front of her chest, then a circular shape. She appears absorbed in sensing.]

ME: Okay. So, it's very solid or dense—

ANNE: —Right in the center.

ME: Yeah … and then around it, it's less dense.

ANNE: Yeah.

ME: Great. Excellent.

Session Notes: Beginning Experience,	"Shame"
Location	*In the chest area (inside and little bit outside)*
Size & Shape	*Oval*
Sensation Quality	*Dense line in the center, less dense around it*

Finding the Authority: The "Hidden Player"

ME: So we've already talked about how it wouldn't be possible to get to an experience like this [shame], without some sense of having violated an authority, or rules or standards, right?

ANNE: [She nods 'yes,' smiling.]

ME: Okay. Now with this next question I'm not asking for a conscious mind opinion....

There can just be a sensing here in the chest [the location of the experience of shame] ... and sensing in and through here [the area in the chest] ... from the sensation here, notice ... *"Where* is the location of whatever *this* is trying to please or satisfy?"

And just notice whatever location comes into awareness ... [Anne's eyes are closed, and she's nodding as she is listening to me.] ... And what do you get?

ANNE: ... [She pauses, waiting for an answer.] ... Around here in front of my face and my forehead. [She draws an oval in front of her face with her right hand.]

ME: Okay. So, around the face, forehead. Great. And what's the size and shape, approximately? You're sort of showing us....

ANNE: Yeah, it's kind of oval again.

ME: It's kind of an oval.

ANNE: Yeah. And it's very red. [She smiles, as if surprised.]

ME: Okay... [I smile and chuckle.] It's funny, sometimes there's a color that just stands out. Lovely. And sensing in and through this oval-shaped area that's red ... what's the sensation quality in and through this area?

ANNE: Okay, so it's not really dense, and it's not airy. It's kind of in between.... It's just there. [She chuckles, as if she can't find an adequate word to describe it.]

ME: Not dense. Not airy. In between. Yeah, great.

Session Notes: The 1st Authority	
Location	*In front of face and forehead*
Size & Shape	*Oval (Gestures for size)*
Sensation Quality	*Red, not dense, not airy, in between*

The Chain of Authority Inside

To the Group and Anne: Okay, so now our next step is to find what I call the Chain of Authority inside. Just as there are Chains of 'I's, there are also Chains of Authorities. Because it turns out that usually the first Authority we find is not really a "Final Authority." It might be more of a middle manager or the person who answers the phone, so to speak. And it's just like, if you were calling up a company with a suggestion or a request, the person who answers the phone might not have any real power to make the change, right? So you're not going to get anywhere. But if you get to the CEO (the head of the company), then you're talking to someone with the power to actually make the change.

So, it's important for us to find out: is this a Final Authority or not? Or is this one a middle manager and it's doing its best to fulfill and carry out what another Authority wishes to have happen? So, this is what we're going to check for now.

Finding the Second Authority

ME: [To Anne:] So, going back to this location here [I gesture to the location of the first Authority relative to my body.] ... this that's oval-shaped in front of the face and forehead, that's not dense and not airy ... sensing in and through this ... is there the sense that this is a Final Authority?

ANNE: [She shakes her head "no."]

ME: Or ... when you check, is there a sense that there's something else ... in some other location ... that this is trying to please or satisfy?

ANNE: Um hum. [She nods definitively.]

ME: So, sensing in and through here [I'm referring to the location of the first Authority, to which Anne is still attending.]

    ... from the sensation here, that's not dense, not airy ... from here, where is the location of whatever this is trying to please? ... Yeah, and you've already got it.

ANNE: Yeah ... And it's like a curved rectangle that's weighing down on my shoulders. [Eyes closed, she traces a curved rectangular shape in front of her chest. She then taps on both shoulders.]

ME: So, it's resting on your shoulders?

ANNE: It's resting on my shoulders ... It's hard.

ME: Great. And how thick is it?

ANNE: It's about that thick. [She indicates thickness with her right thumb and forefinger, and then chuckles.]

ME: Got it. Yeah. Maybe a couple of inches or whatever your measurement is. About half a thumb? Half a forefinger maybe? [Anne and I laugh about this.]

    ... Sensing in and through the space of this ... What's the sensation quality here?

ANNE: ... It's like a thick cardboard.... It's very still.

ME: Okay, great. So, thick cardboard, very still.... And is it fairly dense?

ANNE: [Anne nods.]

ME: Okay. Great. And is it that way all the way through?

ANNE: Yeah. [She nods definitively.]

Session Notes: The 2nd Authority	
Location	*On shoulders*
Size & Shape	*Curved rectangle, a couple of inches thick*
Sensation Quality	*Hard, like thick cardboard, fairly dense*

Finding the Third Authority

ME: Okay, excellent. So now we're going to ask the same question again to find out if there's another Authority.

So, sensing in and through this that's kind of dense, like cardboard, check: Is there the sense that this is a Final Authority? Or ... is there the sense that this is also attempting to please, satisfy something else in some other location?

ANNE: [She nods 'yes,' indicating another Authority.]

ME: So, sensing in and through this here, that's kind of like cardboard, where is the location of whatever this is trying to please or satisfy or serve?

ANNE: ... I've got a sensation of something behind me that's kind of pressing into here. [She gestures to her mid-back.] It feels like it's quite large.

To You/Reader: I ask Anne the questions about size, shape, and sensation quality, and we discover that this Authority is located behind her back and head. It's large, curved, and rectangular, with more substance at the bottom, and vaporous towards the top.

Session Notes: The 3ʳᵈ Authority	
Location	*Behind her back and head*
Size & Shape	*Large curved and rectangular*
Sensation Quality	*More substance at bottom and vaporous towards the top*

Finding the Fourth Authority

ME: Okay, great. Beautiful. So now sensing in and through the space of this, the sensation here ... is there the sense that this is a Final Authority?

... Or is there the sense that this is also trying to please or satisfy something else, in some other location? ...

ANNE: [She nods "yes."]

ME: Yeah ... And where's the location of that?

ANNE: [She continues nodding as she raises both arms above her head to show the location.]

ME: So above and a bit around…. So, what's the size and shape?

ANNE: It's a bit like a plane. Not an airplane, like a dimensional plane … that just goes up. [Her hands open out near the top of her head and then her arms go up higher.]

I can't sense where it ends.

ME: Okay, it goes up. Don't know where it ends …

ANNE: Or how far it goes this way. [Her arms extend outward to both sides.]

ME: Okay, so it's pretty wide. And it extends quite far up. You don't know how far exactly. Okay, lovely. So, sensing in and through this, the area of this, what's the sensation quality here?

ANNE: … Just kind of misty … Misty, yeah. [She pauses. Her hands open briefly in a delicate way, and then she nods.]

Checking for a Final Authority

ME: Great. And sensing in and through this that's misty … Is there the sense that this is a Final Authority?

ANNE: Uh-huh. [She nods "yes."].

ME: Okay. Lovely. So now we've got the whole Authority Chain.

Session Notes: The 4th/Final Authority	
Location	*Above head*
Size & Shape	*A plane that goes up and extends wide*
Sensation Quality	*Misty*

Finding the 'I'

ME: Now we're going to find the 'I' in relation to all of this. So you can be aware of all of this at once, right? That place in the chest area,... then the place around the face and forehead that's not so dense,... the place resting on the shoulders,... the place behind you that's larger, and this vast place above ...

You can be aware of all of that at once, right? ... So "Where is the perceiving of this happening from?" or "Where's the 'I' that notices [this]?

ANNE: [She gestures above her head.]

ME: Great. ... So, the 'I' is above—

ANNE: Yeah. And to the back. About here.... [She extends her right arm above her head.]

ME: Great, beautiful. And what's the size and the shape?

ANNE: It's as if it was an actual eye ... but as if it's looking down. It's creating a triangle shape as if it's the field of vision. Does that make sense? ...

[Anne's eyes close as she tries to put her experience into words.] ... As if it's a field of vision looking down over the whole thing. [Her arms are out wide above her head, indicating the shape of the "seeing field" for this 'I' above her head.]

ME: Great. So, sensing in and through this —that looks kind of like an eye— ... Sensing in and through the space of this ... What's the sensation quality in and through...? [My voice becomes soft.] ...

ANNE: It's—it's quite light.

Session Notes: The 'I'	
Location	*Above the head and towards the back*
Size & Shape	*Like an eye looking down*
Sensation Quality	*Quite light*

Inviting the 'I' to Integrate as Awareness

ME: So now we're ready to begin the integration phase and find out what happens. Are you ready for that? [Anne smiles and gives two thumbs up.] Okay, awesome.

So, sensing in and through this here, that looks like an eye, it's quite light.... Does the sensation here welcome the invitation to open, relax, dissolve, melt... in and as the full field of Awareness? [Anne nods slowly.]

... Okay. And there can just be a relaxing into the happening of that.... When we get a "Yes," we can just allow it to go ahead. And just allow this to integrate however is natural ... opening, relaxing, dissolving and melting ... Or perhaps sometimes all of Awareness comes to it ... Or even the Awareness already present in this location waking up to itself, or something else.... Yeah ... and you can allow that to happen however it happens.

And then whenever things settle, you can let me know....

ANNE: [Her breathing slows and deepens as she follows my guiding, eventually a soft smile appears, along with a nod.]

ME: Yes ... And what's the experience of that?

ANNE: [She smiles warmly and laughs, giving two thumbs up, eyes still closed.]

ME: Well put. [I chuckle.]

Inviting the Fourth (Final) Authority to Integrate

ME: Okay, great. And now we're going to go back the way we came.

We're going to that last Authority, the final one, which before was "above and quite light." And how is it now? Is it the same or a little different?

ANNE: It's different. [She's nodding.]

ME: And how is it now?

ANNE: Hmmm…. It's thin—like not much to it. [Anne seems curious about the change. She draws a thin line in front of her with her thumbs and index fingers, to show how it is now.]

ME: Thin, not much to it. So, it sounds like it's already begun to integrate on its own. And we're just going to invite it to continue. So, sensing in and through this that's already kind of thin, not much to it … we can invite this to integrate however is natural…. [Anne looks increasingly more relaxed.]

Yes … and it looks like it's already happening…. [Anne is breathing more deeply and seems to be experiencing a delicious relaxation.] and that may be a kind of dissolving and melting in and through the field of Awareness…. Yeah … is that how it works well, for this one?

ANNE: Uh huh. [She nods smoothly.]

ME: Okay. And if that feels easy and natural, I won't offer the other options. There are other options that sometimes are wanted. But if this feels like a really good fit, we're just going to go with this. [Anne nods.] Okay. Lovely. Then there can be just a relaxing into the happening of this.

ANNE: [Anne sighs, her chest moving as the release continues.]

ME: Yeah … and sometimes when I do this, I just kind of take a deep breath…. Because it's easy to just let go of conscious control, any effort to make anything happen, or even to track anything happening. [Anne breathes deeply again.]

And just let whatever wants to happen, happen. Because the essential elements are here now. We become aware of the sensation of this. And Awareness itself is present here in this location. So, there can just be an opening and relaxing, however feels natural. Yeah….

ANNE: [Her eyes are closed, head nodding peacefully.]

ME: … And when everything is settled, you can let me know.

ANNE: … [She appears deeply immersed in the process, allowing it to happen. Then she begins smiling softly, and nods.]

Me: Okay. Lovely…. Anything you want to share about the experience of that? You don't have to. We can just go right on.

Anne: [Her breathing deepens even more, as she appears to continue processing, deeply immersed inwardly. She just smiles and nods.]

Me: Yeah, great. We just go right on.

To You/Reader: It's clear from Anne's nonverbals that useful changes are already happening. I'm checking if there is anything Anne can easily share in words. She prefers to just stay with her felt experience, and it's important for me to honor this.

Inviting the Third Authority to Integrate

Me: Okay, now we go to the one before, which before was this curved rectangle resting on the shoulders. And what's there now? Is it the same? Or is it a little different … or even significantly different? Just notice what's there now.

Anne: It's just a lot less.

Me: A lot less. Okay. Great. So, sensing in and through this, that's a lot less … whatever is here right now … we want to sense in and through this, and invite this also to open, relax, dissolve, melt, to integrate in whatever way is natural for this. [Anne takes a few more deep breathes, she gently stretches/rolls her shoulders as her chest becomes more open and relaxed.]

Yes, beautiful…. And just letting that happen however it happens…. [If it wants to dissolve into Awareness … if it wants Awareness to come to it … or if the Awareness already present in this area wakes up to itself.] … Sometimes the integration happens in some unpredictable or unusual way. And we are just giving permission for it to happen, however it really wants to happen. And then the wisdom of the system can just express itself. [A relaxed smile spreads across Anne's face. She looks deeply calm.] Yeah, yeah….

ME: And you can let me know, whenever it's had plenty of time to complete itself, when things have settled....

ANNE: ... [A wide smile emerges, and she nods a few times.]

Inviting the Second Authority to Integrate

ME: Okay, beautiful. So now we go to the one before that, which was behind you. Before it was this sort of curved rectangle with more substance at the bottom, more vapor at the top. So, what's here now?

ANNE: [She pauses to check.] ... It's almost gone.

ME: Okay, it's almost gone. So, it's a significant change already, and you can still find something. And, we want to be sure we include everything remaining....

So, sensing in and through whatever remains here, there can just be this gentle invitation for the aliveness here now, the sensation here now, to open relax, dissolve, melt.... That's right ... in and as the full field of Awareness, that's all around and throughout. And/or however it naturally wants to integrate, can just be allowed to happen.

Sometimes what wants to happen is it wants to merge with the one before it. Sometimes what wants to happen is it wants you as Awareness to relax into and as the sensation of this, or to let this come to you as Awareness. [Anne is smiling widely.] So however it naturally happens, we're just relaxing into the happening of this....

ANNE: Hmmm ... [She says with a sigh, her body releasing. Then she smiles and nods.]

ME: Yeah, right. Beautiful. And you can take all the time you need, and let me know when everything settles.

Inviting the First Authority to Integrate

ME: So now we're going to check in with the one that before was around the face and forehead. That was between dense and airy.

And how is this now? ... What's here now?

ANNE: It's just almost see-through ... cloudy, less substantial.

ME: Cloudy, less substantial. Okay, so sensing in and through this, that's cloudy and less substantial ... Notice what happens when this is invited to dissolve, melt, ... into the full field of Awareness that's all around and throughout the body.

And there may be a streaming and flowing, sometimes there's a melting and dissolving. Sometimes if there is a streaming and flowing, it happens in unpredictable ways and directions....

And there can just be an allowing ... as this relaxes itself ... of whatever naturally happens ... because that will be exactly what the system needs for this return to wholeness— to Undivided Presence.... Yeah....

ANNE: ... [Eyes closed, she seems deeply immersed in the process, with slow deep breathing, looking relaxed.]

ME: ... And taking all the time you need you can let me know whenever things settle....

ANNE: [She smiles and nods, indicating things have settled.]

ME: Okay, beautiful.

Inviting the Original Feeling to Integrate

ME: And now we go to the place we started which was the chest area.... What's there now? Is it the same, or different? What's present now?

ANNE: Well, the hard center bit is gone. There's just a bit of a sensation there. But much, much less substantial. [Anne's hands move in front of her chest, as she is sensing into this original feeling area.]

ME: Okay, lovely. So, a lot has already shifted and—

ANNE: [She raises her left hand indicating she wants to speak.] Can I just say—the horrible emotion that I had with it before is gone. There was something [inaudible—face scrunches up to indicate unpleasantness] before, and that's just gone. [She looks relieved.]

ME: Ah….

ANNE: There was actually a yucky emotion with it, and now it's gone.

ME: Yeah, and isn't that interesting? And it kind of makes sense, because once the Authorities have dissolved, it's like there's nothing—no rule structure for our feeling to get its juice from. Not in the same way anyway. So, that's lovely.

So, sensing whatever remains here, we want to include everything that's still present. And so, sensing and in through the sensation of this now—even without necessarily understanding it or needing to label what's there—the sensation itself is invited to also integrate in whatever way is natural.

So whether that's a dissolving and melting, an opening and relaxing, streaming and flowing … however that naturally happens can just happen. [My voice is soft and gentle.]

ANNE: [Anne looks peaceful as she processes. She takes a really big breath, with a final release, then smiles and nods.]

ME: Yes. Okay. And has this had all the time that it needs now?

ANNE: Yeah. [She nods again.]

Checking in with the Original Situation

ME: Okay, beautiful. So now we're back to the beginning. And we're going to check in with this situation itself.

So, being this way, with the Authorities integrated, the 'I' integrated, the beginning sensation integrated … how is it now when you think about being in this situation?

ANNE: ... I can't even think about it. It's just gone. [She lifts her head higher, blinks repeatedly and shakes her head a few times, as if to express surprise, perhaps amazement.]

ME: Okay. All right.

ANNE: It no longer has any relevance. [She closes her eyes, lowers her gaze, and nods a few times.]

ME: Uh huh. I see. Yeah, that sounds like a pretty complete statement. Okay. Thanks so much, Anne.

ANNE: Thank you.

ME: Yes. Okay. And has this had all the time that it needs now?

ANNE: Yeah. [She nods again.]

ME: And is there anything else you want to say about your experience of this?

ANNE: [Her face lights up with a smile.] One thing that was especially interesting. The one that was here [she gestures in front of her face] when you invited integrating—my awareness went to it. And it just kind of went poof! [Her hands are close together and then open quickly, as if expressing a quick and sudden bursting outwards.]

    So, first it became really bright. And, like, literally all my attention went into it. But then it just all went poof! [She seems surprised, fascinated.]

To You/Reader: Anne seems to be describing two directions of integrating happening in sequence. As the integrating begins, all of Awareness flows into the area of the structure we invited to integrate. This is the second direction of integration. Next there is a "poof" where everything dissolves or dissipates outward, into the whole. This is the first direction of integration, happening quite quickly.

ANNE: So, it was different. The other ones that were all kind of flowing, and softening. This one was much more "whoosh" ... everything went into it [she brings her hands together.] ... and then it just went like that .... [Her arms quickly open out wide showing a sudden bursting or spreading.]

ME: Yeah, I appreciate you sharing that. It's an example of how it's helpful to know the three directions of integration.

When we know the three directions of integration, it helps create permission for the integrating to happen however is needed—however feels right, easy and natural.

ANNE: [Anne gives a brief beaming smile.]

ME: Thank you so much. Okay. Enjoy. And you can just notice now what it's like. Sometimes when we make these changes with Authority, the shift goes to areas we don't expect. It makes—

ANNE: It feels pretty big—like freeing. [She nods and opens out her arms.]

ME: Yeah. Okay, beautiful.

Full Session Notes: Reclaiming Inner Authority

Beginning Experience:	*"Shame"*
Location	*In the chest area (inside, and a little bit outside)*
Size & Shape	*Oval*
Sensation Quality	*Dense in center, less dense around it*

1ˢᵗ Authority	
Location	*In front of face and forehead*
Size & Shape	*Oval (gestures for size)*
Sensation Quality	*Red, not dense, not airy, in between*

2nd **Authority**

Location	*On shoulders*
Size & Shape	*Not very thick (a couple of inches), curved rectangle*
Sensation Quality	*Thick, hard, fairly dense cardboard*

3rd **Authority**

Location	*Behind her head*
Size & Shape	*Large, curved and rectangular*
Sensation Quality	*More substance at bottom and vaporous towards the top*

4th **Authority**

Location	*Above head*
Size & Shape	*A plane that goes up and extends wide*
Sensation Quality	*Misty*

'I'

Location	*Above head and towards the back*
Size & Shape	*Like an eye looking down*
Sensation Quality	*Quite light*

flowchart
the authority format

In the following flowchart, you can see the main steps of the Reclaiming Authority Format in one image.

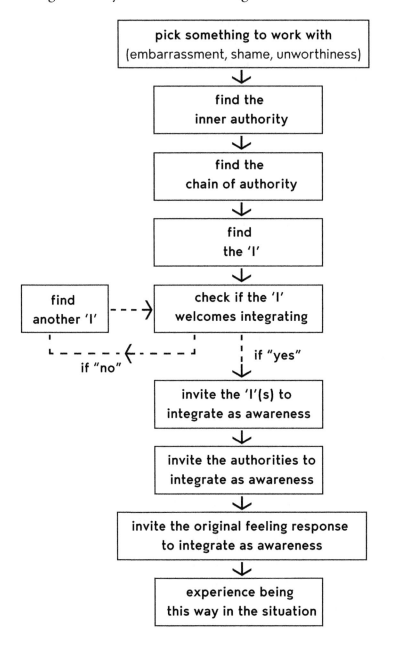

overview
& pointers

Do you feel ready to experience this yourself? If so, you can jump to the next section—the Step-by-Step Guide. If you'd like a few pointers first, read this section.

Step 1: Pick an experience of embarrassment or shame—and step in and notice the feeling response.

The first time you do this exercise, be sure to pick something mild to medium. You can choose a recent experience, or something from the past—childhood even.

Once you've selected an experience, I'll ask you to step into the experience, to notice the feeling response. *You don't need to access this experience fully.* It's ok just to access a small amount of the feeling—just enough to notice the location, size, shape, and sensation quality.

Step 2: Find the Authority or rule-setter related to this feeling.

This isn't something you can find by thinking about it with your conscious mind. Instead the script will guide you to start by sensing the feeling response itself. You can just notice the sensation quality of this feeling. Then, while you're sensing this, you'll ask "Where is whatever this is trying to please or satisfy?" This makes it easy for the location of an inner structure that's been unconscious to make itself known to you.

* * Be Ready for the Unexpected * *

Were you surprised by the Authority Structures that Anne found in the demonstration? Our unconscious Authority Structures are usually quite different than what we might expect. Often they've coalesced at the unconscious level in a form that doesn't look/feel like any person in our life, and that may not make any sense to our conscious mind. This is fine—I'm telling you this so that you're prepared to notice whatever emerges within, rather than expecting anything in particular.

Step 3: Find the Authority Chain.

Usually the first Authority you find turns out not to be a Final Authority, one with the power to make change. As I mentioned earlier in this section, it's like when you contact a business about something. The person who answers the phone usually isn't the CEO. They might not have the power to make a change. So if you can get to the CEO, then you get to an Authority that has the power to actually make the change. On Step 3 you'll be guided in finding the Chain of Authority on the inside, that has been holding the starting feeling in place.

Most Authority Chains have two or three "layers" of Authorities, although you might find up to five, and on rare occasion even more.

* * A Few Tips about the Final Authority * *

- **It can be dense or not dense.** Don't be surprised if the Final Authority you discover is dense. Sometimes the final one is dense, other times not. Either will work well. The first time I did this process with myself, the Final Authority was super dense. I thought, "Oh no, how is it ever going to integrate?" I was accustomed to working with 'I's and usually a dense 'I' isn't able to integrate.

   However, I tried asking this dense Final Authority if it welcomed integrating. To my surprise it did! It even happened easily. I tried this out with other people, and noticed it worked the same way for them. The Final Authority might be quite dense, but if it's truly the Final Authority it will still be able to integrate.

- **It can be dark or light.** The Final Authority might be dark, it might be light, or it might be neither. However it is, is fine.

- **It can look like a person—or not.** Sometimes the Authority you find inside looks like a person. If this happens, just treat it as you would if it had any other shape and form. Just notice what it looks like then let go of the image and sense in and through the space for the sensation quality. (See the Q & A Section later in this chapter for more about this.)

Steps 4 & 5: Find the 'I', and then invite it to Integrate.

Often it would be possible to integrate the Authority Chain without this step, but finding and integrating the related 'I' makes the whole process gentler and easier—and more complete.

Steps 6 & 7: Invite each Authority to integrate—beginning with the "final" or last one.

Did you notice in the demonstration that when I invited an authority to integrate, I offered some new choices? When I started inviting my own inner Authorities to integrate, I noticed that sometimes they wanted to integrate in a different way than the 'I's usually did. So in your script, I've included the main choices that I've encountered in myself or in my clients and workshop participants.

New Choices for Integrating

Here are the main options you'll find in your script: The sensation/ energy of the Authority might want to:

- Dissolve into and as all of Awareness
- Merge with the Authority just before it
- Allow "You as Awareness" to relax in and as the sensation of the Authority

The first two options are easy to understand, right? But you might wonder what that third option means. What does "you as Awareness" mean?

This is much easier to explain in a training session where you can watch my gestures. But I'll do my best in written form. We've already been exploring Awareness. Awareness can be described as the capacity to experience that's in and through the space all around. Or we can just describe Awareness as the experience of spaciousness that's throughout the body and all around.

The experience of "me *as* Awareness" is a little different. I'm not just noticing Awareness (or the spaciousness all around), but I'm BEING Awareness. There isn't a separate 'I' noticing. And this experience of BEING Awareness has a center in subjective experience, and that center is my central column. That's why I'm using the words, "you as Awareness." It's not a separate self that's noticing Awareness; you are actually *being* Awareness. And yet there's a center to this experience of being Awareness. And *this* is what can "lean into" or relax into, the location where the Authority is present.

So if "I as Awareness" am relaxing into the sensation of the Authority, it can feel as if I *am* Awareness, and *as Awareness,* I'm just relaxing or falling into the location of the Authority. I might feel myself literally lean into that direction. (I'll go into more detail on this in the Q & A Section.)

If this doesn't make sense to you, it's not a problem. It usually just means this isn't the kind of integrating your system needs right now. You can read the script including this instruction and if something in it makes sense to your being, it will happen on its own—even if you don't consciously understand it.

— A Key Concept —

When you invite the Authorities to integrate, the main thing to realize is this: We're always inviting each inner structure to integrate *however it wants to*—in whatever way feels natural to it. We're sensing what the Authority wants to do—both *what* it wants to integrate with and *how* it wants to integrate. It's all in the Step-by-Step Guide script, so you can just read it and not think about it much. The script includes the main options that work for most inner Authorities.

 You can use the Reclaiming Authority Worksheet to jot down notes when you guide yourself through the process. You only need a few words or a phrase to remind you of each "aspect." To access this resource, use the QR this code or go to www.thewholenesswork.org/BookResources.

step-by-step guide
reclaiming inner authority

Okay, are you ready to experience this yourself? You might like to allow 30 or 40 minutes of uninterrupted time, the first time, so you can explore this fully. Once this format is familiar, it may happen luxuriously in just 10 minutes. As you continue your practice of the Wholeness Work, you'll discover the amount of time it takes for you to do each process in a comfortable relaxed way.

Read each of the following steps. Pause after each step to notice your experience.

Step 1: Choose an experience to work with—step in & notice the feeling response.
Think of an experience of shame or embarrassment. You can pick a present experience or something from the past. (If you can't think of one of those, you can pick another experience involving authority, such as unworthiness, guilt, or the need to defend or prove something. However, I strongly recommend starting with shame or embarrassment.)

- *Step into the experience just enough to notice how you feel.*
- *Notice where the feeling [_of shame, embarrassment, etc._] is located.*
- *And what is the size and shape?*
- *And what is the sensation quality in and through this location?*

Step 2: Find the "Inner Authority."
It wouldn't be possible to feel [shame/embarrassment] without a sense of violating some kind of rules or standards, right?... So sensing into this sensation in [_location from Step 1_], from there, check:

- ***Where is the location this sensation is trying to please or satisfy? Where is the Authority for this? The one who sets the standards? The rule-maker?*** *I'm not asking you to name a person. I'm asking for a location in space in or around you.*

It may or may not be related to a particular person. Another way to ask the question is: **Where is this feeling/experience here in [_location from Step 1_] orienting toward? What location is this experience checking with?**

- *We'll call this the Authority.*
- *Notice the size, shape, and especially the sensation quality in and through this location.*

Step 3: Find the Chain of Authority.

Check if this is the Final Authority.

Now sense into the sensation in [_location of the Authority_], and notice, "Is this a Final Authority? Or is there the sense that this, here, is trying to please or satisfy something else in another location? Is there some other location that this here is orienting towards, or checking with, or acting in the service of?"

If this Authority is trying to please or satisfy something else:

Find the next Authority.

- *So sensing into this sensation in [_location of the Authority_],... from here ... check:* <u>*Where is the location this is trying to please or satisfy?*</u>
- *Notice the size, shape, and sensation quality of this next Authority.*
- Check if this is the Final Authority. *Sensing into this, is this a Final Authority... or, is the sensation here also trying to please or satisfy something else, in some other location?*

Continue until you get to the Final Authority. (Most Authority Chains have three to five layers.)

If this is the Final Authority: Go on to Step 4.

Step 4: Find the 'I'.

And there can be a noticing of all of this at once, right? ... [Take a moment to simultaneously notice each of the Authorities and the beginning experience.]

And where is the perceiving of all of this happening from?... Notice the location, the size and shape, and the sensation quality.

Step 5: Check if the 'I' welcomes integrating.

Notice the sensation in the location of the 'I'. Does the sensation here, welcome the invitation to dissolve, melt, in and as... the fullness of Awareness... that's all around and throughout?

If "Yes":

Notice what happens when the sensation of this 'I' is invited to open and relax as the fullness of Awareness that's all around and throughout.

If "No":

Find another 'I'. Do this until you find one that's ready to integrate.

(Or, you could check if the Final Authority is ready to integrate.)

Step 6: Invite the Final Authority to integrate.[1]

Now let's return to the last/Final Authority.

- Check in this location. *Is it the same now? Or a little different? ...*
- Now check: *What does this [_the sensation of the Final Authority_] welcome integrating with? It may want to dissolve as all of Awareness... it may want to merge with the Authority just before it ... or it may want to merge with "you as Awareness."*
- *You can just allow it to integrate, dissolve, merge in whatever way wants to happen. If it wants to integrate directly with you, it may want you as Awareness to relax into it ... or it may prefer to come to you, or some of each.*

    (Just allow whatever happens to happen, until things naturally settle.)

---

[1] My experience so far is that the Final Authority is essentially always willing to integrate with something. If it doesn't want to integrate, check for another Authority.

Step 7: Invite each Authority to integrate.

Beginning with the second-to-last Authority, invite each remaining Authority to integrate as follows:

- *Checking in the location of this Authority, first notice how it is now. Is it exactly the same as it was before, or is it a little bit different? Either is fine. It's just useful to notice how it is now.*
- *Check with the sensation in this location. What does it want to integrate with? It might want to integrate with the Awareness that's all around, or with the Authority just before it, or with you as Awareness.*
- *And this can be allowed to happen in whatever way feels most natural.*

Step 8: Invite the original feeling to integrate with Awareness.

Now check what's present now in the location of the original feeling. Is it the same or a bit different?... Whatever is there now can be invited to open and relax as all of Awareness. And/or all of Awareness can be invited to flow in and as the sensation here now.

Step 9: Check for completion and experience in context.

Checking inwardly, does this feel complete?

If "Yes," Experience in the Context:

Take a moment to experience what it's like being this way (with the energy of the Authorities and the 'I' merged with all of Awareness) *in the situation you began with....* (If this feels resourceful, explore one or two additional situations.)

If "No," Ask:

What else is there? (You can check for another 'I' or perhaps a Reaction. In rare cases, there may be another Authority Chain.)

Sharing Experiences

Here are a few experiences that people in Wholeness Work training sessions shared about doing this exercise.

"As soon as all the Authority parts appeared and I invited them to relax into Awareness, it all, like, crumbled at the same time—very, very quickly. And there was a feeling of great joy. Like, yeah, great, great joy. It was wonderful!"

"I worked with feeling embarrassed. It was a racy stress feeling in my heart area. And all that dissolved. Now the same area just feels sort of flat—neutral. It feels fine."

"It's this ongoing trickle of relief. Tears of relief."

"[Doing this exercise] I have experienced the deepest sense of self forgiveness I have ever had."

"That was an amazing journey for me. And I also noticed humor—this sort of cool liquid underneath the experience— by the end. I was very surprised."

"I feel as if my heart has grown, and it is there, beating. It was as if my heart has been compressed, and [through this exercise] it was allowed to expand."

"What surprised me was that I needed to go much slower with integrating the Authorities than when I was inviting the 'I's to integrate. I needed to give them more time."

"My late grandmother had abandoned my father as a baby—I never met her, but [doing this exercise I discovered] she was weighing on my back and shoulders. Through the exercise she was released and now I can breathe. ... NOW I AM. Life is being generated."

Later Reports of Results

The previous reports are drawn from what workshop participants shared immediately after doing the process. Next are two stories of how the transformations carried over into day-to-day life.

Rena's Boss

After doing the Authority Process on a situation with her boss, Rena noticed feeling more "equal" and at ease saying what she thought. Rena said, *"My boss wanted an ill co-worker to come to work anyway. I couldn't believe I was able to tell him very calmly that I disagreed and considered this worker had a right to get better. I was surprised when my boss accepted my point of view. This was not something he did normally."*

Vera's Construction Worker

Vera had been having problems with a worker she'd hired to fix her roof. She was very upset and angry at the worker. He wasn't completing the job as promised, and didn't come to work each day, as he'd agreed.

After doing the Authority Process with this issue in a training, Vera was beaming; she reported that the stress had melted away and she was feeling deeply peaceful. She was surprised by the fact that the peaceful feeling was still there the following day. She said, *"Even my husband noticed the change in my behavior. I was so calm. And the man came early to finish the job he'd started 4 months ago."* She guessed that the change in her led to the man's change in behavior.

reclaiming our power
understanding the authority format

In our process of Awakening or coming to Wholeness within, integrating Authority produces a different kind of transformation than integrating the 'I's.

When you invited an Authority to integrate, what did you notice? Was your experience of integrating Authorities different from when you integrated the 'I's?

For many people, integrating Authorities has a different feeling quality, compared to integrating the 'I's—at least some of the time. Frequently people describe experiencing inner shifts such as "I feel more substantial, more grounded." One woman described it as "It felt like something pouring into me—like calcium was pouring into my bones." It's fairly common to have a visceral experience of more substantialness in and through the body.

This makes sense because the Authorities are representations that literally contain lots of strength and power. Yet this power is something that's coded at the unconscious level as "not us." It's coded as not belonging to us. So when this powerful energy is invited to integrate, we can again experience this power as "us"—rather than separate from us. We are literally reclaiming our power.

Often the Authority energy is experienced as dense or substantial in some way. When this substantialness is integrated, the "power" in it is now part of us, rather than something perceived as "not us."

When we integrate Authority Structures, we're literally reclaiming power that was always "us."

Another typical shift is that before integrating, the "Authority Energy" is often rigid—literally rigid. After integrating, the Authority Energy usually transforms into something experienced as substantial yet somehow flexible in a grounded way.

Remember that however you experienced this exercise is fine—in fact, perfect. Your experience might be completely different from what I'm describing. The processing will always work best for you when you stay true to however it's unfolding for you. As long as you're gently inviting and not forcing anything, it will happen in the way that's natural and that's best for your system.

** A Visual Representation of the Authority Format **

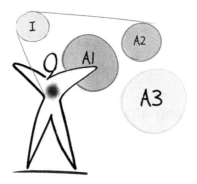

You might find an 'I' or an Authority either outside or inside the body; they can be anywhere.

the significance
of this change

The Wholeness Work Authority Process can potentially bring about a quite profound level of change. And there's a "why" behind it. A "science" if you will.[2]

This process helps us integrate something fundamental within our psyche that we didn't have a way to reach before. When most

---

[2] Here I am using "science" to mean that we have a specific, precise and experience-based map and understanding of how our unconscious structures work, and procedures that are possible to reliably repeat and test with research. Some people think of Science as meaning having existing research support. Wholeness Work has preliminary research support already, and much more to do!

therapeutic approaches work with embarrassment or shame they work with the *feeling* of embarrassment or shame. But these feelings are just the *consequence* of having an unintegrated (and unconscious) rule structure. With Wholeness Work we are finding and integrating the *source* of these feelings—specifically, the inner construct holding an unconscious rule structure in place.

When another therapeutic approach does go beyond working with the feelings of shame, etc., to work with an experience of authority, it's usually attempted through content. For example, if you've explored therapeutic approaches, you may have been taught to communicate with your "Parent" inside. That kind of approach can have benefit. However, Wholeness Work goes farther in the following three ways.

1: Working with Authority at a Level Deeper than Content

As mentioned earlier, most methods of working with "authority issues" deal with content. We talk about our relationship with a person in our life who was an authority for us, and try to come to a new, more adult relationship. When working at the content level, change tends to be slow and incomplete.

Wholeness Work shifts out of content to the process level. We find the Authority Structure(s) inside that keep our feelings of embarrassment or shame in place. When we find these structures inside, it turns out that often they are no longer represented as a specific person in our life. They don't look like Mom, Dad, or Grandpa.

You might have discovered this when you did the exercise in this chapter. If your Authority Structure inside appears as a dense cloud of dust, or a file cabinet, or something else, it means that just talking to Dad or Mom on the inside won't address what's actually going on inside now. Often we're not responding to Mom or Dad any longer, but rather to a more generalized inner representation of authority—for example a dark dense cloud or even a glowing sun. With Wholeness Work, when we shift out of content we can easily find the energetic Authority Structures that exist today at the unconscious level.

We are working at the level of internal structure.

2: Finding the Chain of Authority

If other methods include dealing with inner Authority, they generally address only the first level of authority, and never get to the Final Authority. This makes change more difficult.

With Wholeness Work it's easy to find and include the *entire* Authority Chain and get to the Final Authority. This is what makes the change process sometimes quite profound—and at the same time simple. Using the Authority Process it's possible to experience a deep transformation quickly and fully in a way that also feels kind and gentle. This is an important breakthrough—as far as I know, this has never been done before.

3: Integrating—Not Just Communicating

As we've discussed, with Wholeness Work we actually integrate the Authority Structures. Just learning to communicate better doesn't accomplish integration if our experience of Authority is still separate from "us." Having a separate Authority Structure inside leaves us susceptible to ongoing internal struggles between the "rule-makers" and "us." Once the Authority Structures are integrated as "us," we discover a newfound ability to act from a different kind of "morality" that's based on the Whole. (See the section on "new morality" at the end of this chapter.)

So with Wholeness Work we go beyond talking about it or changing the meaning. *We actually integrate something that was separate.* This is how the deepest level of change happens.

Authority Structures are involved with many life issues.

At the beginning of this chapter, I gave you a checklist of life issues where an Authority Structure is likely to be involved. Any issue that includes a sense of how you "should be" or how others or the world "should be" is going to involve inner Authority Structures. If someone feels anxious or depressed, often a background sense of how things "ought to be" comes into play. These rule structures are a fundamental part of maintaining many difficult-to-change issues. Once we bring these unconscious rule structures into conscious awareness, and know how to process them, it's a different ballgame.

Inner Authorities are involved in maintaining many problems that can seem difficult to change.

During the Advanced Wholeness Work trainings (Level II and beyond), we learn more about how and when to utilize finding the Inner Authority as part of the flow of inner work. Most people find this work quite liberating. It's freeing you to become more of who you really are.

answering
your questions

Can't Find the Inner Authority

Q What if I can't find the Authority?

A If you can't find the Authorities inside, I encourage you to join a live training (either online or in person), or work with an experienced Wholeness Work coach. In the trainings people almost always find it easy to notice the Authority inside. This is because you have a trained staff to help you, plus you get to watch and listen to someone else going through the process. This can make a big difference in your unconscious "getting it" easily.

If you're working on your own, you can also try "just pretending." You can pretend you know where the Authority is located, and find out what happens.

The Authority looks like a person.

Q What if the Authority looks like a person?

A An Authority can have any shape and size. It might appear as a non-descript blob in space, or it might look like a person (perhaps a parent, or teacher, or someone else from your past). It doesn't matter how it appears. If it looks like a person, you treat it the same as if it's just a nondescript cloud. You notice what it looks like, of course, and then— letting go of how it appears—you let there be a sensing in and through the space of this, that looks like whomever.

If it looks like a person, it's important to realize that what you're integrating isn't the other person. You are integrating part of your own consciousness, part of your own energy. It is part of your mental structure that you have formed into something that looks like that other person. However, that person isn't here. They aren't in the room with you. So it's not really them you're integrating. It's your representation of them. When you sense into the sensation quality in this area, this makes it possible for you to integrate the "aliveness" that is actually you, that you had been using to make this inner thought structure that looks like them.

The Authority Won't Integrate.

Q What if the Final Authority doesn't want to integrate?

A In general, the Final Authority will always want to integrate. If the Authority you found doesn't want to integrate, most likely it's not actually the final one. Sometimes I've found an Authority inside wants to present itself as the Final Authority—as if it's trying so hard to act like the "real boss," when it really isn't. Then if I just stay with it a little while being kindly present, eventually it allows me to "know it" more completely. It allows me to sense in and through more completely and it becomes ready to acknowledge it's not the final one.

The structures we find also really yearn to be known for who/ what they are. They yearn to be acknowledged and experienced by—and as—the field of Awareness. This is inherently a kindness. So you can kindly and gently check again. Let there be a sensing in and through the sensation in this area ... Ask: *"Is there something else, in some other location, that this here is trying to please or satisfy?"*

Occasionally, if a final authority doesn't integrate, it's because the person has a reaction to it. There may be a sense of hating this authority, or rebelling against it. In this case, it might be necessary to work with that reaction first, and then come back to inviting the authority to integrate.

As always, it's important not to push or force anything. If you need more help with this, you can contact a Wholeness Coach or join a training.

The Authority won't let me in.

Q When I tried to sense in and through the Authority, it wouldn't let me in. It's as if it didn't trust me.

A If this happens the first thing to do is relax and essentially "back off." With Wholeness Work we never want to force anything. If it doesn't trust you, this is fine. Because "you" don't need to do anything. If you have been trying to sense in and through, it [the Authority] might feel a pushiness and resist.

So it's easiest if we don't do anything, but just allow the field of Awareness itself to sense in and through. When we allow it, it's actually the field of Awareness that can gently sense whatever is present. The field of Awareness, by its nature, has no judgment. So the structures we find inside generally like becoming "known" by the field of Awareness itself. "You" don't need to do it. Because the field of Awareness naturally does this in a gentle and kind way. That's just its nature.

The Authority is dense and/or dark, not light or airy.

Q What if the sensation quality of the Authority is dense and/or dark? Will it still integrate?

A Sometimes the Final Authority is dark and dense, and other times it's light. When the Authority Chain starts out dark and dense, sometimes each new Authority is darker and denser until a really dark Final Authority is revealed. Other times it "flips" from a dark/dense chain to being light and less dense. Either is fine. And you might find something different from either of those options.

It's valuable to open ourselves to whatever is actually there.

And of course, as I mentioned before, even if a Final Authority is dark and dense, it WILL still integrate. If it's the Final Authority, it will always integrate.

Authority Integrating with Awareness vs. "You As Awareness Merging with Authority"

Q What's the difference between the Authority integrating with Awareness, and "you as Awareness" merging with the Authority?

A Let's imagine the Authority is located somewhere outside the body. The Authority integrating with Awareness is usually experienced as whatever is out there (the location of the Authority) melting and dissolving from there into the Whole. So there's a gentle flowing outwards in all directions.

Now let's talk about "you as Awareness" merging with Authority. Here's how I'd experience this…

Right now, Awareness is all around me, and if this Awareness has a center, it would be along the central column of my physical body (the location of my spinal column). Let's say the Authority I'm working with is located outside of my body, in front of me. It has another center within it. When I invite "myself as Awareness" to integrate with this Authority, I'm inviting a merging of these two centers (and these two experiences), to become one. So this experience of

Awareness with its center in my body along the central column, merges or integrates with the sensation in the location of the Authority.

We can think of this as the merging of the two centers. The two centers begin in two different locations. When they merge, there is just one center. "I as Awareness" might even lean forward a bit, almost as if I'm "falling into" the energy of the Authority.... Just letting go of anything that held itself separate.

Or the Authority might flow into "me as Awareness," and from there melt into everything and everywhere.

With the first type of integrating—the Authority integrating with Awareness—there is only one center in a sense. The Authority is located wherever it is. And it integrates with Awareness all around it.

With the second type, there is the experience of two centers that you are accessing at the same time and allowing to merge/meld/integrate however is natural, until the experience is only one center.

If this doesn't make sense, that's fine. Just invite whatever feels natural.

The Authority Is "God."

Q If I get to an Authority that says it's "God," is it the Final Authority?

A Sometimes people discover an Authority inside that says it's God, or they just know it's God. This doesn't happen for everybody, but has happened for quite a few people—even people with no religious beliefs. It's easy to assume that if the Authority says it's God this means it's the Final Authority. But keep in mind, these structures we find inside are our unconscious representations of something. Not that thing itself.

If you get to an Authority that appears as God, for this exercise, just treat it the same as any other Authority. Get the sensation quality and ask: "Is this a Final Authority, or is there something else this is trying to please or satisfy?" Quite often the Authorities identifying as God do have another Authority that they, too, are trying to please or satisfy.

Keep in mind that we don't need to understand what we find inside. This isn't primarily about gaining mental understanding of philosophical questions. However, when we find "God" structures inside during this exercise, these are likely to be unintegrated experiences formed in our attempts to understand when we were a young child.

The Authority is me.

Q What if the Authority is me?

A Usually we experience the Authorities we find within ourselves as a force that's "not me." We experience them as an outside force. However, occasionally someone tells me, "This Authority is *me.*" You don't really need to label which it is. Whether an Authority you find inside is experienced as "you," or as "someone/something else," it's always experienced as separate from the wholeness of consciousness that is you. So either way, you can just notice what is there and invite it to integrate.

Having Authority Structures inside can be functional in a certain stage of life. As children we need to orient ourselves in relationship to authority figures in our life. When we are children, they do have authority over us. However, as adults they don't have this authority, yet we may continue to act as if they do—and they aren't even here! It's a representation that we are carrying around with us (that sometimes even looks like them) that we're orienting to.

indicators for the authority process
clues for when to use this format

Here are the main indications that the Authority Format is likely to be useful or needed. (You can learn more about when and how to include an Authority Process in the trainings.)

Content Indicators: Embarrassment, Shame, and Unworthiness

The Authority Process will always be useful for deep healing of these issues. It's also likely to be useful when working with anything involving "should's," or "have to's," anger, feeling right, feeling wrong, etc.

Process Indicators: Density & Darkness

Density

When we encounter a structure inside that's dense (meaning when we sense in and through, it's the opposite of airy), this almost always indicates the presence of a related Authority Structure or Chain. This means it's almost always useful to ask for the related Authority Structure and include it in the work.

Darkness

This isn't as reliable an indicator as denseness. However, when darkness is present, one can ask if there's a related Authority Structure.

— An Important Caveat —

Be sure to experience the Wholeness Work Basic Format and Meditation Format *before* you use the Authority Format. Even if you're working with an issue you know involves an Authority, start by learning and experiencing the formats from Chapters 2-4. (Other kinds of meditation or inner work won't give you the background you'll need.)

acting from the whole
a progression from rule-based morality

With Wholeness Work, we are shifting from rule-based morality to something else. It isn't amorality, but it's something that is no longer rule-based. We begin operating out of an organic experience of the Whole. We could call it the natural morality that's present within. The rigid rules dissolve, and what remains is the capacity and inclination for greater compassion and kindness towards ourselves and those around us—even the world itself.

When we are operating out of rule-based morality, we do things that are "good" because the rules tell us to. But when we are experiencing Wholeness we don't need to do that.

How it Works
Consider this. I don't need a rule to make sure I don't drop a hammer onto my own foot. And yet I don't do it. This is because I *know* that doing so would cause pain. It would hurt. I know that because I experience my body as a single whole. Since my body is a single whole, I don't need a rule to tell me doing that would be wrong or bad, and I don't need anybody else saying "Connirae, be sure not to drop that hammer onto your foot."

With Wholeness Work, we gradually begin experiencing as "the Whole of things." We experience the wholeness of our own consciousness, and increasingly this comes to include the other people around me—and even the earth upon which I live. When I experience all of this as one whole, and in some sense I *am* this whole, then I also don't drop a hammer on your foot, and I don't need a rule to tell me it's wrong. I don't do it because I can already sense the pain that it would cause. This is the kind of consciousness we are developing as we do Wholeness Work as a practice.

This shift from rule-based morality to the natural morality that happens when we experience ourselves as "the whole of things" is quite significant. It means we have less stress in life—because we're no longer worried about whether we're good enough, or meeting someone else's standards. It means we have more joy in life and can connect more fully and intimately with others having fewer rules standing in the way.

As rigid rule structures fall away, we may discover more impulses of kindness and compassion emerging. The compassion first emerges towards all parts of ourselves—all of our desires, impulses, and needs can be included. When all of our needs, emotions, thoughts, etc., are included and integrated, then we tend to come to a natural clarity about what we want and need and are willing to be part of. What many people call "clear boundaries" tends to happen automatically. Plus we more easily recognize when we are called to contribute and want to do so.

The more all of our own emotions, desires, impulses, and needs are included in the integrated way that's possible through Wholeness Work practice, the more it becomes possible and even inevitable that we begin experiencing the Whole that's wider—*more* than just me as an individual. We experience being this larger whole that we are part of—that we in some sense *are.* From this consciousness of the larger Whole, we are naturally inclined to do things that create more joy in the world, more kindness, more happiness for others as well as for ourselves. Because we *are* this Whole that experiences the joy, and the kindness.

how the authority format helped me

I've used the Authority Format many times, and it's made a positive difference in many areas of my life. You may also find that it's a process well worth repeating.

Earlier in this chapter, I told you I used to get easily embarrassed. Sometimes I would feel myself turning pink, and I wasn't even sure what I was embarrassed about. On one level this wasn't a big deal, but on another it was. It was a sign that there was something in me always trying to meet some kind of rules or standards—trying to be a "good person" or trying to be "right" about things. That was a subtle strain on my system even if I wasn't consciously aware of it.

After doing this process I noticed I didn't get embarrassed as much. It happened gradually as I worked with more authority-related issues. And then "not as often" turned into "almost never." It's easier for me to just be myself now.

Another change I've noticed is that when interacting with another person, I used to try to sense what that person might want or value, and then try to fit into that mold. Now I feel more ease in just being myself, and I notice that most people like that better, anyway. Because I'm being authentically me, I'm not trying to make myself into what I think someone else wants me to be. It's a lot more relaxing for me, and easier for me to make natural connections.

I continue to use this format if I notice an area in my life or situation where I feel boxed in by rigid standards or rules of some sort.

Again, Wholeness Work isn't about just leaving the rules behind and doing whatever I want. This way of dissolving rigid rule structures brings us gradually into more contact with the Whole. The whole of ourselves, and perhaps even a larger Whole that can easily include the rest of this world we all live in together. That's been my experience.

It's easier for me to experience empathy *for* and awareness *of* the needs of others, yet without feeling that I have to fix everything—or *do* anything. Whatever I might do for another person is then done out of authentic desire to do it, not out of obligation.

An Indispensable Tool for Healing

Recently a close colleague—a coach and therapist—exclaimed to me,

"The Authority Format is a true game changer!" She went on, *"Virtually every time I see a client having difficulty making changes in their lives, inner Authority Structures are playing a key role in keeping things in place. This is true for depression, complex anxiety, and just run-of-the-mill ordinary problems that people have such difficulty changing.*

Since learning this method, I finally have a way to help them. My clients are getting results so much faster now."

She continued—*"There simply isn't anything else like this available anywhere. This method helps us access and heal important elements of our nature that nothing else that's come before has had a way to touch. … It has the potential to do for the field of transformation what the internal combustion engine did for transportation."*

I always get amazing feedback about this format from students and coaches alike. And, each time I teach this method, or guide a client through this process, and witness the powerful transformations, I feel the same kind of inspiration.

I hope that you use the Authority Format to find and transform Authority/rule Structures that have been living within you since childhood. Although they formed for a positive purpose—to help you carry an understanding of the rules you were expected to follow—now you can have more choice. This method can help organically reveal what is authentic for you now.

The following quote from the Sufi poet, Rumi beautifully describes the radical transformation that comes when we make this shift beyond rule-based morality.

> *Out beyond ideas of wrongdoing and rightdoing,*
> *There is a field.*
> *I'll meet you there.*
> *When the soul lies down in that grass,*
> *The world is too full to talk about.*
> *Ideas, language, even the phrase 'each other'*
> *Doesn't make any sense.*
>
> *– Rumi*

Dissolving these rule structures into Awareness gives us the opportunity to shift to the next level of consciousness, where we are acting out of awareness of the Whole. We become more directly responsive to the people and the world around us, rather than just being responsive to rules. Imagine how the world might be different if more people operated from the whole. Personally, I am loving how this shift is making my life easier. I hope you will too.

In the next chapter, you'll learn another *new* Wholeness Work format that will enable you to transform feelings of emptiness, loss, or yearning—and invite you to enjoy a more fulfilling way of being.

CHAPTER 6

THE "WHAT'S MISSING" FORMAT

Nourishing Fullness Within

I was in the middle of an individual session with a client I'll call "Rita." Rita had come to me because she was troubled by a strong "pain in her heart," which she said she'd had "all her life." As she described it, it was literally a feeling of fairly intense pain in her heart area. Using this as the starting place, I guided Rita through the Wholeness Work Basic Process. We found the Chain of 'I's related to this, and invited each to integrate. I'd guided many other people in working with body pains, even chronic pain, often with positive results. But "pain in the heart" seemed somehow different.

Things seemed to be going smoothly and at the ending step I asked "What's the sensation in your heart area now?"

Rita checked her heart area. "There's nothing there," she said, in perhaps the most unexpressive and flat voice tone possible.

I asked, "So there's no pain there any longer?"

"No, the pain is gone. It's not there," Rita confirmed, still in an unexcited monotone.

I was puzzled. Rita was telling me that the life-long pain that had troubled her was completely gone, yet she seemed almost despondent as she reported this to me. I wondered how this made sense.

So I asked, "So the pain is gone... and what's in this area now?"

"Nothing. It's just empty," Rita explained.

When someone discovers "emptiness" on the inside, it's generally one of two kinds. The first is the kind of "void" or "spaciousness" that spiritual teachers describe, that's actually positive. It might be experienced as a limitlessness, an expansiveness, with nothing tangible filling it.

Watching Rita, it was clear to me that the "emptiness" she was noticing was not that kind. Rita's emptiness was the second type: the experience that something was missing. It was the experience of "lack"—the sense that something should be there but isn't.[1]

I immediately intuited what was needed for Rita and guided her in a series of steps that led her to experience a sense of fullness in her heart and throughout her entire being. That's the format we'll explore next.

How does this apply to you?

You might never have experienced an ongoing pain in your heart. I hadn't. Yet I quickly realized that Rita had helped me become aware of another "universal structure"—something that lives within each of us.

We could call it an experience of emptiness within. Or a sense of "something missing" that we long to have completed or filled. Even though the experience of "lack" or of "something missing" is universal, for many of us, it's not something we're consciously aware of. And yet it can drive behaviors and feelings that leave us unhappy, or get us into trouble.

Noticing this structure offers the next "doorway" to wholeness.

So let's talk about how you might be able to find it in your experience, and use this format for your own benefit. An experience

---

[1] It's important to recognize the difference between "emptiness" that's the experience of undivided whole, and when it's an experience of lack that comes from separation on the inside. I've watched more than one spiritual teacher not recognize this distinction. One teacher I recall had a student ask what to do about an "emptiness" inside. It was clear from the student's expression, that this was an experience of lack. It wasn't undivided space. Instead it was an experience of separation between the empty space within, and something else. Because of not making this distinction the teacher told the student that this "emptiness" is the fertile void and it's a good thing. Not surprisingly, this advice didn't seem to help, and the student was left hanging.

of being incomplete, or lacking something, can manifest in different ways.

In Our Relationships

Perhaps you have, or have had a partner in life or business…. And if you don't have one now, would you like to have one? If so, here's something to consider. When we choose a life partner, we choose them because we love them. But if we're honest, we might also recognize that in some way we're hoping they'll "fill up" something that's missing in ourselves. This isn't necessarily a bad thing. It's valuable to find a partner who complements our strengths and brings something different into the relationship—whether it's a personal or business partnership. Yet when we're drawn to someone from a place of lack, needing them to supply something we haven't found within ourselves, inevitably there comes a time when we're disappointed. Our partner isn't filling the need we wanted them to satisfy. We can easily start blaming them and things might get uncomfortable for both of us. We're dissatisfied with them because they aren't who we "need them to be." And they're unhappy because we don't appreciate them for who they are.

This dynamic changes completely when we do the Wholeness Work method you'll learn in this chapter.

Once the emptiness or neediness is "filled from the inside," we can better appreciate and maximize our partnerships. Without this inner work, our relationships can often sour when our partner doesn't fill the need we had hoped they'd fulfill.

Grief and Loss

It's not possible to get through life without experiencing loss. This format has helped many people in a deep healing of the emptiness and sadness that often accompanies loss. One woman had lost a beloved pet about five months before she attended a workshop I was leading. When she volunteered to do the process, I could see immediately that this loss had been profound for her. She described how she'd been unable to recover from her sorrow, no matter what she tried.

At the end of doing this process she looked strikingly more alive and present, and said, "I feel as if the blood is flowing through my veins again." She was gesturing towards her arms, and I could see that the skin color in her arms had changed significantly. When we started, her skin tone had been a greyish dull hue, and now her arms looked pink and vibrant. It looked as if blood was literally flowing through her veins again.

Another workshop participant said she'd felt a "hole inside" ever since her brother had died when she was still a young child. After doing this process she reported feeling more complete than she could remember experiencing in a long, long time.

When we lose a significant person or relationship—or anything we hold dear—it's common to suffer an emptiness inside that can leave us feeling bereft of wholeness and vitality. This process offers a gentle and effective way of transforming the experience of emptiness and loss to one of discovering the inherent abundance present within.

Food Cravings

Do you ever feel compelled to eat when you're not really hungry? If so, this experience can be satisfying to explore. It can be especially useful if there's a specific food you crave, in a specific circumstance. For example, maybe you find the candy at the grocery store checkout counter difficult to resist, or you go for ice cream when you're bored.

Other Compulsions

Many of us have what I call "mini-compulsions"—things we feel *compelled* to do, such as binge-watching TV, playing video games, shopping (online or otherwise), gambling, etc. Perhaps we feel "pulled into" doing it, almost as if we don't have a choice. If there's something you feel compelled to do, you can explore it with this format.

For this exercise, work with minor compulsions only. When dealing with major compulsions or addictions, I recommend starting with Core Transformation[2] (CT). After using CT, then consider exploring the same territory with Wholeness Work.

What You Can Pick to Explore

It can be rewarding to explore any of the areas I just described to discover if we've been unconsciously seeking something outside ourselves in order to feel complete. When our behavior comes from a sense of incompleteness and lack, then we are living from an imbalanced place. Our partnerships and other things we cling to are then based on an insecure foundation rather than sufficiency or abundance. So doing this inner work is tremendously helpful. As we use the What's Missing Format to heal and integrate these vulnerable or needy parts, a deeper wholeness and freedom is revealed. We can actually experience and live from the feeling of completeness we've been seeking.

Find something to work with that will make a difference for you. Here's a summary of what you might pick...

Feeling of emptiness inside
Feeling needy or incomplete
Grief, loss, or sadness
A food craving
A minor compulsion

The key is to start with anything where you can notice an experience of emptiness or missing something. As usual, the first time through pick something medium to mild in intensity, especially since you'll be guiding yourself. (In the training sessions, where we have backup support, people frequently pick significant issues and this method works really well to transform and heal those at a deep level.)

Before trying it out yourself, read the following demonstration; this will prepare you to experience the method more easily and fully.

---

[2] Core Transformation is a companion method to Wholeness Work. It works at a similarly deep level, and research shows it to be effective with a wide range of issues. See the book *Core Transformation: Reaching the Wellspring Within* by C. Andreas and T. Andreas.

what's missing format in action
demonstration

Sneak Preview: The Results for Nina

"I can just feel it. This intense joy....

It's like, I just love everything....

*I don't think there are any other
words apart from 'thank you.'"*

Finding an Experience to Explore

ME: Okay. So, Nina, you already have something in mind you'd like to explore?

NINA: Yeah, I do.

ME: Okay, great. And are you comfortable letting me know what kind of experience you're choosing—if it's a loss, or a partnership, or something else?

NINA: Yeah, there's a kind of sense of grief in me that feels like it's missing something. [Her face flattens, and her right hand circles near her chest.]

ME: Okay, a sense of grief.... "Feels *like it's missing something.*" [I repeat Nina's words to acknowledge the experience.] And you don't really know what it might have to do with, is that right?

NINA: I think it's probably from very young. I think I've always had it. [Nina's eyes open briefly, yet she appears to be attending to her inner experience.]

The Starting Place: Stepping into the Experience

ME: Okay, that sounds perfect for this. So Nina, you can just take a moment, and eyes open or shut, whatever is comfortable. [I begin speaking more slowly and softly.] … And just let yourself notice this experience that you told me about … this experience of grief, of missing something…. And where is this experience of missing something? Where is it located?

NINA: [Closing her eyes.] … It goes from the top of my chest to the bottom of my chest area. [She gestures with her left hand to show the location.]

ME: Okay…. Top to bottom of chest.

NINA: Yeah. And it comes out as wide as my shoulders in—like an oval. [Nina's hands touch her shoulders, then her right hand traces an oval around her chest.]

ME: Okay. "As wide as my shoulders—like an oval." Okay. And do you have a sense of how deep it is? The other dimension?

NINA: It's about two inches inside my body and one inch outside my body at the front.

ME: Okay, so it's partly in and partly out. Two inches in, then one inch out. Great…. So now, Nina, sensing in and through the space of this … What's the sensation quality here? [I speak more slowly, with gentle emphasis, as I invite Nina to notice the sensation quality.]

[To Nina and the Group:] And you know, this is a really a special moment, when we do Wholeness Work. It's always a special moment, we're actually making this shift to directly encounter something. We're beginning to include it in a different way. And this itself, it's a kind of intimacy that is very, very special. And it is kindness, in a way, just to let ourselves notice something and sense something directly….

[To Nina:] And what's the sensation quality here?

NINA: Yeah, so it feels soft … and squishy and warm. And it gets wetter and wetter towards the center. [Her eyes close. Nina moves her hand gently outward and back toward her chest a few times as she senses.]

ME: Okay, soft, squishy, warm ... and wetter towards the center.

NINA: Yeah. [Her eyes are closed and she nods almost imperceptibly.]

Session Notes: The Beginning Experience, "Grief"	
Location	*Top of chest to bottom of chest, extending out to shoulders*
Size & Shape	*Oval (2" inside and 1" outside body)*
Sensation Quality	*Soft, squishy, warm; wetter towards center*

Finding "What's Missing" (M₁)

Finding "What's Missing" (M_1)

ME: Okay, excellent. So now we get to take things to the next level.

So, sensing in and through here, sensing in and through this, that's warm, that's squishy, that's soft, and wetter towards the center ... From here ... From *here*, [I repeat for emphasis.] ... *where is the location that this is seeking something from?* [I speak this question with a gentle emphasis.]

NINA: So, it's a big area behind me. And it starts out kind of diagonally, like that. [She lifts her right arm up and out and then her left arm, extending both and smiling shyly.] Yeah, and then goes around me at that height. It's almost like an arc shape.

ME: So, it's behind and around.... So, it's a fairly large area, isn't it?

NINA: Yeah, it is.

ME: Okay.

To You/Reader: Nina is showing me with her gestures that she's very aware of the location and extent. Because she's already noticing, I don't need to ask her for more details. And I have enough information about the location that I'll be able to guide Nina's attention back to this location when I need to. I know it's behind her, around her, and fairly large.]

ME: [To Nina:] So back now to this, that's the behind and around. Yeah, now sensing in and through the space of this, the area of this, what's the sensation quality, in and through?…

NINA: [She pauses, eyes closed] … So, the far edge is airy. And then as it gets closer towards me, gets denser, kind of like dense and fuzzy or fluffy, as it gets towards my skin.

ME: So, it's more airy around the edge. And then as it gets closer into you, it's more dense and fuzzy, or fluffy.

NINA: That's it. Yeah.

ME: Okay.

NINA: And it's warm again.

ME: And it's warm, too. Great.

Session Notes: The 1st "What's Missing" (M_1)	
Location	*Behind and arcing around her body*
Size & Shape	*Fairly large*
Sensation Quality	*Airy (far edge); dense, fuzzy, fluffy, warm (closer to her)*

Checking if (M_1) is Complete or Missing Something

ME: Now we're going to do something similar to the Authority Process, yet different because we're dealing with a different kind of structure.

So, sensing and through *this here* [location of M_1] … that's kind of fuzzy, that's fluffy, warm … Let's just check … Is there a sense that this is complete in itself? Or, when you check here, is there a sense that the energy of this is *also* missing something, or yearning for something, or seeking something?

NINA: [Her eyes are closed.] … Yeah, it's missing something.

Finding the Second "What's Missing" (M₂)

ME: Okay, great. So, sensing this, [in the location of M_1] … this that is seeking something … where is the *location* that this is seeking something from? [I am again speaking slowly, in a cadence that invites turning inward and noticing.]

NINA: It's another quite large area, that's level with my hips. But it extends out either side of my body, a couple of feet by the side of my body. [She is speaking softly, her body staying still.]

ME: Great. Okay. So, take a little time to really register the full area of it, how far it goes in each direction…. [Nina attends inwardly.] Yeah, yeah … And then let there be a sensing in and through the space of this…. And what is the sensation quality?

NINA: So, it's eye-shaped. [Nina traces the shape of an eye in front of her.] And the sensation quality is gray … and woolly, like a sheep.

ME: Gray and woolly. Okay, great. Lovely. [I smile.]

Session Notes: The 2ⁿᵈ "What's Missing" (M₂)	
Location	*Large area level with hips*
Size & Shape	*Eye-shaped, extending out either side of body (~2 feet)*
Sensation Quality	*Gray, woolly*

Checking if M₂ is Complete or Missing Something

ME: So, we can pause for a moment…. And just sensing in and through this, the sensation of this … that's gray, that's woolly … just sensing this, really letting there be an intimacy with this…. And then we can check: is there a sense that this is complete in itself? [I'm speaking slowly.] … Or is this also seeking something or yearning for something?

NINA: It's complete in itself, Yeah. [She says softly, with clarity.]

ME: So, this is complete. Great. Okay, so now we have the whole What's Missing Chain. We've gotten to something that's complete in and of itself.

Finding the 'I'

ME: And Nina, you can be aware of all of this at once, right? [Nina closes her eyes and turns inward.] ... Yeah ... there can be a noticing of all of this at once. So, this experience in the chest ... the top of the chest to the bottom is squishy, warm, wet ... then this larger thing that's behind and around, it's airy, dense, fuzzy, fluffy, warm ... and then also this large area that's lower down, that's gray, woolly, eye-shaped. It's possible to be aware of all this at once, right? You could say: "*I am aware of this.*" So, where's the 'I' that notices all of this? Where is the noticing of all of this happening from?

NINA: Just between my right cheekbone and ear. [Nina's right hand reaches towards her ear, fingers cupping her cheekbone.]

ME: Okay, right cheekbone, ear.... And what's the size and shape?

NINA: ... So, it's roughly ball-shaped, roughly a sphere. And it's about two inches in diameter. [She traces a circle around her cheekbone with her right index finger.] Part goes into my ear, part into my cheek.

ME: Okay, lovely. And so, now gently sensing in and through the space of this ... What's the sensation quality here?

NINA: It's quite hard. And then there's a tiny bit at the center that's hollow, or empty.

ME: Okay ... it's mostly hard or kind of dense. [Nina is nodding.] And then in the center it's hollow.

Session Notes: The 'I'	
Location	*Between the right cheekbone and ear*
Size & Shape	*Roughly a sphere, 2" in diameter*
Sensation Quality	*Quite hard (dense), tiny hollow area in center*

Checking if the 'I' Welcomes Integrating

ME: So now ... you can also be aware in this moment of the whole field of Awareness, right? ... that's everywhere throughout the body and all around.

    So let's check with the sensation of the 'I' that's kind of hard.... There's this hardness here, and yet the hardness always has its own molecules of hardness ... so there can be a sensing in and through the whole thing.... And what we want to do is check: ... Does the sensation of this 'I', does it welcome being invited to open, relax, melt into the whole field of Awareness that's all around and throughout? It doesn't have to, but if it does, you can let me know.... Yeah.... [My voice is slow and soft as I'm watching Nina.]

NINA: ... Yeah

ME: Okay.... And there can just be relaxing into the happening of this. [I'm speaking softly and kindly.]

NINA: [Long pause as Nina processes. She looks increasingly relaxed, and her breathing softly slows.] ... Yeah.

ME: Yes ... letting it happen however it happens, and taking all the time that it does, you can just let me know when things settle.... Yeah....

NINA: [Nina's face is almost glowing.]

ME: **To the Group:** And I don't know about you guys ... I'm going along for the ride with Nina. She's letting this lovely dissolving and melting happen. So I just let myself go along for the ride.

    [To Nina:] Yeah. Okay. Great.

integrating the second "what's missing" (M₂)

ME: So now, we check back to that area that was large, in the hips, shaped kind of like an eye.... And is that the same now or is it a little different?

NINA: Little bit smaller.

ME: Okay, a little bit smaller. Great. So, sensing in and through the area ... we can check for what the energy of this wants to integrate *with*. It may be that it wants to integrate with the one before [M₁, that was arcing around the body]. It may be that it wants to integrate with the full field of Awareness. And if so, it may want to allow itself to dissolve and melt into the whole field. Or it may want Awareness to come to it, to flow into and as ... opening, relaxing as the energy here.

NINA: [She speaks promptly, without a pause.] It wants to merge into me. It wants to merge into my body. [Her eyes are closed, head slightly turned down.]

ME: Okay, lovely.... And that's kind of like letting this merge with *"me as Awareness"* ... letting this dissolve and melt in and as *"me as Awareness,"*

To You/Reader: When I say *"me as Awareness,"* by this I mean that Nina can be experiencing *"herself"* as Awareness," and allowing "herself as Awareness" to merge with the sensation in the hip area.

ME: [To Nina:]... Yeah. Centered on the whole physical body. Yeah just letting that happen, how it happens. Great. And letting it luxuriate in the process ... however it happens.... You can just let me know whenever things settle.

[Now I'm just quietly present, giving Nina plenty of time.]

Lovely. Yeah. And it's nice how just letting ourselves breathe through the process, it just kind of allows the system to really let it happen in its own way, doesn't it? Yeah. Okay. And what is the experience of that? If there's anything you'd like to share, you can, and if not, we'll go right on.

NINA: Yeah. It felt like it was dissolving into my body as "*me as Awareness.*" [Her hands rise and wave gently to show the dissolving.] There was a sensation of tears and laughter at the same time. [She speaks softly and appears touched, like something meaningful is happening.]

ME: Lovely. Beautiful.

Integrating the First "What's Missing" (M₁)

ME: So, now we check with the one before that, which was behind and around. And how is that now? Is that the same? Or is it a little different?

NINA: Yeah, the bit at the edge is gone. It's just a bit … the half layer on my body is there.

ME: Okay, great. So, sensing in and through how is it now, and whatever remains … Yeah, letting there be this kind, gentle sensing in and through the energy of this that remains. That's right. We can invite this to also integrate in whatever way is natural.… And that might be also merging with you as Awareness. Letting yourself as Awareness fall into this sort of opening and relaxing into you as Awareness, or something else.… Whatever feels natural.

NINA: [There is a lengthy pause as the processing happens.] … Yeah. [Nina smiles and chuckles.]

ME: Yes. Lovely. And if you'd like to share the experience of that, you can.

NINA: Yeah, so it was very different, and it didn't define one direction. It felt like everything you offered—all of it was happening, every direction at once. And I couldn't really distinguish it. [Her eyes are closed and hands moving back and forth.] And then there was a sense of like, "Oh! this has been missing and it's come back,"… and then yeah, wanting to laugh again. [She laughs.]

ME: Yes, beautiful. Yeah, your smile says even more.

NINA: [She bursts into laughter.]

Inviting the Original Sensation to Integrate

ME: Okay, so now we go to the place in the chest.... Yeah ... and find out what's there now. Is that the same or is it a little different or a lot different? How is it now?

NINA: Yeah, it's like the same shape is there, but it's completely moved. It's moved from being flat there, and it's kind of curled up on its side now.

ME: So, it's kind of curled up now.... Okay ... And sensing in and through the space of this, notice the sensation quality of the energy here now. And it might be same, it might be different, but however it is now.

Yeah ... we want to invite this to integrate however feels natural. And this may want to dissolve and melt into Awareness. It may want Awareness to flow in and as the sensation here ... it may be that it wants you as Awareness to relax in and as the sensation here, and/or this sensation here to open and relax into you as Awareness ... or something else.

NINA: [More laughter with tears come.] Yeah, it just wants everything.

[She's laughing, and wipes a few tears. Her expression looks like relief—letting go. It's a full body experience with a quality of sweetness.]

ME: *"It just wants everything."* Yeah. Thumbs up there. Why not have everything and everywhere? Yeah, lovely. And there can just be a letting go into the happening of this. And when there's this *letting go into the happening of this*, it's like the sensation meeting Awareness and Awareness meeting sensation ... whatever wants to happen, happens in its own way. And we don't need to track it, we don't even need to understand or know what that is.

Sometimes for me it's almost like there's a sense of the '*me*' as I usually think of myself, just kind of disappearing and releasing into the happening of this. And whatever is happening is happening and I have no idea what it is, but something knows and is just allowing it to unfold in its own way ... Yeah, beautiful ...

... Yeah, taking all the time that it takes ... luxuriating in the process and then letting me know whenever things have settled.

NINA: [There is a long pause.] ... Yeah. [Nina begins laughing and raises both hands to her eyes wiping them quickly.] Cool, I can just feel it, this intense joy.

ME: Yeah ...

Checking How It Is Now

ME: And now just sensing this ... *Being this way,* with all this integration ... What is it like now, being this way ... moving through life?

NINA: It's like, I just love everything ... Yeah. [She looks peaceful and alive.]

ME: Okay. Beautiful. And is there anything more you'd like to share about the experience of this? And there doesn't have to be anything, you can just sit with this if you'd like.

NINA: ... Yeah, I don't think there are any other words ... apart from "thank you." [She gently wipes both sides of her eyes with her fingers. Nina looks glowing and radiant, visibly experiencing "being Awareness itself."]

ME: That's totally good. Totally good.

To the Group: You know, the field of Awareness is not chatty. [I chuckle.] It doesn't require a lot of words really. But we get it, when we're in each other's presence like this, and we share the experience, you know, I go along for the ride with Nina and I get it, too.

Thank you very much, Nina.

Full Session Notes: Integrate What's Missing	
Beginning Experience: Feeling of "Grief"	
Location	*Top of chest to bottom of chest, extending out to shoulders*
Size & Shape	*Oval (2" inside and 1" outside body)*
Sensation Quality	*Soft, squishy, warm; wetter towards center*

M$_1$	
Location	*Behind and arcing around her body*
Size & Shape	*Fairly large*
Sensation Quality	*Airy (far edge); dense, fuzzy, fluffy, warm (closer to her)*

M$_2$	
Location	*Large area level with hips*
Size & Shape	*Extending out either side of body (~2 ft), eye-shaped*
Sensation Quality	*Gray, woolly*

'I'	
Location	*Between right cheekbone and ear*
Size & Shape	*Roughly a sphere, 2" in diameter*
Sensation Quality	*Quite hard (dense), tiny hollow area in center*

Pointers and Observations about the Demo

How many "What's Missing" layers are typical?

For Nina, the second "What's Missing" layer was already "complete in itself." Most people find three-five layers. So don't be surprised if you discover another layer or two.

What about the 'I' being dense?

The 'I' Nina found was quite hard (dense), yet had empty space in the middle. Because of the denseness around the edge, I didn't know if Nina's 'I' would welcome integrating. However, it did, and the integrations were quite powerful and full. If the 'I' hadn't welcomed integrating, I would have chosen to find the related Authority Structure. As we discussed in the last chapter, when we find something dense on the inside, it can be useful to use the Authority Process.

flowchart
the what's missing format

In the following flowchart, you can see the main steps of the What's Missing Format in one image.

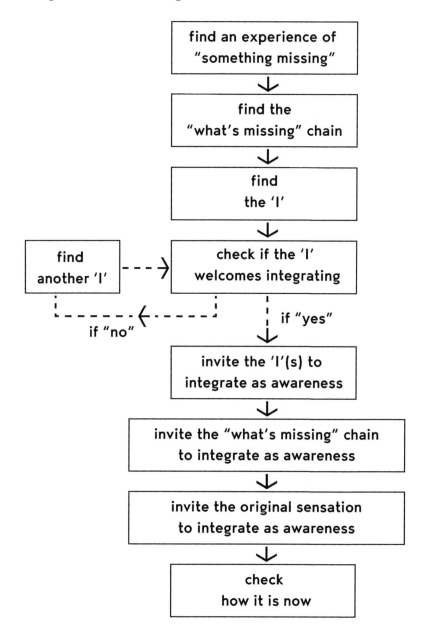

step-by-step guide
integrating what's missing

Now try it out yourself. You can use the following steps to guide yourself through the process.

 If you'd like, you can use the "What's Missing" Worksheet to jot down notes. You only need a few words or a phrase to remind you of each element you find inside. To access the worksheet for this process, use this QR code or go to www.thewholenesswork.org/BookResources/.

Step 1: Choose an experience to work with—then step in.
Pick a situation where you experience missing something or wanting something. For example: a sense of emptiness or loss, of craving something, or of seeking approval, acceptance, or love.

- *Step into the situation, so that right now you are experiencing missing something or wanting something.*
- *Notice the location of the experience of missing something.* [Usually this is a feeling in the body or close to the body.]
- *And what is the general size & shape?*
- *Sensing in and through, what is the sensation quality?*

Step 2: Find What's Missing.

- *Sensing into the sensation here* [_in the location of "missing something" you found in Step 1_], *what is the **location** that this is seeking something from? Another way to find this is to ask: "What direction is it orienting towards?"*
- [We'll call the answer 'M$_1$'.]
- *And notice the size & shape.*
- *And notice the sensation quality.*

Step 3: Check if this is complete, or if it's also missing something.
Sensing into the sensation here [_in the location of 'M₁'_] .... Is this complete, satisfied? Or is this also missing something?

> **If complete:** Go to Step 4.

> **If it's missing something:** Use the questions in Step 2 to discover the next location ['M₂'], the size & shape, and the sensation quality.

Continue until you get to something that's complete in itself.

Step 4: Find the 'I'.
- *Ask: "Where is the perceiving of all of this happening from?" …* Notice the location.
- *Notice the size & shape.*
- *Notice the sensation quality.*

Step 5: Check if the 'I' welcomes integrating.
Does the sensation here [in the location of the 'I'], welcome the invitation to dissolve, melt, in and as… the fullness of Awareness… that's all around and throughout?

> **If "Yes":**
> *Notice what happens when the sensation of this 'I' is invited to open and relax as the fullness of Awareness that's all around and throughout.*

> **If "No":**
> Find another 'I'. (If you prefer, you can instead check if the final What's Missing wants to integrate.)

Step 6: Invite the "What's Missing" Chain to integrate.
Check with the last What's Missing. Does the sensation in this location welcome integrating with all of Awareness? … Does it want to integrate with what's just before it in the chain? … Does it want to integrate with you as Awareness? … Invite the sensation in this location to integrate in whatever way feels natural."
Do this for each of the 'M's in the chain.

Step 7. Invite original sensation to integrate.
Now return attention to the location of the experience you started with [in Step 1]. Is the sensation here the same as it was before ... or is it a little bit different? However it is now, notice what happens when the sensation here, is invited to open and relax ... as all of Awareness.

Step 8: Check how it is now.
Being this way (with the 'I's and the original feeling integrated with Awareness), notice what it's like now, when you imagine being in the situation you were working with.

Sharing Experiences

Here are a few experiences that people in Wholeness Work trainings shared about doing this exercise.

Healing from Death of Brother

"This exercise was extremely powerful for me. When I was just 18 months old, my brother died of leukemia. It created a hole that impacted my life in many ways, even though I have no "conscious" memory of him. Through the years, I'd done several NLP processes related to this issue, with positive outcomes. Even so, there still seemed to be more. My brother's loss would come up when working with seemingly unrelated things.

"When I did the Wholeness What's Missing Format with this, I found a roundish hole in my chest and solar plexus area. After doing the process, I felt more complete than I had in a long time. It was extremely powerful.

"Now, [7 years later] I can report that I still feel solid, grounded and complete, more like me 'all the way through' ... a very satisfied and comfortable feeling."

Relationship with Wife Transformed

"I felt irritated with my wife. Somehow, how she was in our relationship left me disappointed with her in an ongoing way.

After reading the chapter on What's Missing I followed the instructions to work with myself. I discovered my What's Missing Structure had left me feeling a residue of neediness that neither she nor anyone else could fill. The feeling felt quite old, as if it had been with me my entire life. After working with What's Missing all of that relaxed. The hole in me filled in, and I could now fully enjoy how wonderful my wife actually is."

Healing Relationship with Mother

"In the training I had no idea what to work on. Then I remembered a quote from Bert Hellinger, who said something like 'What's missing is always mother missing.' So I worked with my relationship with my mother.

"The integration from doing the process brought a profound sense of compassion for my mom's weaknesses, deep forgiveness and love. Now I can look at pictures of my mom without an adverse reaction. That was a huge shift."

Walking normally again...

"When I was 7 or 8 years old, all my classmates had this fountain pen that was very fashionable, and very expensive, but I didn't. This was very distressing to me at the time. So I started the process with the representation of missing this. I went through the steps and was surprised to experience a filling in within my left hip, which had been hurting and stiff for a year due to osteoarthritis. Even after two months of physiotherapy, it had improved very little. I could not walk at a normal speed, as I had to pay attention to how I put weight on my hip while walking.

"After doing this exercise, I was surprised that I could walk normally again. I didn't think the improvement would last, but this happened about forty days ago and I am still walking normally, with no stiffness at all.

"The experience was quite intense and profound for me."

tips
the what's missing format

Here are a few tips to help you use the What's Missing Format in a way that will give you the best results.

Select the optimal wording for <u>you</u> on Steps 1 & 2.
Consider seeking, yearning for, longing for, wanting, hoping for… For most Wholeness Work formats in this book, I encourage you to use the scripts *exactly as written*. This will help you get the best results. However, with the What's Missing Format, beginning on Step 1, there's one word that sometimes needs to be changed so that the questions you ask match your experience.

When you discover the place of lack or emptiness within, you can check if it's "seeking" something, "needing" something, "yearning for," "longing for," "wanting," or "hoping for" something. Just notice the word that best describes the experience of the energy in this location. It's OK to change this word to match the experience. For example, you might end up asking the inner question: "Where is the location that this is *'longing for'* something from?" or "Where is the location this is *'needing'* something from?"

Notice how this format is similar and different from the Authority Format.
This process is structurally quite similar to the Authority Format that you just learned in Chapter 5. Here's what's different:

To find the What's Missing Chain, we use a different question. We ask: *"Where is the location this is seeking something from?"*

We also use a different question to know when we're at the end of the chain. Instead of asking, "Is this a Final Authority," for the What's Missing Format we ask: *"Is this already complete in itself?"*

* * *A Visual Representation of the What's Missing Format* * *

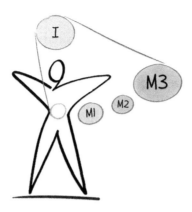

Each of these structures can be located either outside or inside the body.

answering your questions

Can't find the location of the first "what's missing." (M1)

Q I asked, "Where is what you are seeking?" and it didn't know. What do I do now?

A Here are several tips that usually help…

It can help to take time to get to know the "empty" space as sensation before asking it any questions. To do this, just start again. Return to the "empty" place that's seeking something, and this time slowly and intimately *sense in and through* to experience the sensation quality of this that's missing something.… *Then*—once you've become intimately familiar— gently ask the question again. You may find it's become easier for your system to reveal the answer.

Notice the "direction" of the yearning sensation. Return your attention to the "empty" space. As you sense in and through this area, attend to the sense of longing or yearning for something. Notice if there's a sense of direction to this longing. Often it's as if it is reaching out or *leaning* toward a direction in space. This can be a clue. Is it leaning forward, back, up, or somewhere else? The location from which it's seeking something will be in that direction.

It can help to realize that for this to be missing something, or yearning for something, there *has to* be a knowing of what is yearned for or missed. Otherwise it wouldn't know to yearn. What it yearns for might be vague, but there has to be a sense of what it is that's worth longing for. And this means there is some representation of it. And if there's a representation of it, it has to be in some location. So where is this located?

Sometimes What's Missing is close, sometimes it's a little farther, and occasionally it's *very* far away. Some people have reported that it's "in the next galaxy." So if it doesn't appear at first, it may be useful to expand the distance where we're checking.

It's given up.

Q I asked the empty place inside: "*Where is the location of what this is seeking something from?*" and I didn't get an answer. It was as if this empty place had given up. This part feels hopeless that it will ever find what it's hoping for. It doesn't think it's possible to get what it wants—so it's not seeking anymore.

A When this is the situation, here's how I might talk to this empty place inside: "*I get that you've given up. I get that this place inside doesn't think it's possible to get what it wants. That's okay…. And yet it's clear that the energy here does feel a sense of emptiness or lack.*

And when there's a lack, there's also something that's wanted. So we're not really asking whether or not it might be <u>possible</u> to get what's wanted. We're asking something else. This energy probably gave up a long time ago. So now we're asking, before it [the part] gave up, **'Where is the location of whatever it was seeking something from?'"**

Another way of wording this could be: **"Even though you don't think it's possible to get it or have it, where is the representation of it? Where in your personal space is what you are wanting?"**

These are just a couple of options; there are additional ways to discover the answer if the way you try doesn't fit. And these are some of the subtleties we learn in the training sessions.

Healing Minor Compulsions

Q You mentioned doing this method with "minor compulsions" like shopping, or watching TV, or gaming. Are you saying that if we do those things, it's a problem and we should change it?

A No. It really depends on you, and how you experience each activity. Doing these things can be fun and/or useful for you. However, if you're doing an activity more than you want to, or you feel driven to "have to" do it, then it might be a useful example to explore with this method. When we do something based on a fundamental neediness, or from a sense of incompleteness, this is a place where this method is likely to be helpful. Because it helps us uncover and experience what we're truly seeking through those behaviors.

Afterwards, you might do more or less or the same amount of the behavior—but you're more likely to be doing it from a sense of fullness, balance, and happiness, rather than from a sense of lack.

clues
when to use the what's missing format

Assuming you've already practiced the formats in the earlier chapters of this book, here are the content and process indicators for when you're likely to find the What's Missing Format useful.

Content Indicators
These indicators include the situations listed at the beginning of this chapter such as feelings of emptiness, neediness, grief, loss, food cravings, or compulsive behaviors such as binge-watching, shopping, gaming. (Please start with mild compulsions only. For more significant compulsive or addictive behaviors, it's best to start with Core Transformation, and then use the Wholeness Work.)

Process Indicators
If you encounter an inner structure that just feels empty—like an unwanted void—this is a good time to use the What's Missing Format. The experience of emptiness almost always means the What's Missing Format will be beneficial.

The remaining process indicators include grayness, dryness, tears/moisture within, or location in or around the heart. When you find these experiences within, you can check to find out if it's an experience of something missing. It's not a certainty—so it's important to check.

In the training sessions we learn how to check in a gentle way, and respond to what our system wants us to do. We also learn what needs to happen for a gentle and natural transformation.

A Frame
When you begin learning this format, you don't need to think about the process indicators at all. You'll probably find it easiest to just use the "content indicators" I've just described, to identify experiences you'd like to explore using this format. I encourage you to start with using the experiences that are obvious to you, and easy for you to find.

After you've been practicing for quite a while, you might find it useful to return to the following list of content and process indicators, to notice if it enriches your understanding and ability to use this format. Understanding these elements can be helpful when you're putting everything together, and learning how to flow in response to your experience in the moment.

Indicators Summary

<u>Content</u>	<u>Process</u>
Sadness (grief and loss)	Emptiness or a sense of vacuum
Longing	Heart area location (pain or other sensation)
Neediness	
Cravings (such as food cravings)	Grayness of a structure within
	Dryness within
Compulsive behaviors (mild)	Tears (and/or moisture within)

If an indicator is present, just check and notice if there's a sense that something is missing. If so, the What's Missing Format is likely to be useful. Again, this only suggests a likelihood; it's not a certainty. The trainings teach ways to become sensitive to "the wisdom of the system."

An Example: Using the What's Missing Format "in the Flow"

Here's an example of how I used the What's Missing Format, in the middle of guiding someone in another Wholeness Work format.

I was guiding "Elaina" through the Authority Format exercise (from Chapter 5), and the first several Authorities that emerged were black and dense circles. After this, the next Authority was gray and not very dense. When something is gray, this can indicate that there's something longed for or missing, rather than another Authority. So I asked Elaina to check which fit better. "Checking with the energy here, is there the sense that this is trying to please or serve another authority, or is it more that the energy of this is missing something or longing for something?" She said, "As soon as you mentioned missing something, this part immediately responded. That fits."

This shows how you can respectfully and gently check for whether the What's Missing Format is a fit for what your system needs in the moment. Often gray indicates loss/missing something. However there may be other "types" of gray that indicate something else. So it's important not to assume, but to ask, as I did with Elaina.

With Wholeness Work we always offer possibilities in a gentle way, and notice what your system responds to. It's never useful to impose or push or force something.

why the order matters
why we integrate inner authority before we integrate what's missing

The order in which I'm presenting these formats to you isn't random. This material in this book is carefully sequenced to guide you in a kind, gentle, and effective process of evolution. Learning the Wholeness Work Basic Process, *and then* the Authority Format, paves the way (lays the groundwork) for you to experience the benefit of the What's Missing Format.

Why?

The presence of rule structures can often get in the way of fully receiving the value of the What's Missing Format. For example, I might have an empty place inside that yearns for a feeling of love or fullness or completion. But I might also have an internalized message that "I don't deserve that," or "I'm not good enough." This is why we learn the Authority Format first. Once we've begun transforming our inner Authority Structures, it becomes easier to actually absorb the nurturing and love, or whatever positive "energy" these places inside have been yearning for.

You may notice that the What's Missing Format often produces an even deeper resolution of shame and unworthiness. Unworthiness often accompanies shame, and within unworthiness is often a sense of lacking something. Once the related Authority Structures are integrated, it becomes possible—and easy—to transform this and feel whole.

experiencing the fullness of our being
understanding the what's missing format

The experience of emptiness or lack is a universal human experience, though most of us try not to notice it. It's not fun to experience this—especially when we have no way to heal it or transform it.

These experiences of lack are talked about in attachment theory, in grief therapy, and by those attempting to deal with addictions and compulsions. This Wholeness Work method offers a way to heal and transform this fundamental experience at the level of the nervous system. Why do I describe it that way? If you've tried the exercise yourself, you may already understand. For me—and for the thousands of people who've done this in trainings and coaching sessions—the experience of integrating "what's missing" is a deeply-felt experience. It goes beyond content—beyond changing our thoughts about things. When doing this process, people experience the change very viscerally. Something that's been needed fills in… *in and through the body*—literally—it can sometimes feel quite physical.

We can finally feel the fullness or love that we may have been missing from early childhood. At long last, we can feel what attachment therapists describe as being so important to experience, and critical to forming the foundation for positive and healthy relationships. We can feel what makes life more joyous to live.

If you didn't feel much yet, I want to offer you some perspective—and encouragement. Yes, I'm going to talk about myself again.

When I first used the What's Missing Format, I found it quite difficult. I resorted to "just guessing" or "pretending" a lot. I did get some results from this, but they were minor—quite subtle. Not as strong as many of my clients reported.

I discovered that I needed more integration of other inner structures before I could fully absorb what I was missing and wanted, in a visceral way. I especially needed more time doing the Authority Process. I also found it valuable to take more time going through the processes you can learn in Wholeness Levels II, III, and IV (if you choose to go on). After doing that, I cycled back to the basic wholeness formats in this book and got more value. I could finally absorb what I had been missing and feel it viscerally. At times what fills in for me feels like love and nurturing that's almost physical. Other times what fills in feel more energetic in nature—something that's at perhaps a deeper level than the physically felt love of one person to another. I encourage you to just notice what fills in for you.

The What's Missing Format enables us to discover, transform, and heal another structure that's within each of us—a structure that most of us have no idea is even there. As we've discussed, we often have life contexts where we seek to complete ourselves with something from the outside. This Wholeness Work format offers a way to resolve these basic issues of "incompleteness" or lack—and find more fullness within. It's particularly helpful in resolving loss or emptiness, and transforming relationship issues including feeling needy, wanting to be liked, or seeking fulfillment through a partner.

In the next chapter, we'll be exploring how to use Wholeness Work to sleep better and get more restorative rest.

CHAPTER 7

BETTER SLEEP AND REST

Replenishing the Mind-Body System[1]

*"Insomnia was a lifelong problem for me dating back to early childhood.
It's been two years since I learned the Wholeness Work with Connirae.
It works like nothing has ever worked—and I have tried it all! Furthermore,
the process can be used to resolve other issues and to heal deep wounds.
I now fall asleep calmly and easily almost every night. I look and feel younger,
am shedding excess pounds, and am experiencing more congruency on a
daily basis. I give it 5 stars."*
~Cate[2]

Have you ever had difficulty falling asleep? Or times when you woke up in the middle of the night and had trouble going back to sleep? What about waking up too early—you know you're not quite rested but here you are, awake? If so, you're not alone. Almost everyone has difficulty sleeping at some point in their life, and increasingly large numbers of people report having some kind of sleep difficulty on a regular basis.

One of the most common benefits people report from doing Wholeness Work is sleeping better. Even lifelong insomniacs often find that Wholeness Work helps them when nothing else did. The Wholeness Work was extremely helpful to me when I was having difficulty sleeping. In fact, my trouble with sleep was one of my main motivators to develop these processes.

---

[1] This chapter was written in 2017 and revised in 2023.
[2] Cate reported these results after a single 80-minute Wholeness Work coaching session with Connirae. Most people find more sessions are needed to get this level of results.

In this chapter we'll focus specifically on how you can use Wholeness Work to sleep better and have more energy during the day.

First, I'd like to ask you a question. When you did the exercises in this book so far, did you ever experience feeling more relaxed at the end than you were at the beginning?

In my trainings, everyone usually answers "yes" to that. If you did as well, you probably already sense how using Wholeness Work can support better sleep. And yet, for you to get the most benefit with sleep and sleep issues, the tips in this chapter are likely to be helpful.

In this chapter I'm *not* going to teach you a new format. But the material you'll learn here is important. I'm going to show you how to use everything you've learned about Wholeness Work so far to get better sleep and rest.

about sleep
six interesting things

When a client comes to me and says, "My sleep is terrible. Can you help me?" I reply, "Well, Wholeness Work has helped A LOT of people get better sleep. So most likely, yes." What I say next might surprise you.

"Sleep might not be the essential thing you thought it was..."
That's what I tell people.

Okay, you might be thinking I've lost touch with reality here. We all know there's *a lot* of research showing us that getting a good night's sleep is *very* important. And I personally recognize the value of sleep. So why would I tell my clients it might not actually be necessary? I hope that you stay with me and read on to discover why I say this, and how this is helpful to my clients.

After using Wholeness Work for sleep—and experiencing their own sleep quality improve—quite a few people have told me, "You know, one of the biggest things that helped me was when you said that *sleep isn't actually necessary.*" Sometimes they add, "That helped me to not feel so stressed about something I didn't think I could do anything about." This message made it easier for them to actually *use* Wholeness Work, in the way I'll describe in this chapter, to get better rest and sleep.

There is a connection between restorative sleep and health.

Before I tell you more about that, let's talk about sleep studies and what they actually show. Research on sleep shows a very clear *correlation* between sleep and many desirable outcomes such as health, longevity, and more. People who sleep a reasonable number of hours tend to be healthier and live longer than people who don't. That seems clear. Very clear. But the sleep studies don't actually show causation.

When people sleep, they usually experience a deep relaxation and resetting of the nervous system, right? So what if *this* is what people actually need, rather than the physical sleep itself?

And what if it's possible to get this deep relaxation and resetting of the nervous system, even while being physically awake? If we can do this, perhaps we can experience the sleep benefits more reliably. This is what Wholeness Work Meditation helps us do.

The Problem with Trying to Sleep

Lying in bed thinking, "I *have* to get to sleep because I read this research! Everything will be terrible if I don't sleep right now!" is a good way to stay awake all night, right? Those aren't exactly sleep-inducing thoughts.

So *trying* to sleep better is usually counterproductive. It just leads to more tension and stress about not sleeping well. Trying to sleep better is inevitably doomed to fail. It can't work. And the reason is because *sleep is one of those things we cannot do on purpose. It just happens.*

But the good news is we *can* do Wholeness Work on purpose. And Wholeness Work becomes an easy bridge from something we can do on purpose, into that effortless zone—that land of no effort.

This is because Wholeness Work gently guides us into a letting go of effort.

With Wholeness Work our attention is engaged in a way that consciously includes *everything happening in our experience.* It can even include experiences that might seem counter to sleep. It can include worries that I'm not going to be able to sleep, or that I'm going to feel stressed out tomorrow because I'm not sleeping right now. It can include everything.

Experiencing deep relaxation is a part of all Wholeness Work.

When we do Wholeness Work we already begin experiencing a deep relaxation of the nervous system, whether or not we're physically asleep. This relaxation starts to happen as soon as we shift our orientation from the content (i.e., *what* we're thinking about), to noticing *"Where's the 'I'?"* or *"Where's the One thinking?"* and *"What's the sensation quality there?"*

Then, each time we cycle through a Wholeness Work process and one of the 'I's releases itself, our nervous system relaxes even more deeply. So we can begin to experience the benefits of sleep while we're still technically awake.

We can consciously model what naturally good sleepers do unconsciously.

I believe Wholeness Work gives us a way to consciously do what naturally good sleepers do without realizing they're doing it. When naturally good sleepers lie down to sleep, I'm guessing what happens is an automatic and spontaneous letting go of the 'I's. This happens naturally for them, without effort, and outside of conscious awareness. These sleepers lie down and the 'I's that have formed during the day just naturally dissolve and melt.

Young children are better at this than adults are, because they don't have as many small 'I's built up yet. They just have a few, and the small 'I's that young children have aren't quite so fixed. Their 'I's haven't been in place very long. So for most young children, it's easier to relax into sleep.

And the research supports this. On average, young children sleep well. The percentage of sleep disturbance goes up with age. That is quite an interesting statistic because it's also true that as we get older, our small 'I's have been in place for a longer time and they have become more fixed and rigid. We've gotten into the habit of having this contracted sense of self at the unconscious level. So when we lie in bed with the intention to go to sleep, the older we get the less likely it is that our small 'I's spontaneously and naturally release so we *can* fall asleep.

Wholeness Work guides us in experiencing what is *meant* to happen when sleep occurs naturally and easily. Usually when people do Wholeness Work when in bed at night, they *do* slip into sleep. But it's important to know that it's not necessary to be *physically* sleeping for you to get the deep relaxation and replenishment that is such an important part of our 24-hour cycle. When we're doing the Wholeness Work, before sleep happens—and whether or not sleep happens—there's quite a bit of relaxation and resetting of the nervous system already occurring.

I began to really understand this after doing the Wholeness Work myself for a while. To some extent, the Wholeness method came into being because I was in a challenging phase of my life and, among other things, I was having incredible trouble sleeping. I was exploring everything I could think of to help me sleep better. When I started using Wholeness Work at night, I noticed I was getting an unusually deep relaxation even if I wasn't technically asleep.

Then I recalled something I'd heard about the spiritual teacher Paramahansa Yogananda, the author of *Autobiography of a Yogi*. One of the very first gurus from India to come to the West, he started an ashram community in California. I'd heard that he used to tell his disciples, "You don't need to sleep; sleep is a waste of time." He said, "Instead of sleeping, you should just sit and meditate for five or six hours. After that, you'll be good to go." According to the disciples, that's what *he* did and it did work for him. As far as I know, his students were never able to do that. But *he* could.[3]

The reason this is believable to me is that I started experiencing a shift in this direction as I was doing the Wholeness Work. When I woke up in the middle of the night, I would practice Wholeness Work while I was lying in bed, and I began to feel the deep relaxation that comes from the releasing of the 'I's and "resting as Awareness." And I started to realize, "If I continue this, at some point it's likely to be equally restful as actual sleep—and possibly even more so."

And if we're lying awake at night, it seems like a "no-brainer" that it's better to do something relaxing and replenishing than to fret. By doing the Wholeness Work we can immediately begin meeting some of the mind-body's important needs for deep relaxation and replenishment.

To be clear, I enjoy sleeping. It's not a personal goal to learn to meditate all night instead of sleep. But I'm glad to have a way to use "awake" time for relaxation and restoration, and my own personal evolution.

When Physical Sleep Isn't Restful

Have you ever had the experience of waking up after a night of sleep, but you wake up feeling kind of tense—not really rested? Sometimes people are "technically" asleep, yet their bodies don't fully relax. It's as if the body maintains a certain level of tension through the night.

This is an interesting experience because it shows us that just getting physical sleep doesn't guarantee getting the necessary relaxation of the body and nervous system. In this situation it's possible it would be better to be awake and do the Wholeness Work. We might actually get a deeper relaxation and "reset" that way.

Fortunately, we don't need to decide which is better—because we can do both.

---

[3] At least that's how I heard the story. I wasn't there to watch and see for myself, but I don't have any reason to doubt it. I'm guessing he was speaking honestly from his experience.

using wholeness work for sleep
the simplest version

Here's how it might play out if you use Wholeness Work…. Imagine you've just gone to bed. You're lying in bed, but not yet asleep. You can close your eyes, begin relaxing, and notice what you notice. Perhaps there's a body sensation, or an inner voice, or image. Then you can pause and recognize the point of view (or 'I'), if there is one. And noticing the location, the space it takes up, and the sensation quality there, it can be invited to dissolve into Awareness…

As you've experienced before, these simple steps tend to take us into a state of relaxation—sometimes even a deep relaxation. And in that kind of state, if the body is tired and needs to sleep, it naturally does so. We don't have to *make* it sleep.

Then if you wake up again in the middle of the night, it's not a problem because you can just do more Wholeness Meditation.

If you can't get to sleep, wake in the middle of the night, or wake earlier than you'd like and aren't fully rested, you now have something useful you can do—Wholeness Work—instead of choosing between lying awake frustrated, or just getting up even though you feel exhausted.

Including Thoughts and Worries
It's very common for "worry thoughts" to emerge, if we're lying in bed yet not sleeping. With Wholeness Work, this is totally fine. We don't need to make any inner thoughts or voices go away. We just kindly include them, like this example drawn from my own experience…

I'm lying there awake, and a voice in my head says, "Oh no, I'm awake. This is terrible!" or maybe the voice says, "It's happening again!"

I pause, and just ask inside, "Where is the One saying that?"[4]

And I notice: "Oh, it's right here, to the right of my head."

---

[4] I could have asked "Where's the 'I' that's saying that?" It's the same question. With reactions, I often use the version, 'Where's the 'One' saying that?'

Then I notice the size and shape: "It's kind of round, like a small ball."

And what about the sensation quality? ... "Hmm ... there's a sense of movement. It's a bit dark, but actually there's not much to it. It's sort of insubstantial now that I notice it."

And now I just notice what happens if the sensation of this is invited to dissolve and melt into the whole ... and/or I as Awareness can just relax into and as the sensation of this.[5] ... As I'm doing this now, I'm already feeling more relaxed and peaceful.

It's a whole different territory.

I don't have to fight with myself. I don't have to stop thinking anything. If another thought comes in, such as "Yeah, but I'm still not sleeping. Shouldn't I really be sleeping?" I can simply notice...

"Where is the One who's thinking *this*?"

"Oh, it's here. It's half inside the head, it's half out, and it's a little bit open and airy. I can't really put it into words."

So now, "What happens when the sensation of this is invited to dissolve, melt into everything ... or if I as Awareness just sort of relax into the sensation of *this?*"

... And now I'm feeling remarkably peaceful.

So very quickly, within the space of a few seconds, things have changed. The change really starts happening as soon as I shift out of the content or the story of it. If I'm in a mode of reaction to my circumstances—"Oh no, I can't sleep!" or "I'm going to be in a horrible mood tomorrow"—then I'm in the content and I'm not realizing that I'm *in* the drama. The drama *has* me. I'm acting it out. Once I recognize "Oh, this is something *I* am *doing*," then I can ask, "Okay, *where* is the *One who* is doing it?" "Where is the One thinking this thought?" Then I'm playing a different game, and already there's a beginning of relaxation.

---

[5] You might notice I'm using a slightly different wording to invite integration here. I teach when, why, and how to use these variations in the Wholeness levels II–IV trainings. You can just stick with the usual wording if that feels easier.

Ellie's Inner Struggle with "Mind Clutter"

Here's another example of how you can easily include any thoughts or "mind clutter" that comes up when you're going to sleep.

Ellie asked for help in using Wholeness Work with distracting thoughts. You can see how simple my answer is…

ELLIE: When I try to go to sleep, there's a phrase running through my head. I'm saying to myself, "*I better sleep.*"

ME: So, you're saying to yourself, "I better sleep." [Ellie nods. She's clearly in the experience right now.] Probably everybody has had that experience. So, *Where's the One saying that?*

To You/Reader: The question I'm asking is not just "Where is the speaking happening?" It's "Where is *the One* saying that?" And usually that question will get a different answer.[6] Once you're familiar with Wholeness Work, it's usually more effective and inclusive to find *the One speaking.*

ELLIE: [Ellie gestures to a location around her head, indicating size and shape.]

ME: Now notice the sensation quality in and through the space of that and just relax into and as that. [Ellie nods as she follows my invitation, and is looking relaxed and peaceful.] …
To the Group: And usually that itself becomes an enjoyable thing.

This is a very fast way of including our experience instead of arguing with ourselves. This "*I better go to sleep*" … this is an aspect of ourselves that wants the rest of us to do something and is telling us what to do. So there's a bit of an inner argument happening. As soon as we're just registering location, the space it takes up, and the sensation quality, we're already over the argument. There's no fight

---

[6] The location of the voice itself is the first experience someone usually notices. The "One speaking" is the self structure that is generating this experience. It is possible to use either one as the beginning in Wholeness Work. When it's easy for the person to find the "One speaking," I ask for that. However, if that isn't easy to find, then I go forward using the location of the voice itself.

happening anymore. That in itself tends to be a little more peaceful. And as we shift into sensation quality and invite the dissolving, then it becomes deeply peaceful.

Sleep Issues—An Opening to Heal and Evolve

When people seek solutions to sleep difficulties, they are usually thinking of their sleep difficulty as a problem to be solved. This is totally understandable—because we all want to wake up feeling rested and mentally clear for the day.

However, if you use Wholeness Work for sleep, you're doing more than solving a sleep problem. Because, if you're awake in the middle of the night with thoughts going around in your head, or the body feels a bit "revved up," guess what?

> *The very things that are keeping you awake, are actually aspects of your being that are crying out for recognition and integration.*

So as you're doing Wholeness Meditation in the night, it isn't just about getting to sleep. You're doing much more than that. There's use in it; there's value in it. You won't be awakened in the middle of the night unless in some sense your system needs this. Your system needs you to notice something. Your system is doing its best to bring something to your attention for processing, healing, and integration. The same thing is true if you wake up before you're fully rested. Whatever emerges in the middle of the night that's keeping us awake, these are our issues. These are the keys to our evolution, to our becoming more whole and integrated—more happy and fulfilled and capable beings.

When we shift out of content and we pause to actually notice the direct experience happening in the moment, then our mind-body system can begin to come back into harmony again, which is what our system wants. It's what our system is longing to have happen.

And for many people, nighttime is the easiest time for this kind of processing, healing, and integrating to happen. In the night, it's easier for experience that's usually out of our conscious awareness to begin coming forward. And with Wholeness Work we can kindly meet it. Fortunately, we don't even need to understand the content. We just meet whatever experience arises. If we need to know content, it will be revealed to us. And otherwise it can often be simpler just to allow the processing, digesting, and integrating of experience happen at a level deeper than our conscious mind can understand.

Physical Shifts: Increase in Circulation and "Flow"

When this kind of release begins happening, it's not just that we are in a better emotional state. Most people describe physical shifts as well: feeling more relaxed, and perhaps even feeling a deep relaxation in the core of our being.

Many people describe a feeling of more *flow* through the body, after doing Wholeness Work, and I feel this as well. I don't know exactly what is happening on the physical level, but I often have a strong subjective experience of a kind of flowing that feels quite physical. It makes sense that as muscles relax, blood can flow more freely through the body and most likely our other circulation systems can also work better.

The body has many circulation systems: the circulation of blood through arteries, veins and capillaries that brings oxygen and nutrients to the cells of the body; the circulation of lymph fluid that's involved in removing waste; the circulation of cerebrospinal fluid around our brain as well as around our spinal cord, and the flow of fluid within each cell.

As I do Wholeness Work and the 'I's release, I can feel subtle muscle tensions relax through deeper and deeper layers of my physical body, and it makes sense that when this happens all of these circulation systems can work better. This may be an important part of the replenishment that is meant to be happening at night in our 24-hour daily cycle. It's even possible that this can happen more fully when the 'I's dissolve through Wholeness Work, than if we were to physically sleep but our 'I's haven't opened and relaxed.

The possible physical effects of Wholeness Work haven't yet been examined through research, and I hope that begins happening soon. I anticipate it will confirm what most people doing Wholeness Work have already been experiencing: that when this deep relaxation and flow happens, the various circulation systems work better and the body can more easily repair and replenish itself on the physical and cellular level.

As I mentioned at the beginning of this chapter, I regularly receive reports from workshop participants and clients who thank me for giving them the message: *"It's not physical sleep you need, it's the deep relaxation of the nervous system. So if you do Wholeness Work, you'll be okay whether or not you sleep."* They tell me that this message helped them let go of "trying" to get to sleep, which had been keeping them awake.

There is room for considerable research to test the hypotheses about sleep and rest described in this chapter. My experiences—both personally and with clients—leads me to believe that systematically testing these hypotheses could lead to some significant advances in our understanding of sleep and its purpose.

tips
for sleep & rest

When on your way to sleep, start by using the Wholeness Meditation Format, in Chapter 4. Here are a few pointers to make it easier.

1. Practice during the day first.
This way you'll be familiar with the steps.

2. You don't need to use the script.
Reading a script would keep you in a more "awake" mode of consciousness.

Once you've practiced the method a few times during the day, the process will feel familiar and you'll be able to do it without needing to read the script. Simply lie down, close your eyes, and "feel your way" from one step to the next.

3. No need to take notes
Note-taking would also keep you in a more "awake" mode, so no need for this.

4. No need to track or remember things
At night, you can flow through the steps in the simplest most relaxing way. If you find a series of 'I's, just invite the last one to integrate. It doesn't matter if you remember the rest; your system will keep track for you. If anything remains that you need to notice, it will still be there. So you can just check for anything still present.

If you don't notice anything, that's fine. As the integrating settles, just continue resting as Awareness. And if a new sensation, image, or voice emerges, this can invite you into a new round of processing and ever-deepening relaxation.

5. No need to finish or complete anything
At any point in the process, you might be feeling so relaxed that you drift off to sleep. That's fine. Nothing needs to be finished. For example, you might find a Chain of three 'I's, invite the third to integrate, and then the next thing you know, you're waking up. This can be quite lovely, and it really doesn't matter if you officially finish with the other 'I's, or even remember them.

6. Continue both daytime and nighttime practice.
Many people find it helpful to go back and forth between using Wholeness Work during the day *with* notes, and then at night just letting it happen *without* notes. You'll gradually get the feel of it.

A Practical Tip
When you drift off to sleep, are you ever kept awake by thinking of something you need to do the next day? "Oh, I just remembered I need to call so-and-so tomorrow!" If this happens for you it might be helpful to keep a pad by your bed to write down any "to-do's". Once

it's written down, if you still find the thought going through your head, you can do Wholeness Work with "the One who's thinking the thought," knowing you really don't need to keep the thought in your mind. Your note will be there in the morning to remind you.

wholeness work for sleep and restorative rest
a guided experience

There are many ways to use Wholeness Work for sleep. Here's a brief script guiding you in an easy way to get started. It's a simplified version of the Meditation Format. Use this only after you've practiced the formats in Chapters 3 and 4.

Step 1. Close your eyes, and relax. Let go of everything that easily releases... and notice what remains.
If nothing emerges in Awareness, just relax into experiencing Awareness itself ... the full field of Awareness that's all around and throughout.... You can continue doing this as long as happens effortlessly.

Step 2. If a body sensation, a constriction, or an image, thought, or inner voice comes into Awareness, then notice...

Where is it located?
How much space does it take up?
Sensing in and through, what's the sensation quality?

Step 3. Find the 'I'.
Notice where the perceiving [of whatever you noticed in Step 1] is happening from. Notice the location, how much space it takes up [the size & shape], and sensing in and through, notice the sensation quality.

Step 4. Check if the 'I' welcomes integrating.

Now gently sensing the sensation quality of the 'I' … does the sensation here welcome being invited to open and relax, in and as, the fullness of Awareness, that's all around and throughout.…

If yes: *This can be allowed to happen now.*

If no: Then find another 'I' until you get to an 'I' that welcomes relaxing as Awareness. (See Chapters 3 and 4 for how to do this, i.e. how to find the 'I' Chain.)

After the 'I' integrates, go straight to Step 6 and Rest as Awareness. Or do Step 5 first. Do whatever feels easier, kinder, and more natural in this moment.

Step 5. Check with the starting experience.

Notice what's there now. Any remaining sensation can also be invited to dissolve into Awareness, and/or you as Awareness can relax into the sensation of this.

Step 6. Now just rest as Awareness.

This phase can be deeply restorative, so there's no need to rush. You can just enjoy this. If—and whenever—another sensation, image, or inner voice or sound emerges, you can cycle through these steps again.

Pointers to Keep in Mind

You may find yourself relaxing into sleep before you finish all the steps. That's fine.

You may discover that nighttime is an especially good time to use Wholeness Work, to process whatever thoughts, feelings, etc. emerge. Nighttime is when the 'I's tend to dissolve on their own, so Wholeness Work follows this natural inclination.

When we do Wholeness Meditation at night—either when going to sleep or in the middle of the night—anything unfinished from the day tends to reveal itself spontaneously. For example, we might see the image of a person's face with whom we had a difficult conversation that was left unresolved. Any remaining stressful thoughts or feelings tend to emerge naturally, and Wholeness Work gives us a kind and gentle way to process these.

Gently including reactions—whatever thoughts, feelings, etc. emerge in your experience when you turn inward to rest or sleep— is important. There are several examples of how to do this earlier in this chapter. You can find more information on how to notice and include reactions in Chapter 20 of my earlier book on this subject, *Coming to Wholeness: How to Awaken and Live with Ease.*

When using Wholeness Work for sleep, start by using the simplified Wholeness Meditation Format I outlined for you in the guided experience. Then, if it feels easy and natural, you might find yourself adding the Authority or What's Missing Formats when your inner experience needs them.

In the beginning, most likely the formats you learn in this Wholeness Work Level I book will be more than enough to meet and process your experience. If you continue using Wholeness Work as a nourishing and restorative nighttime practice, eventually you may find some of the formats in the later Wholeness trainings useful. If/when you learn the formats in Wholeness Work Levels II – IV, you can also draw upon these to meet whatever emerges in your nighttime experience.

 If you'd like to listen to me guiding you through a short version of this meditation that's designed to reduce stress and encourage relaxation, use this QR code or go to www.andreasnlp.com/nlp-support-resources/meditation/.

Sharing Experiences

Here are a few examples of what people have shared when they used the Wholeness Work to sleep better at night. These comments are from people in trainings with me or other Wholeness Work trainers.

"I used to not sleep well at all. I had to follow a very rigid routine to try to get even a modicum of sleep. But after I did the Wholeness exercises and dissolved just a few 'I's, I could get off sleep medicine and all the sleep teas and all the rigid routines and just go right on to sleep. It happened quickly—and this was after years and years and years of struggling with sleep."

"I tried this out last night, and went to sleep right away. When I woke up I had a lot of energy. More than usual. I think I got better rest than usual. So 'thank you.'"

"When my husband is out of town, generally I'm quite scared, sleeping alone. I get up and check for sounds, and I don't have a restful sleep. But now [using Wholeness Work] I just slept like a baby. I had no fear."

"I had a sleep issue for a long time, and I used to have cramps in my calf muscles. I would go to sleep and then wake up in the middle of night at 3:00 am. And then, it was very difficult for me to focus on anything. I knew meditation, but it didn't work. So it used to take half an hour, one hour, two hours for me to get back to sleep. But now, since I've done Wholeness Work, that issue is not coming up. I'm sleeping restfully, and [the cramp thing is] much different. It's much lighter. The discomfort is not there. And sleep in general has improved a lot."

"After yesterday's session I was much more relaxed, slept well, rested more and woke up with much more energy. I am surprised and grateful. I hope everyone can experience this."

"D" had been having difficulty sleeping after his divorce. He said, "I want to tell you that I was able to sleep like an angel again. I feel my muscles are loose. Wow. Thanks for this incredible experience."

q&a
using wholeness work to improve sleep

Will this help with daytime tiredness?

Q Will Wholeness Meditation help if I'm tired during the day?

A It definitely helps me when I'm tired during the day. If you're tired you might enjoy taking a short break to do the Wholeness Meditation Process. You can experiment and find out what happens.

You can also tune into your body and sense what it needs. If your body is tired, does it need this relaxation and resetting of the nervous system? Do you need some time to process something stressful? Wholeness Work will help with both of these needs. You're likely to feel deeply refreshed after 10 or 20 minutes of Wholeness Meditation.

Other times the body actually needs movement and exercise. And sometimes it needs good quality food to maintain energy. Wholeness Work helps us become more in tune with our actual needs.

Will this help in the middle of the night?

Q What if I'm awake a long time in the middle of the night and don't go back to sleep even after doing Wholeness Work?

A Usually doing the Wholeness Work results in deep relaxation which typically leads to sleep. However, sometimes a person might find themselves awake for quite a while, even as they're doing Wholeness Work. If this happens for you, consider that it can sometimes be a positive thing.

Personally, I find the middle of the night the easiest time to practice Wholeness Work. It's as if in the middle of the night, the 'I's are ready to relax and dissolve into the whole—and other structures are as well. So the middle of the night can be an excellent time to do this kind of meditation. Remember, Wholeness Meditation is doing more than helping us deeply relax and reset our nervous system. We're also processing, healing, and integrating our Being. We're evolving.

So I just trust the process. If I wake up in the night, I shift into Wholeness Meditation. I might continue processing for an hour, or two hours, and then I usually fall back asleep again. (As you do this over time, the way you use Wholeness Work will change; the steps you flow through will be different. I address this in more detail in the trainings.)

I have heard from more than one spiritual teacher that the middle of the night is the best time to meditate. These teachers point to somewhat different times as the "ideal"—some say 2:30 a.m. is the best, some 3:00 a.m., others 4:00 a.m., and so on. Some teachers even instruct their students to set an alarm clock and get up at a particular time to meditate. And they have explanations based on their spiritual system for why this middle-of-the-night meditation is important.

Leaving aside any belief systems, I think we can find a simple explanation for this. Perhaps nighttime is a good time to meditate because this is the time when the small 'I's tend to naturally relax and dissolve. We function on a 24-hour cycle for quite a few things. During the day we eat, we exercise, we go to work, we play. Nighttime *isn't* the usual or "natural" time for any of those things. At nighttime, our body organs make adjustments—for example, the kidneys automatically slow down their processing so that we're less likely to need to go to the bathroom. So many things *don't* happen at night. But nighttime *is* the natural time for the small 'I's to relax. So the Wholeness Work goes along with what the system is naturally wanting to do anyway *at that time.*

I advise people not to set an alarm clock for it. You can trust the wisdom of your mind-body system. If you sleep through the night, then you probably don't need to be doing this work in the night. However, if you wake up and do Wholeness Work and you remain awake for a while, this may be exactly what needs to happen. This may actually be the wisdom of the mind-body system. It may be that our mind-body system is attempting to process something that can't be processed when we are asleep. Perhaps our system is attempting to deal with the small 'I's that have formed as a natural part of growing up as a human being on this planet. We need to be awake/ present for these contractions of consciousness to be recognized and included and integrated. And yet in the night is when our system is in a mode for this dissolving to happen more easily.

Sometimes the difficulty sleeping becomes so intense we have no choice but to devote real attention to it. And then the Wholeness Work offers a way to give it this attention in a constructive way. We get both the dissolving of the 'I's that the system wants, plus we get the deep relaxation of the mind-body system that we also need.

Will I need less sleep?

Q If I do Wholeness Work, will I need less sleep?

A Sometimes people report that their sleep has become more restful, so they need less of it. So it's possible that might happen for you. But it depends on the needs of *your* mind-body system. What we can be sure of is that Wholeness Work will help you get whatever sleep you actually need, and to wake up feeling more rested. For some people that might translate into less time sleeping, but for others it might mean more sleep—at least at first.

Today's culture has placed a value on sleeping less, and having more hours to "do things." So there are people who've been sleep deprived for years, even decades, without knowing it. Those people might discover they're sleeping more, after doing Wholeness Work. As the 'I's let go, more beliefs and assumptions let go. And the ways we're trying to impose our ideas on reality, on ourselves, and on the world, *that's* what's dissolving. Doing Wholeness Work allows the way things *actually are* to be known and to be experienced more.

If the reality is that your system is sleep-deprived, then as the 'I's relax, there may be a phase when you actually sleep more. On the other hand, if you've already been getting adequate rest, then as the 'I's dissolve there is the possibility that either you'll sleep less, or you'll experience more energy during the day. You're likely to experience one of these effects.

What we can trust is that as the 'I's dissolve and we become more integrated, our mind-body system will come into balance and we'll naturally do what's best for us.

One thing to check is whether you have a belief that it's *better* to need less sleep. If so, then that's something you can consider exploring with Wholeness Work. It's a pretty common idea in modern culture, "Oh, it would be really cool to just need four hours of sleep, or no sleep at all." People try to cut back their sleep as little time as possible, with the idea that they're going to somehow get more out of life this way. If we can find "the One who believes this," then it's going to be tremendously useful to invite this 'I' to integrate.

Getting less sleep isn't necessarily a useful goal. It assumes a need to pack more into life somehow. That we'd be happier or more fulfilled or a better person if we could squeeze more out of each day. With Wholeness Work, these kinds of beliefs and attachments start dissolving. (In Level II training we learn a specific format for finding and dissolving attachments.)

Sleep vs. Meditation

Q Is it better to meditate at night rather than sleep?

A Personally, I like sleeping. And I think it's best not to "try" to do anything. If you're awake at night, then do Wholeness Mediation. Your system is waking you up, so you can flow with it this way. If you sleep easily and don't wake up, then great. Enjoy that. I don't recommend trying to force yourself to do something different from what your mind-body system is doing on its own.

The more I do Wholeness Work, the more I have glimpses of feeling like "Oh! I think I'm starting to experience what Yogananda was talking about." I have the sense that this is as deeply restful as sleep and perhaps more so. And if that would last through the whole night, then perhaps I would have the experience Yogananda did. I don't know. So far, that level of relaxation hasn't lasted through the whole night for me—and it's not a goal of mine. I don't really care.

It'll go how it goes, but it's interesting just to notice these things. I enjoy sleeping, so I'll be content if that's my destiny: to sleep at night. That's okay! I'm good with that.

Will this help me beyond just sleeping?

Q Will using the Wholeness Meditation for sleep have results *beyond* better sleep?

A Yes it will. We tend to start having deeper sleep. And yes, the sleep starts becoming more replenishing, but that's not the only thing. The very work that gets those results can't do so without also influencing your life. It's going to make your life better, too.

This brings to mind a story I shared with you in the Introduction, and it's a good answer to this question. Once I was working with a woman who'd been referred to me by a colleague. He'd told her, "You really should work with Connirae. She has a new meditation method and I think it would be good for you."

So I started teaching this woman how to do Wholeness Work. We met once a week, and in between she practiced doing the Wholeness Meditation each day. After three or four meetings, I asked her, "How is it going?" And she said, "Well it's going pretty well, but you know the weirdest thing is happening."

"What's that?" I asked.

"Well, my life is different too." And I was thinking, "Whoa, I wonder what she *thought* would happen?" I had no idea she wasn't aware that was a part of the intention. But she must have been thinking this was just for relaxing—it's "just a meditation." So I asked, "How is your life different?"

She said, "There's less drama. Well, actually there's the same amount of drama, but I'm not pulled into it anymore. There's still drama at work. People do their things, but I just know it's all okay. Now it's not a big deal and I just do my job and it's easier for me."

This woman was a single mom with two kids and she added, "My kids can get into their dramas too, and I just feel like it's more okay. I know it'll be fine. Before I would have gotten caught up in the drama and it would have been stressful for me."

So that's an example of how our life starts coming into balance along with the sleep. You don't need your whole life to be in balance before the sleep gets in balance, but sometimes they happen together, and sometimes it can start with sleep.

If we needed life to be in complete balance before we could sleep well, very few people would sleep well. So to some extent "life balance" and sleep are independent. But in case the sleep doesn't come into place right away, just know that you're also working with these other levels. You're also working with the things that will allow your *life* to work better. So you may experience improved sleep first, or you may experience "less drama" in your life first; the changes can work from either direction.

Complicated Sleep Issues—Including Medication

Q My sleep issue seems complicated. Will Wholeness Work Meditation work for me?

A If you practice Wholeness Work regularly, you're likely to notice that things start sorting themselves out over time. Some things sort themselves out very quickly, other things more gradually.

The sleep experience is a reflection of the sum of all kinds of other things happening in the mind-body system—a composite of the needs, motives, intentions, and interests that are a part of us being alive on the planet as a human being. So to think that one thing is going to instantly, completely sort it all out might be a little unrealistic. But the thing is that with Wholeness Work we're doing much more than just medicating the system.

Sometimes people resort to sleeping pills to deal with sleep issues, and for some people in some situations, medication is likely to be a useful option—especially if used on a temporary basis. But sleeping pills deal only with the symptom, rather than resolving the structure of what may be happening. Some psychological methods essentially function like sleeping pills. They don't have the capability of actually healing and resolving; in effect, they only "medicate."

Wholeness Work is a method that begins to bring the system itself back into harmony, balance, and wholeness. When this happens other things—along with sleep—can start to right themselves.

Asking, "Where's the One Who is speaking?"

Q You said that if we are meditating and an inner voice comes in, we should ask "Where's the *One who* is speaking?" Why not just ask "Where is the voice?" or "Where is the speaking happening from?" Is there a difference?

A Yes, there is a difference. If we ask, "Where is the speaking happening?" we are finding the location of the *experience*. We'll get the location of this inner talking. If we ask, "Where is the '*One who*' is speaking?" we are asking for the location of the "self" that generates the experience. Sometimes the "One who" is speaking is located in an entirely different location than the voice itself, and other times the location is the same or almost the same. If the "One who" is speaking is in the same area as the voice, it's likely to be a bit smaller or larger. Noticing the difference in size can help you recognize the different structure.

When we find the *"One who* is speaking" then we have the inner structure that generates the experience. So the integration will be more complete than if we only include the experience of speaking. This is why I suggest asking for that.

However, just the other day I was working with a client who got confused when I asked, "Where's the One speaking?" But it was easy for her to notice, "Where is the speaking happening?" So we went with the question that was easy for her to notice in experience. It's important to let this work flow in a way that's experience-based, rather than just conceptual—so I went with that.

sleep and states of consciousness

Sleeping and "Awake" Consciousness

I'd like to share an idea that you might find intriguing. It's not essential to understand or agree with it to benefit from Wholeness Work, so if you don't think this makes any sense, that's totally fine. Just skip over it. Here's the idea…

During the day when we are going about our lives, we call this being "awake." However, most of us move through life caught in reaction patterns; we're living and acting out of them. While we call this being "awake," there is a sense in which we are "asleep." We are "asleep" to the reactivity that is happening—the automatic knee-jerk reaction patterns we are acting out of. Our consciousness, or "awareness," isn't present in/as our responses in an "awake" way.

So we are awake in one sense (our bodies are not asleep), but the small 'I's are activated and are not "awake" to themselves. We could perhaps describe this as Awareness having gone to sleep. Awareness is there, but we are not conscious of it or living from it most of the time. When we do Wholeness Work, we are learning to be awake "*as* Awareness" or "*as* Consciousness."

In one sense this is the same as "baby consciousness;" in another, it is quite different because we now have the full wisdom that comes from the sum total of our life experience. The direct knowledge that comes from our experience remains when the small 'I's dissolve. What melts away are the fixed or rigid meanings we make out of this direct experience. The beliefs, "should's" and "have to's" aren't there any longer. This puts us in the position of being able to access maximum wisdom, as insight and creative ideas can form themselves newly in each moment, in full responsiveness to our life situation.

When I was having a lot of difficulty sleeping—and I mean GREAT difficulty—I remember telling close confidants, *"I feel like I'm being required to learn to do consciously what used to just happen unconsciously."* I have no idea how I got that impression. That was before I started exploring meditation approaches in earnest, so as far as I know I hadn't yet read anything on the subject. But I got the impression that I was being asked to do something *consciously*, as though it wasn't enough to just "go to sleep" or "fall asleep" as I'd always done until then.

Looking back, I think Wholeness Work is that "next step" that I was being asked to take. Babies start off in a state of undivided consciousness. Then as we grow bigger we form small 'I's. In our waking life, we are living out of these small 'I's. And these small 'I's, at least some of them, relax when we fall asleep. Then we are meant to go to the next step, where we become "awake as consciousness," as we move through the day. Our body is awake, and also our consciousness is "awake," with the I's relaxed into Awareness, while we move through the world with all the learnings that come from our experience.

But learning to live "as awake consciousness" doesn't happen by itself while we are living our lives. It also can't happen when we're physically asleep. However, it *can* happen through systematically doing Wholeness Work. We notice our rigid structures and invite them to dissolve. And it's possible that this transition can happen most easily in the middle of the night.

— *Two Key Reminders for Using Wholeness Work for Sleep* —

Remember that it doesn't matter if you're asleep or awake—it just matters that you use the time for the deep relaxation and resetting of the nervous system that happens naturally when you do Wholeness Work.

If you wake up in the night, there may be a useful purpose to this. It's possible your system is calling your attention to something that needs to be processed within. And nighttime may be the easiest time for our system to present to us whatever we need to notice. Fortunately we can kindly include and integrate whatever emerges, using Wholeness Work, in order to come to Wholeness and wellbeing.

getting the benefits

From my experience, almost everyone can experience significant benefit from Wholeness Work for sleep. If you have any sleep challenges—or you're just curious how using Wholeness Work with sleep might be beneficial for you—I encourage you to try it out. I've done my best to include in this chapter everything you'll need to successfully use Wholeness Work for sleep.[7]

Some people find it clicks for them right away from the book. Others find it much easier to absorb this practice in individual coaching or trainings. Please do whatever works well for you. Just know that if you encounter questions or stumbling blocks to getting the results people share in this chapter, help is available.

---

[7] For some people, sleep difficulties indicate a medical issue, so consider seeking medical attention as well.

When you're using Wholeness Work for sleep, you're really drawing from *everything* you know about Wholeness Work. So after you've used the method for a while, you may find it useful to re-read this chapter or other sections of this book. You may discover a new section that pops out for you with an instruction or tip you're now ready to take in.

Getting restorative sleep and rest provides the mind-body system with an opportunity to "reset" and refresh—which are critical to physical and emotional wellbeing. Using Wholeness Work principles and methods will enable you to stop *trying* to sleep—and instead relax more deeply by including all of your present moment experience in a direct, deep, and kind way.

In the next chapter, you'll learn how Wholeness Work is really a *complete* system of transformation that can help you continue creating lasting and meaningful changes.

CHAPTER 8

GENERAL Q & A

Understanding More about
Wholeness Work

As you know, most chapters in this book include a section of Questions and Answers specific to the content of that chapter. Here I want to address questions about Wholeness Work that are more general.

Changing the Script—the Pronouns

Q Some of the words in the script seem awkward to me. I'd like to change them when I guide someone else. Is this OK?

A I recommend using the script as is—especially in the places it might seem awkward. Those are often places where the wording is chosen for a specific purpose. For example: When people change the script, one of the first places they do it is adding in extra pronouns. Instead of saying *"sensing in and through..."* they might say *"You can sense in and through..."* or even *"I want you to sense in and through."*

In the scripts I use as few pronouns as possible, and still have the guidance make sense. This is because if we say, "You can sense in and through," this creates a separate self that is going to do the sensing. And we don't want to do that.

If we just say "… and sensing in and through…" we're making it easy for the person we're guiding to just allow the sensing to happen from the Awareness itself. They don't need to create a separate structure inside to do this sensing.

It's not that we need to completely avoid using pronouns. Sometimes I've included pronouns in the script—in places where we need the pronouns for the other person to understand the instruction. But if there's a way to offer the instruction without adding the pronoun, I generally do it that way.

There are also other ways we've noticed people changing the wordings that weaken the process, and that's why we recommend sticking with the wording as it is.

When Emotions Emerge During the Process

Q When an 'I' integrates, sometimes an emotion or memory comes up. What does this mean, and do I need to do anything about it?

A Emotions emerging is a natural part of the process. Here's how I think about it. Often an 'I' (or other inner structure) was formed as an attempt to deal with an emotional response that wasn't ok to express at the time. We might have had a strong feeling, but didn't feel ok to just express the feeling at the time for whatever reason. Instead we dissociated a bit and formed an 'I' inside, and the emotion may have become stuck within.

When the 'I' is invited to integrate, this naturally releases any emotional response that may be related. A related emotion often naturally releases at the same time. So it's a good thing.

All you need to do is just let this emotion be experienced "as Awareness" too. The 'I' is already relaxing back into Awareness, so there's a natural tendency for any related feeling to also be experienced as Awareness and relax back into the flow of things.

And there's something really special about allowing it to happen in that way.

Emotions are meant to be temporary experiences. We feel something in a particular situation, and the emotion is meant to be a temporary thing, flowing through our body/mind system. It's only if the emotion is blocked in some way that in a sense it may become stuck in our body-mind system.

Releasing the 'I's is what makes it possible to easily access these "stuck" feelings and release them. Once the 'I' has released, it's possible to fully experience the sensation as Awareness. And when Awareness experiences the energy that forms this emotion, AS SENSATION, this releases it back into the whole.

It's a positive thing to allow any feeling that emerges, to flow through the full physical body. It's usually been stuck in a smallish location. When it's allowed to flow through the full physical body—or as much of the physical body as naturally happens—as Awareness, then it tends to naturally dissolve.

And the Awareness that we are can acknowledge the emotion in a deeper and more complete way than any person could do—because Awareness is completely free of judgment. It naturally "loves" whatever arises within it. And this allows the natural dissolving back into the Whole.

Note that this is completely different than just reliving the feeling *without* experiencing it as Awareness. … Doing it that way would tend to entrench the old emotional response, whereas experiencing an emotion as Awareness, releases it.

Integrating—Its Meaning in Wholeness Work

Q Many therapy methods use the word "integration." You use the word "integration" in Wholeness Work also. Is it the same thing?

A In Wholeness Work, "integration" has a unique meaning. It's actually very useful to understand this difference. In Wholeness Work, "integrating" means that something that has been separate from the Whole of our consciousness becomes one with the whole. For example, the 'I' structures are a constriction of our consciousness, which creates inner tension and stress. Integrating means the energy that's formed into this 'I' relaxes and again becomes one with the Whole.

We go through the same process with other structures within.

With most other kinds of coaching or therapy, this "integration" is not explicitly invited—so it's more of a random event. In these other kinds of therapy, "integrating" might mean the merging of one part with another, for example. That results in a larger part, but still isn't the same thing as these parts merging with the whole.

Other times "integrating" is used to talk about ways to apply a learning in one's ongoing life. With Wholeness Work we don't emphasize this, because when the 'I's and other inner structures are merged with the whole of our being, there is a natural expression of our new way of being. We don't have to do anything extra to get that result.

How Integrating Might Feel Viscerally...

Q When I invite something to integrate, sometimes the experience surprises me. It can feel different than anything I've felt before, and I wonder if it's ok.

A The experience we have when these contractions of consciousness dissolve into the Whole, can be quite different from time-to-time, and different for different people. The most common experience is just a subtle relaxation.

People who have a lot of 'I's located outside of the body tend to experience less of a visceral response when the 'I's dissolve and integrate. If the 'I's are located within the body, the person is more likely to experience the integration in a more visceral way. It's not better or worse. It's just different. And your experience might be different than I'm mapping out here.

As more of the 'I's located outside the body integrate, the experience of integrating tends to become more visceral. It might be experienced as...

a deep relaxation (sometimes subtle, sometimes stronger)

vibrating

flowing of aliveness/energy (there can be various flow/circulation patterns). A flow or circulation pattern might or might not fit with known theories of how chi or energy is thought to flow. You can trust that when you release 'I's and authorities and other structures, whatever flow happens will be whatever needs to happen for your body/mind system.

sensation of electricity

bubbling or percolating (as if tiny particles of energy are percolating)

When the shift is subtle, it's usually easy to assimilate. If the experience is more intense, you might find yourself having a reaction to it—perhaps even feeling startled, or a bit frightened. If so, it's helpful to kindly include the "One reacting" using Wholeness Work. This makes it easy to again relax into enjoying the shift that's happening.

If you experience strong shifts and have any concerns, I encourage you to schedule a session with a trained Wholeness Work coach to help guide you safely and comfortably through the process.

Feeling Resistance to Practicing Wholeness Work

Q What does it mean if I feel some resistance to doing the practice?

A Feeling resistance to doing the practice almost always means that there's something that wants to be noticed that you're not yet aware of. We're caught in content, without realizing it. For example, if I wake up in the middle of the night and I just feel like *"Oh I don't wanna practice!"* what is calling out to be noticed is this 'One who' is going "Oh I don't want to practice!" If I shift out of content, into process, and notice what's actually happening, then I can notice its location and sensation quality, invite it to integrate, and things become easy again.

When we can shift out of content—noticing what's actually happening and processing it—there is no such thing as resistance. So experiencing "resistance" can be a good thing. It just means it's time to pause and ask "OK what's actually happening right now in this moment?" Once we recognize the program that's operating in the background, we ask "Where's the One running this program? Where's the One doing this?" And then we're back into processing what's happening, rather than reacting to the content of what's happening. Often there's an immediate shift to feeling more at peace, the moment we shift into noticing the "One who" instead of being caught in reactivity.

What if the practice stops working for me?

Q What if the practice stops working for me?

A If it stops working for you, this usually means one of two things…

You need to notice whatever is in the way. Often there's something emerging from within your system that needs noticing and attending to. This may mean a reaction or meta-response that you haven't yet included using Wholeness Work. (By "meta-responses" I mean a reaction like "trying to figure this out," "trying to do this right," or "trying to make change happen.")

Your system is ready for and needs some of the more advanced practices. You can gain access to these in Wholeness Level II and beyond.

differences from other approaches

Participants sometimes ask how Wholeness Work relates to other methods of change. Feel free to skip over any of the next questions if they aren't of interest to you. If you're ready to just dive in and do more self-practice, I encourage you to go for it! The self-practice produces more meaningful understanding than anything I could explain.

Differences from "Parts Work"

Q Is Wholeness Work "parts work?"

A The short answer is "no." I describe these structures we find inside as "constrictions of consciousness" instead of "parts." That description fits better with what we are doing. We notice the sensation quality, and invite the constriction to relax. We can also call a particular constriction an 'I', or an Authority, etc., when that fits.

Parts work involves different assumptions. In most forms of parts work, we're encouraged to personify an aspect of our experience and have conversations with this "part." We don't need to do this in Wholeness Work—instead we go directly to the sensation quality of the experience. Conversations aren't needed, because we're working at a deeper level of change. And when we invite Awareness to meet the sensation of the 'I', as one example, this invites an acknowledgment at a deeper level than conversation could ever produce. When we invite the sensation of the 'I' to integrate, this again produces change at a deeper level than could happen through conversation.

It would be possible to call an 'I' a part. We could even call the other structures we find inside a "part." It's just a name. However, there are so many differences between Wholeness Work and what's known as "parts work," that I encourage you to let go of that way of naming things when you practice Wholeness Work.

If you use the terminology from parts work systems, this tends to unconsciously bring along the assumptions and presuppositions of those other ways of working. This reduces the impact of Wholeness Work because this work goes to a deeper level of change than most forms of parts work can go.

Core Transformation (CT) is a unique parts method because it works at a deep level like Wholeness Work does. CT begins by communicating with parts, and then utilizes content, the conversation, to discover a Core State of being. This Core State is similar to Awareness, and is what makes it possible to integrate the entire part into the Whole, similarly to Wholeness Work. We recommend using parts language when doing Core Transformation, and switching to Wholeness Work language when doing Wholeness Work.

Is working with "Parent Parts" the same as the Authority Method?

Q Some forms of parts work include finding "parent parts" or "judging parts" within. Isn't this the same as what you're doing with Wholeness Work?

A Great question! It's actually quite different. In parts work, when we find a parent part within, it tends to be personified. It's as if we're imagining that person, now talking to us.

The structures we access through Wholeness Work are usually quite different. It's important to use the unique questions I've laid out in this book. And if you do, when you find an Authority inside, it's likely to be different than if you were doing parts work. It's likely to be located in a different place, and have different properties. Often the Authorities don't look like a person—it's more a literal contraction of consciousness that we are finding within.

Equally important, with Wholeness Work we discover the Chains of Authority. This is what makes easy and *complete* transformation possible.

Differences from "Submodalities Work"

Q Is Wholeness Work "submodalities work"?

A People with NLP training background sometimes think Wholeness Work is a type of submodalities work. It actually isn't. While I consider submodalities (SMs) Work to be quite useful, Wholeness Work is not a type of submodalities work, and what we find with sensation quality is not the same as submodalities. Here are the main differences:

SMs are *codings on experience* that we can utilize to make change. (For example, we can make an image brighter or closer if we want to have a stronger feeling response; we can change its location, so that we unconsciously categorize the experience differently; etc.) Sensation Qualities (SQs) are *direct* experience. They aren't codings added onto an experience to categorize it or change our feeling response. Wholeness Work involves working at a deeper level.

SMs are generally surface qualities. We're noticing what can be noticed from the outside of something. With SQ we're sensing in and through. Just noticing surface qualities isn't sufficient for doing Wholeness Work.

When noticing SMs, we are observing from the outside. In Wholeness Work, when noticing SQ, we are inviting our experience to become increasingly associated. The more we do Wholeness Work the more we begin to experience it as if "from the inside."

SMs are treated as a list of discreet attributes—brightness, color, opacity, etc. With SQ the intention is to notice it as one thing, even if we use several words to describe it.

Eye focus: When we are asked about SM's, our eye focus becomes sharper, as we notice something in more detail. When we notice SQ, we tend to defocus. The experience is different enough that our physiology is different.

Words used: Words to describe submodalities have some overlap with Sensation Quality words; so it's easy to think they're the same thing. But the overlap isn't complete. In submodalities, an experience might be either 2-D or 3-D. In SQ there isn't any such thing as 2D.

In Wholeness Work, when discovering the SQ, we generally begin by offering examples of what could be considered more tactile experience, i.e. "it might be dense, airy, smooth, rough, vibratey, etc." However, I don't ask about color. Sometimes color emerges spontaneously, but often there is no sense of color that's relevant. Submodality work is different, i.e. one would usually ask about color, and expect to have a visual aspect to the experience.

If we call what we do in Wholeness Work "submodalities," this would put it in a box and bring up other assumptions related to submodality work that aren't necessarily true of Wholeness Work.

In general, Wholeness Work operates at a deeper level of experience than submodality work, and makes possible a deeper level of change. Submodality work is valuable in its own right— there are times when I use it and consider it the best fit for the needs of the client—or myself.)

Dissociation

Q Does Wholeness Work teach people to dissociate more?

A It's actually quite the opposite. Wholeness Work results in people becoming *more* fully associated than they've ever been before. I started out as a fairly dissociated person. And have been enjoying becoming increasingly associated.

Wholeness Work provides a way to discover the dissociation that already exists in the body/mind system. The 'I's are examples of dissociations that currently exist within us, at the unconscious level. With Wholeness Work we find these existing dissociations and invite them to integrate. This leads to gradually becoming more associated.

When someone goes through the complete Wholeness Work system—Levels I–IV—it's almost inevitable that they describe fully inhabiting their body. Often beyond what they can recall ever having experienced before.

Differences from Hypnosis

Q Is hypnosis the same as Wholeness Work?

A People do go into a deep state, with their attention turned inward when they do Wholeness Work Meditation. So this has some similarities to what people call a "trance state" or "hypnosis."

However, there are some differences that matter. With hypnosis, one bypasses the conscious mind to get to the deep inner state. With Wholeness Work we don't need to do that. We can use whatever experience is happening as the doorway to the deep state of consciousness.

There are different types of hypnosis. Hypnosis is just a name, of course, and it depends upon what you mean by hypnosis.

Hypnotic Language in Wholeness Work

Q Are we using hypnotic language patterns (or Ericksonian Language Patterns) when we do Wholeness Work?

A Yes and no. It doesn't work to just import hypnotic language patterns, even Ericksonian Language Patterns, into Wholeness Work. I encourage you to stay with the script as written. Adding in other hypnotic language patterns is likely to dilute the process just a little bit, and reduce the potential effectiveness.

The reason is that most of what's taught as hypnotic language patterns operate at a different level of change. Ericksonian Language Patterns, and most hypnotic language patterns, are developed with the understanding that to get change, we need to bypass the conscious mind. With Wholeness Work, we don't bypass the conscious mind.

Instead we integrate it. All our conscious mind reactions thoughts and meta-responses—they're all easily included and dissolved using Wholeness Work. The result is that gradually we have less separation between conscious mind and our unconscious processing. It becomes one thing—one undivided consciousness. This is what makes the work ultimately more complete, easier, and more stable.

Hypnotic language patterns are usually developed with the assumption that the Guide needs to influence the process. It's the Guide's (or Hypnotist's) job to at some level steer the client into feeling better or more resourceful. There's a time and place for that kind of work. But Wholeness Work is different.

With Wholeness Work we don't utilize language patterns in an attempt to get the client to do anything. Instead we use language patterns to help uncover what the person's system wants to do. The guide's role is quite different.

Combining Hypnosis with Wholeness Work

Q I'm a hypnotist and I often put people into a trance before doing changework. Will it help if I put someone in a trance before using Wholeness Work?

A Hypnosis can be great for lots of things, but it doesn't help to put someone in a trance to do Wholeness Work.

The Wholeness Work formats are designed to give you the simplest, easiest, and most direct way to open to our "true nature." The process guides us to our deep level inner experience, which already longs for undivided wholeness. So we simply invite the system to do what it wants to do. If we add additional trance instructions, it can be misleading. (It gives the impression that it's necessary to exert a subtle influence or force to "get" our system to make these deep changes.)

Wholeness Work is designed to invite people to greater trust in the wisdom they easily find within. It gives us a way to find and trust the guidance from within ourselves. If there is a hypnotic trance induction first, this can lead people to trust the hypnotist, rather than their own inner wisdom.

With Wholeness Work we are systematically dissolving inner divisions, including the division between conscious and unconscious experience. As we melt the barriers between the two, we increasingly experience being an undivided presence that includes more. This is in part what gives rise to the increase in creativity and ease in solving problems that people report from doing Wholeness Work.

Somatic Therapy and Wholeness Work

Q In somatic therapy the client notices body sensations too. Is this the same thing as Wholeness Work?

A Some forms of bodywork or somatic therapy are very aligned with Wholeness Work, for example in attending to body sensation. There are also two ways Wholeness Work is different from most of these methods—and makes a unique contribution.

One is that with Wholeness Work we start with whatever is easiest for the client (or for you) to notice. If you're aware of a sensation in the body (i.e. a somatic experience), we start there. But if what you're noticing is a persistent inner image, we can start there. And if you're aware of an inner voice, we start there. It's easier for you if the change method can engage with what you naturally experience. And you can get the same deep transformation with any starting place.

The second difference is that instead of focusing on the somatic experience, we find the 'I's that have been holding these somatic experiences in place. Once the 'I's have been released (and sometimes also related Authority Structures), the somatic experiences tend to release themselves. So Wholeness Work is a very direct way of releasing the emotionally charged experiences our body has been holding onto. We are going deeper than content, and even deeper than the felt body experiences, to noticing and including the unconscious structures that have been holding these somatic experiences in place.

CHAPTER 9

WHOLENESS WORK:
A COMPREHENSIVE SYSTEM

A Path of Healing and Radical Transformation

Congratulations! If you've gotten this far, you've now learned and experienced the scope of material included in Level I of Wholeness Work. If you've tried these processes, you may already know that they can be powerful ways to transform your life. If you use these methods in an ongoing way, you'll inevitably make progress—significant progress—in your personal transformation and growth.

Wholeness Work is a comprehensive system for spiritual growth and emotional healing. It can walk us through a process of inner discovery and transformation that enables us to go beyond fixing problems to evolving as human beings.

With these processes, Wholeness Work kindly guides us through our unconscious, shining a light in areas that might otherwise remain hidden. And it all happens in a way that the transformation feels kind and organic.

Sometimes (and for some people) these changes can be dramatic and profound in the moment. However, for many of us it may feel like a very gradual unfolding. It's been that way for me. Yet the changes are real and lasting. Each bit of "separation" you find inside, and invite into the whole, means a shift at the level of beingness.

an organic sequence of transformation

The sequence in which I've shared these Wholeness Work methods with you is not random. It's carefully designed to match the way our psyche is organized—so that transformation can be kind, gentle, and easy. In exploring within myself, plus teaching many others, a natural sequence emerged for how we can invite deep—even radical—transformation, in a kind and gentle way.

On the physical level, there is a natural sequence for an infant to grow and develop into a full adult. The infant moves through crawling, to walking, and then to running and jumping, and more. It doesn't work to try to run before learning to walk. In the same way, there's a natural sequence to our inner growth and development. If we follow this sequence, it tends to flow easily.

The Wholeness Work books and trainings follow this natural sequence. This book provides a reliable sequence that has worked well for many people already, and most likely it can work for you.

I want to emphasize that this sequence didn't come to me through mentally analyzing things or from my mind figuring things out. It emerged from my experience. I felt a strong desire for deep transformation within myself. So I began doing the inner work, and as I went along, I noticed what my system still needed. I noticed what emerged next and longed for inclusion. And this gave rise to another Wholeness Work format. My experience with thousands of clients and workshop participants confirmed that the sequence that emerged organically was the best sequence for most people.

However, reflecting back on it afterward, the inherent "logic" of the sequence became clear to me. And I'll spell it out for you here.

1: Dissolving the 'I's—Dissolving Distortions, Beliefs, and Filters on Reality

We begin with dissolving the 'I's. The 'I's are many individual structures, as you've experienced through these exercises. Yet we could call all of the 'I's together the "perceiving self." We could also call it the experience of "limited self" or "small self" that's present every moment. Dissolving this can be quite profound—and even lead to experiences that spiritual teachers might call Awakening— yet it's simple and easy and gentle for most people to do.

When we do this, the experience of Awareness shifts from something that I *perceive,* to something that I *am.* I AM the experience of Awareness. We begin to experience ourselves AS Awareness.

Initially this shift (from perceiving Awareness to BEING Awareness) is often the strongest when we're in the middle of integrating an 'I' or other inner structure. As we continue the practice, and more 'I's have been integrated, this experience of BEING Awareness becomes easier to relax into, and gradually we just ARE Awareness.

The Effect: Experiencing "Reality as it is" and Uncovering our True Nature

As soon as we begin dissolving the 'I's, this dissolves filters we have unconsciously placed on reality that we didn't realize were there. Yet these filters distort reality. So when we dissolve the 'I's we become more able to experience reality as it is. This increases our emotional intelligence, and our ability to problem-solve and be creative in a way that fits with circumstances in the outer world. It also increases the "fullness" of how we're able to experience Awareness. With each 'I' that dissolves into Awareness, our experience of Awareness becomes a little bit richer and fuller.

2: Integrating Authority—Reclaiming our Natural Strength and Finding our "Inner Axis"

Dissolving the 'I's enriches our experience of Awareness, and this readies us for the next step: finding and integrating Authority Structures.

Authority Structures on the inside create unpleasant emotions (embarrassment, shame, guilt, etc.). Having unintegrated Authority Structures inside, also keeps separate from us some of the "energy" and vitality that actually belongs to us.

The Authority Structures inside are how we keep track of all the "should's" and "have to's" that unconsciously guide our actions, and how we see others. Do you ever find yourself judging other people, or yourself, almost reflexively? Most of us do. And doing this creates rigidity and stress inside. It literally results in body tension and stress that isn't great for our health, and gets in the way of our emotional wellbeing.

After integrating at least some of the 'I's you have inside, you're in a good position to find and integrate Authority Structures in a gentle and kind way. You can regain strength, dissolve rigidity, and become even more able to experience "reality as it is" without the filters of assumptions and pre-judgments.

The Effect: More Groundedness and Energy

When you invite the Authority Structure(s) to integrate, you're likely to feel a visceral shift in your body. Perhaps you'll feel more groundedness, or substantialness, and definitely a release of rigidity and tension. This is a confirmation that something useful happened, whether or not you have any recognition of what rules have dissolved. Keep in mind that these Authority Structures were formed when we were quite young. And as a young being, we probably didn't have a clear understanding of what we were internalizing. Sometimes it's just a sense that we must somehow try very hard to meet some rules or standards.

3: Healing Emptiness—Restoring the Natural Love and Nurturing

Integrating Authority Structures readies us to include and integrate structures related to emptiness: places within ourselves that feel a sense of lack, and that (in ordinary language) long for and need nourishment, affection, even love. The experience of these is different—person-to-person and structure-to-structure. However, most of us need at least some dissolving of Authority Structures before we're able to fully absorb the love, nourishment, and fullness that we long for. This is because most of us have internalized judgments about ourselves, that are some version of "I'm not good enough" or "I don't deserve that." Or we might have internalized rules for how we have to measure up *before* we're allowed to experience these natural and positive feelings. This is why it's important to do some work with dissolving inner Authority, before we attempt to fill inner emptiness.

If you're doing the What's Missing Format and you encounter a difficulty, you can check if there's a related Authority that's still unintegrated, and include it first.

The Effect: A Significant Shift in our Beingness

The Authority Format shifts us from rule-based morality to relating from the whole. The What's Missing Format gives us a similarly significant shift in our consciousness. Instead of seeking completion from the outside, we have a knowingness of the fullness that's already present within. This is an experience of an alive essence that *is* us, that is already complete and doesn't need anything.

This leads to a completely different relationship with others and the world. When we experience how we're already complete, and don't "need" something to be fulfilled at this basic level, we feel so much better and we have the capacity to contribute more to our relationships, our community, and our world.

Our actions become an expression of this beautiful Whole that we are, and we can contribute based on what actually adds something, rather than based on our inner experience of need.

a new theory of personality

Implicit within this sequence is a new understanding of the structure of personality. Because what we are systematically uncovering are the universal structures of the unconscious that hold our limitations in place. Wholeness Work maps out these universal structures in a clear and precise way, for the first time.

Through Wholeness Work we can understand the structure of personality at a deeper level, and in a more precise way. We see that each of us has within multiple experiences of "limited self." These are quite literally structures that we can find within. And these structures are usually nested—organized in layers or chains.

Next we can notice that each of us has Authority Structures within. Again, these are literally structures we can find within, and they also are organized in layers or Chains of Authority.

And next we can notice the Emptiness Structures within—the structures related to the nurturing we may have missed in our own childhoods, and that can open to an experience of our natural fullness. Again, these are literally structures we can find within, organized in layers or chains.

Being able to find these structures makes the Wholeness Work theory of personality unique. It isn't just about having a mental concept about what's within us. We have a carefully designed set of questions to actually find these structures. And then we have the procedure for healing and transformation—for deep integration.

After developing and practicing Wholeness Work for some time, it dawned on me that the structures I was finding inside are the same personality structures that have been described or at least hinted at by the "greats" of psychology, in addition to the "greats" in spiritual traditions. For example, the Authority Structures are getting at what Freud described as the "super-ego" and what Transactional Analysis talks about as the "parent."

And, this new theory of personality includes additional structures that aren't included in this book, but you'll get to meet them and understand them in future books. Or you can learn about them right now in the trainings.[1]

> ### *With Wholeness Work, what was hinted at becomes explicitly mapped out.*

The contribution of Wholeness Work is that…

---

[1] You can also learn about these additional structures in Wholeness Trainings, Levels II and beyond.

We have a way to actually find these structures within. To be able to change something, the first step is obviously to find it.

Once we know how to locate these structures, it's easier to discover more about them. We can recognize they are organized in chains or hierarchies. This recognition is essential to a gentle, easy, kind, and *complete* healing and integration.

This is the first time all of these structures have been mapped out in a clear way as a system, including where they're located, their relationship to each other, and a simple way to transform—or reintegrate—them.

You may wonder what happens to the structure of our personality, when the 'I's, the Authorities and the What's Missing become integrated. What remains when we do Wholeness Work and these universal structures of the unconscious become integrated? We increasingly become one undivided Whole. The process is similar to what happens when we eat and digest food. Before the food is processed through digestion, it's separate from us. Once digested, what used to be identifiable as "food" is now distributed throughout out body, nourishing the whole of us. Similarly, when our inner contractions of consciousness are processed, digested, and integrated, this nourishes our system, and we become an undivided Whole.

In Wholeness Level II we'll talk more about that, and about how the Whole is the same but also different than the Whole we experienced as baby consciousness.

Wholeness Work is a comprehensive system, not just a single method. Right now (2024), the Wholeness Work material is organized into trainings Levels I – IV, which teach over 20 methods. After that an ongoing Wholeness consultation group provides support for self-practice and coaching others.

While there is already a comprehensive system with many existing resources to support your journey, Wholeness Work is *continuing to evolve*. My personal journal already includes additional material—

more formats and understandings—that will be included in future Wholeness training levels.

I welcome you to participate in whatever way works best for you. In the next and final chapter, I'll describe the changes that happen when you use Wholeness Work *over time* and ways you might choose to continue *your* explorations and transformation.

CHAPTER 10

THE CONSCIOUS JOURNEY TO WHOLENESS

Becoming Present as Awareness
Throughout the Body and Space
All Around

When people use Wholeness Work as a daily practice, they begin experiencing positive shifts in many, many areas of life. It does fix problems. You might already have experienced some positive changes in your relationships, in sleep, etc. It's easy to talk about specific problems that are resolved. What's more interesting, but harder to describe, are the changes in our Being. We might experience this as changing at an energetic level.

This is the more important shift that happens through Wholeness Work. We become increasingly present *as Awareness* throughout the body, and throughout the space *all around* us.

What do I mean by this? Well, at the beginning most of us experience Awareness through the body and all around. But it's as if there's an 'I' that notices this space. As we dissolve more and more 'I's, we start *BEING* the space that's throughout the body and all around. There isn't a separate 'I' that's observing it.

I'm letting you know about this so you can recognize when your experience starts shifting in this direction. However, it's important not to rush it. There's nothing to be gained by pushing ourselves, trying to *be* the space throughout the body and all around. That just takes more effort. If we find ourselves efforting, we can get real value from finding the "One who" is trying to be the space all around, and invite this to integrate.

I've found this very gradually happening for me. When I began this work, I was fairly dissociated. I wasn't really "in my body." If you have an NLP background you'll know what I mean. This just means I was often experiencing things as if I were an observer in my own life. Lots of people experience life this way, whether or not they're aware of it.

Also, when I began relaxing into experiencing the Awareness that was present through my body and all around, at first the Awareness didn't seem to "penetrate" through my entire physical body. My experience of my central column was dark, and I couldn't experience it as Awareness. And my head felt literally quite separate from my body.

The more I practiced, the farther in and through the space of my physical body I "as Awareness" could penetrate. The experience of my central column became richer and fuller, and one unified thing.

This is actually the Front Page News about Wholeness Work. Often people come to Wholeness Work because they are seeking a way to resolve their personal issues—emotional and relationship issues, behavior issues, etc. And that's good. That's using our life as our teacher. When we use Wholeness Work, we get more out of resolving the problem than we might have imagined. That's because through Wholeness Work, the problem becomes a pathway "into the arms of the beloved" (to use the words of Rumi). We are solving problems by changing who we are at the beingness level. The fact that many problems are solved is the byproduct.

the impact of practicing over time

If you do this work on a daily basis, or with some regularity, your practice will inevitably change. This is because *you* will be changing. While each of us is unique, here are some of the ways that the work often shifts as we use the process over time.

Early Phase	Middle Phase	Later Phase
Words	Wordless	
'I's	Reactions, roles, identities, personas, authority, etc.	*This is intentionally blank because your practice will continue changing; and, I think it works best if people don't have specific expectations of how things will change.*
Follow a process/ format	Follow our experience	
We do the process	The process does us	
Begin with what to dissolve	More time just resting as Awareness/ Consciousness	
We are fixing something.	Everything is OK as it is. All reactions & feelings are already OK.	
Do at a separate time	Do as living life	
Many layers of 'I'	Direct integration of whatever arises (perspective, "the One reacting," etc.	
Integration in field of Awareness (outside body)	Integration is felt through the body	

Here's a little more explanation of what I mean by each category in the previous chart...

Words ➔ Wordless

Be sure to use the scripts at first. You can trust the scripts to help you get the fullest results. After doing this many times, the experience of Wholeness Work may begin to feel familiar. It's almost as if your system anticipates the next question and begins answering before it's asked. When this happens, you can just go with this, and let the process unfold wordlessly.

Again, please DO use the scripts at first. They guide you in a specific way, and if you drop the words too soon, you might unknowingly shift to doing something that isn't Wholeness Work and won't give you the same reliable deep benefits.

If you shift to a wordless practice, I suggest occasionally returning to the scripts and noticing if this adds anything to your experience.

'I's ➔ Reactions, Authorities, etc.

It's useful to start with finding the 'I's and the 'I' Chains. It's possible to do this for quite some time with lots of benefits. Then you're likely to begin noticing and processing more of the other constrictions we find inside. You'll notice reactions, Authority Structures, etc. (For some people, reactions begin emerging right from the start, and in this case, of course that's where you'll start your work.)

Following the Process/Format ➔ Following Your Experience

The formats in this book are intended to give you an easy way to begin processing, integrating, healing, and evolving. I still return to them frequently. You may find it useful to systematically go through each of the formats, in order. Perhaps you want to spend a week on the Basic Process in Chapter 3. Then, a week on the Meditation Format in Chapter 4, and do the same with the Authority and What's Missing Formats. After doing this, you may discover it's easier to just notice what your system wants to do, and follow that.

We do the process ➔ The process does us

When learning Wholeness Work, most people experience that "I'm doing this process." As time goes on, and the formats become more familiar and natural, it may begin to feel more that the process happens effortlessly. Nobody is doing anything—it's more that the process "does you."

Beginning with Something to Dissolve ➔ Resting as Awareness

At the beginning, most people are aware of many specific feelings, reactions, and experiences they want to transform and heal. This is good. As time goes on, and many 'I's, Authorities, etc. have been integrated, you may discover that when you relax and turn inward, nothing immediately shows up to work on. It's effortless to just rest as Awareness. It's useful to recognize that Awareness itself is open to any experience that could arise within it. Awareness itself has no preference for whether you're just resting as Awareness, or processing something.

Fixing Something ➔ Everything is OK as it is

When difficult emotions emerge, most people automatically think, "This is something I need to fix." As we do this inner work, our ongoing experience shifts, so we begin welcoming whatever emotions emerge instead of judging them. We have the sense that "Everything is OK as it is" even before we've processed the emotions that arise.

Doing at a Separate Time ➔ Doing As We Live Life

It's useful to pick a specific time for your Wholeness Work practice. As time goes on, you may find yourself also practicing as you live life. Sometimes when I go for a walk, I might notice a feeling, or a stress response, and it's easy to do a simple Wholeness Work process right then, as I'm walking. When I clean, do the dishes, etc., if I become aware of something, I might find myself processing it.

Many Layers of 'I' ➔ Direct Integration of What Arises

When you do this practice over time, you may find there are fewer and fewer layers of 'I' inside. This is because many 'I's have already been integrated.

Integration in the Field of Awareness → Integration through the Body

If most of your 'I's are located outside the body, when the 'I' dissolves into Awareness, you might not feel the shift very strongly—because more of the change is located outside of your physical body. If the 'I's are located within your physical body, you're more likely to experience the integrating through your body. Either way, the integrating is making an equal change in your mind-body system. It's just a matter of how much you feel it.

As more 'I's are integrated, you may discover that you begin experiencing the integration more strongly throughout the body.

The Results

By doing Wholeness Work over time, the results that matter most are that...

- ❀ We become increasingly associated *AS Awareness.*
- ❀ We are more in touch with reality as it is. We're more in touch with how things are, instead of how we believe them to be, want them to be, or are afraid they might be.
- ❀ Should's, must's, and have-to's fall away.
- ❀ Negative beliefs and beliefs in general fall away.
- ❀ We're more present in life as it is, in a more fluid way.
- ❀ Many aspects of our life spontaneously improve.
- ❀ Drama falls away.
- ❀ We have easier and greater access to creative solutions.

More About the Changes for Me

At the beginning of this book, I described the life crisis that propelled me to discover the Wholeness Work—including the debilitating physical symptoms I'd been experiencing. Throughout the book I've shared examples of how I've used Wholeness Work, and how it's helped me. I'd like to come full circle and tell you more about the physical part...

For me, finding Wholeness Work was a godsend. It helped me in so many ways. But I don't want to give you the impression that using Wholeness Work resulted in everything being "perfect."

What's more true is that I'm no longer searching for "perfect." I have more contentment with life as it is—more readiness to lovingly accept however things unfold. I think that's an important part of the learning, the wisdom, that we increasingly have access to through Wholeness Work. We realize it's not about having a perfect life. It's about recognizing that no outer circumstances can harm the essential "me" that's within. This is something we begin to know viscerally, from the core of our bones, and on out.

And, I find I'm no longer afraid of dying. There's a story about American Spiritual Leader and Guru, Ram Dass, that resonates with me. Ram Dass describes speaking with a spiritual teacher named Emanuel, through a channel. Ram Dass asked, "What should I tell people about dying?" Emanuel answered, "Tell them it's absolutely safe!" "It's like taking off a tight shoe."[1] [2]

It's the same message that many living spiritual teachers impart, and that I've come to subjectively experience as true. Put simply— there is some essence of our being that is eternal. And this essence can't be harmed by circumstances.

I've told you about many of the benefits I've experienced in terms of psychological and emotional healing. More ease in my relationships, etc. These benefits continue to accrue. On the physical level I've experienced benefits too (as I mentioned in the Introduction). I do still have some unusual symptoms. And I have no idea if these are purely energetic symptoms or if they are more physical. It matters less to me, because I don't fear death as I used to. (I wouldn't be surprised if when I actually make that transition, an additional layer of fear might emerge, but I don't fear that either. I feel a sense of "leaning in" to meet it, if and when, as it's something that can be loved also.)

To continue with the physical benefits, I've already shared how I gained significant stamina after using the Authority Process. Much later, I fell—breaking several small bones in my foot—and Wholeness Work helped me process the pain and get to a place of

---

[1] The story appears here www.youtube.com/watch?v=dhRZKmPCO6U
[2] A video of Ram Dass speaking about this. www.youtube.com/watch?v=OArVDb1B9fE

comfort. I've used the Wholeness Meditation when having major dental work, and it's made the experience much easier.

It's also helped me with other physical gains as I recovered from the challenging experience that led me to Wholeness Work. These include that I'm much more able to tolerate noise and both visual and auditory stimulation. I do still like quiet and peaceful environments, but I'm more comfortable with sensory stimulation. At my worst, I wasn't able to walk into stores, without feeling as if the barrage of sensory stimulation was grating on me. Now I do that with ease, and can enjoy the same environment that was intolerable before. Before, I couldn't be in the same room if a TV was on, or even if music was playing. It was too much. Now I enjoy music again, and can also enjoy watching TV or movies. Before, my digestion was super-sensitive: I had to avoid many foods, and carefully rotate the foods I could tolerate, or I would be in pain. Now I eat healthfully, but *can* eat almost everything, and rarely need rotation. So many things have improved. It's clear to me that Wholeness Work has been a large part of this improvement. I can experience an immediate transition from being overstimulated, to feeling deeply peaceful and relaxed when I open myself to processing whatever is emerging within—including my reactions and fears.

Increasingly I've come to trust the way life unfolds for me. Having this way to kindly meet whatever emerges in my experience makes it possible for me to experience whatever happens—both within my physical body and in the world outside—from a place of presence. We could call it love.

I consider myself a person "in process." I realize I'm not a fully awakened being. Whatever that might mean, I know I'm not that. My contribution is less about being fully awake, and more about offering precise roadmaps that we can all use, to reliably awaken. We can all become more of *that,* if we choose it.

I wonder what will happen for you—if you choose it.

So, What's Next?

You may be wondering what's the best way to continue your exploration of Wholeness Work. Well, that depends on you... and how *you* like to learn. I'm guessing that after reading this book, one or more of the possibilities below may fit for you:

1. You have a challenging life issue you'd like to transform.
2. You want to practice the Wholeness Work methods in this book on a daily basis and experience additional benefits.
3. You're ready to learn *more* Wholeness Work methods—the next level of Wholeness Work.
4. You may want to become a Wholeness Work Coach.

I'd like to speak to these situations one at a time.

situation 1:
you're seeking to transform a challenging life issue

A lot of people come to me saying, "I have this big life issue and nothing else has worked with it. Will Wholeness Work help me?"

And the answer is, "Probably Yes," But, it's not the "yes" they think it is. Because often they're expecting one "breakthrough" session—like a magic bullet of sorts.

And most of the time, Wholeness Work doesn't work that way.

Okay, *sometimes* people do a single session of Wholeness Work, and the very first time they apply the Basic Process to their issue—even that big issue—it just clears up. And it feels like a miracle. And it *is* a miracle.

Bad News/Good News: The Myth of the Breakthrough Session
However, more often with "life's biggest issues," these issues become essentially a *life teacher* for us. They *require* us to go through the whole process of transforming who we are at the "Beingness" level, a deeper level. These "life teacher" issues are not typically resolved in one "breakthrough" session.

It's important to remember that with Wholeness Work, we're working at a deeper level. Often when people have breakthrough sessions (using other methods), the shift occurs through a little bit of coercion. *And, anytime a change happens through coercion—even if it's subtle coercion—that change is likely to break down at some point.* It's likely to relapse some time in the future and require attention. That's a really important thing to know… that most people do *not* know. Because this truth about change speaks to many situations—from parenting to politics—understanding this is critical because anything that's accomplished with force is not really fully accomplished. Simply put, it's going unravel at some point. And the same thing is true with a "breakthrough" session, if it involves subtle force from the method a coach or therapist is using. Because if force is used to make change, *something remains separate—not fully integrated—within.*

With Wholeness Work, you can't do things with force, it just doesn't work that way; it's completely happening without any force at all—not even with the subtle forcing we could call "effort." So that's why this is an entirely different way of working than has usually happened.

And it's why the bad news is good news.

When people first hear, "Oh, I can't have my one session and everything is magically changed," they think that's bad news. But it's also good news because you get *more* out of this than just changing your one issue. Even though we get tremendous relief from changing our one issue, Wholeness Work guides us through a series of questions *and* series of transformations that change us at the *being* level. It changes our consciousness and how we are in the world.

And the result of that is that so many problems, big and small, do begin falling away. But you can't predict the order of that. And it's rare that your life's biggest issue is one of the first to fall away. But the good news is that so many other changes that are positive start happening in your life.

For example, I've told you about how after doing Wholeness Work over time, I no longer found myself entangled in other people's responses, worrying about how people might think about me, or trying to be the person I thought others wanted me to be. I was so much more able to be present for who other people are and whatever their emotional reactions are, without me taking it personally.

I could go on and on and on about the changes I've experienced with Wholeness Work. But having said that, I've discovered that our "life's biggest teacher issue" tends to remain in our lives—at least for a while. In one sense, it's because it's not just one thing. It's not really just one issue—it involves multiple layers, multiple issues. And when we approach them one at a time to kindly transform them, things start becoming more positive for us. But our life's biggest issue might still be there—at least in part. In a way that's good news because it keeps us on track, it keeps us going. It gives us a focus to continue evolving our consciousness—it keeps us going to continue how we evolve as human beings.

I understand that this can be difficult to really, really take in at the bone marrow level and I can appreciate how, "Yeah, I get it; it all sounds good. But I still am very unhappy that my big issue is not just changing for me in one session." And this is where it can be really helpful to get individual coaching or join a training, to be involved with a community of people engaging in Wholeness Work. With these "life's biggest issues," it can be helpful to have classmates and/or a coach provide you with support and hold the space for you. This way, you don't have to try to stay optimistic about it, you can be wherever you are, and somebody can help hold the space for you and help you move forward. So you can to continue to use your issue to evolve as a human being.

When to Start with Core Transformation

Wholeness Work can help you and others with so many challenges—and yet, there are times when I find it's better to *begin* with a companion method called Core Transformation (CT). Core Transformation is aligned with Wholeness Work; it helps us change at a similarly deep level, yet the approach is completely different. Some people and some issues are better served by beginning with Core Transformation.

Indications It May Be Better to Begin with Core Transformation (CT):

- The person has a strong trauma response. (See the following section.)
- If you find it difficult to shift from meaning and interpretations, to sensation quality, you might find CT easier and more natural.
- If you have found it difficult to relate to Wholeness Work, often it's good to shift to CT and begin there. CT uses meaning and interpretation to get to a Core State, which is similar to the field of Awareness.

Because CT teaches that there's always a positive purpose, experiencing this in a visceral way (through CT) can make it easier for you to feel more comfortable, to trust the Wholeness Work processes. After working with CT, you know that each aspect we find inside has a beneficial purpose, and we don't need to get rid of anything.

Transforming Trauma

If you're working with healing trauma, I recommend finding an experienced and capable coach to guide you in your healing process.

Wholeness Work is very helpful in the full healing of trauma, but it's usually not the place to start. Here's the sequence I recommend for a gentle and complete healing.

If the person is working with an intense trauma, and just beginning their trauma healing, Core Transformation provides a safe, kind, and gentle way to process and heal the strong emotional response. There are other methods that also are effective in processing the trauma response. I usually use Core Transformation because it works at a deep level and offers a more complete healing than just changing the trauma response. You can also start with a method such as RTM protocol,[3] or Eye Movement Integration,[4] and then shift to Core Transformation.

By strong trauma response, here's what I mean: if you can easily be triggered into feeling flooded with an intense emotional response, and you find it difficult to "come back" to a neutral emotional state, that's a strong trauma response. That's an indication to start with Core Transformation.

After using Core Transformation to transform the strong trauma response, and any other strong emotions, the Wholeness Work can be a beneficial next step. It inevitably carries the healing farther, helping to heal aspects of the experience the person might not even have been consciously aware of.

Many people who've considered their trauma already "healed," report that when they processed the same experience using Wholeness Work, they got significantly more benefit. Here's one recent example from a workshop participant:

> *Yesterday I worked on my miscarriage (an incident that happened 15 years ago). I'd worked earlier on it with various NLP techniques and Wholeness Work cleared whatever was left in my awareness just like you said. It felt healed on a deeper level with finally a sense of closure and satisfaction.*

situation 2:
you want to integrate wholeness work into every day

As we've discussed, getting the benefits of Wholeness Work depends on actually *using* the methods. Here are proven practices that can make it easy to do that.

---

[3] Gray, R., & Bourke, F. (2022). The reconsolidation of traumatic memories (RTM) protocol for PTSD: A treatment that works. www.doi.org/10.36315/2022inpact068 Psychological Applications and Trends 2022

[4] To learn more about the Eye Movement Integration Method, go here: www.andreasnlp.com/nlp-method-source-materials/#Eye_Movement_Integration_Technique_EMI.

Tip #1: Develop a daily practice.

You'll get the most benefit if you use these processes as a *daily* practice.

If you'd like to find out what benefits are in store for you through this work, you might ask yourself, what time during the day will a little Wholeness Work feel like a welcome nourishment or self-care? You might choose a time when you like to relax anyway. Your usual relaxation time can become more enjoyable and productive by adding Wholeness Work practice. It might be just 5 or 10 minutes, or it might be a half hour, or even longer. Whatever fits comfortably for you.

Some people like to do Wholeness Work when they wake up in the morning—before getting out of bed. Many people do Wholeness Work when they go to sleep at night. Again, do what fits for you. It's fine if you miss a day, or even many days. You can just begin again whenever you think of it.

So try it out. Take advantage of the free demonstration[5] online and find out if you can do it on your own comfortably just from the book and demos.

I encourage you to try out the exercises in this book *according to the sequence in which they're presented.* You may remember that I mapped out the Wholeness Work sequence organically—based on what I needed next, and then tested it with what my clients needed next. However, reflecting back on it I noticed there was a logic to it. There are reasons why doing things in this order works best for most people. So even if you have an issue indicating the What's Missing Process, you don't want to start with *that* format.

And, as I recommended earlier, please use the scripts as they're written because making adjustments in the language may impact your ability to get the most out of the process.

---

[5] You'll find a guided group experience plus a short demonstration on our free 70-minute Wholeness Video training. Visit www.AndreasNLP.com, click the "Resources" tab, and select the "Wholeness Work Video Training."

Tip #2: Keep a development journal.
This is optional, of course. If you like to journal, you might find it helpful to keep brief notes of what you've worked on, what you've discovered, and future issues you might want to explore. This brief record of your journey of transformation allows you to see the scope of what you've done. You may find noticing your changes (big and small) inspires you to *continue* your daily practice.

Tip #3: Work with a committed practice partner.
It can be easier to create new and healthy habits by partnering with someone who has a shared interest in self-improvement. Find a partner who has read (or is willing to read) this book or has attended a Level I training in Wholeness Work.

Clarify your hopes of working together by discussing what you'd each like to get out of your time together and the support you'd like to receive.

Establish a plan of when and how you'll connect to discuss what you've done, the results, and any obstacles you may have encountered in your explorations.

Please note that this book is intended to offer YOU a precise and systematic guide for self-exploration. This book does NOT provide you or your partner the training needed to capably *guide* others.

Tip #4: Join a training or enlist the support of a Wholeness Work Coach.
If you find it challenging sometimes to do these life-changing practices on your own, you needn't be discouraged. Most people find it MUCH easier to experience these methods in a training, or when being guided by a coach who has in-depth training in Wholeness Work. Common signs that you might need more support include:

- When you sit down to do the practice, you get bored or distracted.
- You get stuck—you encounter obstacles that you don't know what to do about.
- In spite of the best intentions, you don't actually do the daily practice.

There are definitely times when these exercises or sequence needs to be modified to fit the person. Often all that's needed is a simple adaptation. For example, the guide may help you notice and include a reaction. Or perhaps there is an Authority that needs to be included before anything else can really happen.

The Wholeness Work is all about adapting to each person—to *you*—in the moment. The more you learn of it, the easier this is to do.

situation 3:
you want to learn more

In this book, you already have all of the Level I powerful formats for transforming your life. Just learning and using these can bring about progress—even amazing progress—in your personal transformation and growth.

However, there is *more*. At this point in time (early 2024), the *complete* system includes trainings offered through Level IV. Each level includes additional steps that can support you in your growth. Just as the Authority and What's Missing Formats add something beneficial beyond the Wholeness Work Basic Process, Wholeness Work Level II – IV will take you beyond what you've learned in this book about Level I. You'll discover how to find and transform completely different and also important universal structures of the psyche.

To explore your options for learning more about Wholeness Work, visit these websites to discover live-online or in-person training opportunities.

AndreasNLP.com (for Connirae's trainings), click on "Trainings," "Wholeness Work."

TheWholenessWork.org (For international trainings)

Situation 4:
you want to become a qualified coach

If you are inspired by this work and want to learn to guide other people, please go to our websites to see the recommended training sequence to become a qualified guide. Specific additional training is essential to being an effective coach. In the training sessions, you will have an opportunity to:

Observe me and/or other trainers working with different people.

Pair up with various participants and learn from your experiences with them.

Get support from the training staff and coaches if you and/or your partner encounter challenges when doing the different Wholeness Work Formats.

Get feedback on your coaching skills.

To explore your options, please visit:

AndreasNLP.com
TheWholenessWork.org
WholenessWork.eu

So that's it—except for the Resources in the next Section that you may find useful. Thank you for joining me on this journey through the comprehensive system of Wholeness Work. This kind and gentle approach offers us:

a clearer picture of what's "inside the black box" of our thoughts, feelings, etc.

a way to find and transform our experiences at the beingness level

direct doorways to Awakening

As I reflect on the wonderful changes Wholeness Work has helped me make, I wonder what transformations you'll experience. I wish you ease and peace on your journey.

RESOURCES

This section includes additional resources if you want to better understand the following aspects of Wholeness Work.

Wholeness & Oneness Work Presuppositions
Sensation Quality vs. Meaning & Interpretation
Using Wholeness Work with Pain
Worksheets

 If you'd like to download and print resources presented in this section, use this QR code or go to www. thewholenesswork.org/BookResources.

WHOLENESS & ONENESS WORK PRESUPPOSITIONS

Each therapeutic or personal growth method has underlying presuppositions—things assumed to be true. The method is an expression of these assumptions. With the Wholeness Work we are working *at* and *with* a different level of experience, and our methods are an expression of a different set of presuppositions than most previous forms of changework. Knowing these presuppositions can help us better understand what we're doing. It also helps us understand its value—why it can create both ordinary and extraordinary benefit. It also explains why combining Wholeness Work with other types of changework can dilute the results.

Here is a list of the 15 main presuppositions embodied in Wholeness Work[6]. You'll notice that many of these presuppositions are the same as what is taught in spiritual traditions. They align with the esoteric teachings in each of the main religions, and also with non-dual teachings (such as Advaita Vedanta).

What's different with Wholeness Work is that we have a specific precise practice. This practice turns the teachings into a precise "science" of how to get there. So Wholeness Work draws on the precision of classic NLP and the philosophy from spiritual teachings.

These presuppositions guide HOW we do the work; we...

1. **Include everything.** Everything has value and enriches the wisdom of the whole. It's important not to override anything, whether consciously or unconsciously. Everything, including what we don't like, has value, and it's through

---

[6]   From Wholeness Work II manual v 11.6 © Connirae Andreas

including everything that wholeness and full wellbeing become possible.

2. **Use no force.** Instead we invite and allow. It's never useful to *make* something happen. With Wholeness Work we invite and allow the shifts to happen that want to happen. Useful changes happen spontaneously when we're in touch with our complete inner nature. A solution that comes from force can never be a lasting or complete solution.

3. **Find the easy way.** If something isn't easy (e.g. an 'I' or other structure doesn't want to integrate), it means we need to shift attention to the place in our system that is ready to take the next step (i.e. to be recognized, to integrate, etc.).

4. **Don't need to manipulate a change.** We don't need to hide our intention, or trick any part of a person, in order to get change. Instead, our goal is more awareness, to include all that a person is currently noticing, and more. (There may be a gentle shifting of where the attention is focused, without shutting out anything.)

In contrast: Some types of hypnosis teach bypassing the conscious mind, to get to the unconscious patterning and change it. With the Wholeness Work, instead, we also include the conscious mind patterns that would interfere with access. The result is greater integration of the conscious mind with the unconscious mind. We experience undivided consciousness.

These presuppositions are about the philosophy—how we THINK about what we're doing.

1. **Wisdom comes from wholeness.** Solutions arising from the whole are wiser and more "ecological" than solutions generated by the conscious mind, or any "part" of the system. Through including everything—and especially through integrating everything at the beingness level—we come to wisdom.

When we set goals for ourselves they are usually formed from separate 'I's. Wholeness Work helps us find and dissolve these 'I's, so that we can discover the deeper wisdom.

2. **Wellbeing is innate.** Everyone has it. Powerful, deep states of essence, presence, etc., exist within everyone's psyche, and it's just a matter of accessing it. Each of us has an inner essence (Awareness, Core States) that can't be destroyed or damaged.

3. **The solution is easier than the problem.** Problems take effort. Stress takes effort. It takes effort to maintain the problem experience. Discovering and releasing this effort leads to the solution—i.e. to transformation. The solution is easier than the problem.

4. **It's possible to live life as the Whole of Awareness, instead of as a "small/separate self."** Awareness is already present. It isn't necessary to perceive or take action from a small separate 'I'. We can be present as Awareness and perceive or act as Awareness (the Whole of our being).

5. **Everything is already "perfect."** At the deepest level, everything (both within ourselves and without) is already Ok, before we do anything to change/transform it.

   This "field of Awareness" that we are, is already "perfect." This is our basic nature, and it's inherently perfect. This "perfection" is not about judgment. It is beyond judgment. And we don't need to change anything to be "more perfect." The Awareness that we *are,* already experiences things being fully fine. The entire process of discovering limitations and inviting them to dissolve is part of this "perfect process" of unfolding that we're participating in.

6. **The field of Awareness within each of us is *already* Whole,** and the constrictions we discover (the small 'I's etc.) are created from the Whole of our being.

7. **The constrictions we discover *want* to return home to the Whole** and because of this, they are easily willing to do so.

8. **We can experience the Eternal Now.** The more we experience ourselves as an undivided Whole, the more Time is also experienced as an undivided whole. Subjectively we begin to experience what we could call the "Eternal Now." Consciously we are present in the current moment, and the experience is of simultaneous access to past and future. Nothing is separated off. It's the subjective experience of linear time not really existing, or that all moments in time exist simultaneously. So changing one moment also changes all moments.

9. **Transforming/evolving is a process.** There is no endpoint. We continue to evolve and grow. In earlier phases of personal growth we focus on specific outcomes or goals, and how to reach them. The farther we go, the more we recognize that it's a continual unfolding. "We've already arrived," and "we'll never arrive," are both true.

These Presuppositions are about our ROLE in guiding the change process.

These are especially relevant for Coaches & Therapists, and also relevant to how we guide ourselves.

1. **Our role is to help discover what the system wants.** When self-guiding our job isn't to make ourselves change. It's to notice and facilitate what wants to happen, in the system as a whole. (And if we are a coach or therapist, our role isn't to make someone else change; it's to help the other person's "system" discover what wants to happen and to facilitate that.)

2. **We are here as equals.** This is different from a hierarchical relationship of up-down. And even beyond equals, we can experience ourselves as part of the same larger whole.

— A Key Concept —

I've already told you that Wholeness Work is an expression of the presuppositions just listed. There's something more that's important to realize: *Wholeness Work also teaches us these presuppositions.* As we practice Wholeness Work, we begin experiencing the truth of each of these assumptions. We *know* each truth for ourselves. We develop confidence in the wisdom of the system—in the wholeness that we are.

When we directly experience how each of the contractions of consciousness longs for a return to the *whole* of consciousness, we discover that we can trust in the wisdom of our system; we can trust in life itself. And when this happens a deep shift occurs in our experience of life.

 To download and print a copy of these presuppositions, use this QR code or go to www.thewholenesswork. org/BookResources.

SENSATION QUALITY VS. MEANING & INTERPRETATION

In Wholeness Work, we are guided to shifting our experience from content, to what we call sensation quality. Content includes the meanings we give to experiences. It includes emotions, interpretations, and even metaphor. Sensation quality is the direct experience of something. When we find separate structures inside (such as 'I's, Authorities, etc.), shifting to sensation quality makes it possible and easy for this separate structure to integrate.

The following chart shows the difference between sensation quality and interpretation.

Examples of Sensation Quality

warm, cool	soft, hard
light, dark	heavy, light
clear, opaque	moving, still
dense, airy	vibratey, bubbly, buzzy
solid or misty/foggy	smooth, rough

Examples of Meaning or Interpretation

Emotions (how it feels): "It's sad." "It's angry."

Intent (what it's trying to do): "It's trying to protect me."

Function (what it's doing): "It's keeping my head separated from my body." "It's managing everything."

Cause: "This 'I' was formed because my parents beat me." "This 'I' was formed because I had to be nice."

> Consequence: "This is what keeps me awake at night."
>
> Metaphor: "It's an umbrella over my head." "It's a pineapple."
>
> Other: "This is an archetype."

You can find more discussion of why this matters in the book, *Coming to Wholeness*, Chapter 11.

 To download and print a copy of these presuppositions, use this QR code or go to www.thewholenesswork. org/BookResources/.

USING WHOLENESS WORK WITH PAIN[7]

In my training sessions, people often want to know how to use Wholeness Work with physical pain. I have received many, many reports from people telling me how their chronic pain has significantly improved or completely cleared up using Wholeness Work. Sometimes this happens just from using the Basic Format with the pain experience as the starting place. People have reported migraines clearing up, peripheral neuropathy clearing up, etc.

However, sometimes the pain experience involves more than what the Basic Process or Meditation format can fully resolve. If you are working with an experience of pain, here is the sequence I suggest, to kindly and systematically include everything that needs including.

Begin with the Meditation Format as follows:

Notice the sensations that are uncomfortable (i.e. the sensations that you are calling "pain.") Find the Location, Shape & Size, Sensation Quality.

Find the 'I'. (Location, S&S, SQ) Does it welcome dissolving?

If yes, invite dissolving, and then go to experiencing the sensation as Awareness. (So experience being the sensation AS Awareness.)

If no, check for another 'I'.

---

[7] When dealing with any physical symptom, including pain, I recommend consulting your medical practitioner to have your needs assessed and find out if they have recommendations for treatment. Wholeness Work can be used along with any physical intervention you may choose, to support your body's healing and recovery.

Ongoing: Include Reactions whenever they arise.

Often we have reactions to an experience of pain. For example, we might feel frustrated, or annoyed that we feel this pain. We might feel hopeless. We might judge ourselves, and wonder what's wrong with us, etc. We might feel afraid that it's never going to go away. So it's good to be ready to notice and include any reactions. If a reaction is strongly present even before finding the first 'I', then it works best to include it right away.

Ask: "Is there a reaction happening to this experience?"

If yes, "Where is the 'One who' is reacting?" (Notice L, S/S, SQ, and invite this to dissolve.)

Include any and all the reactions that emerge.

The *first* layers of reactivity are likely to include meta-responses like frustration or impatience that this is occurring, or hopelessness that it can ever change. After welcoming these to integrate, it will be easier to notice if there are any emotions or memories that are linked to this feeling of pain. For example, residual feelings from childhood such as hurt, anger, sadness, etc. may spontaneously emerge. If we just include each layer of reactivity that reveals itself, it will work well.

Use the Authority Format if indicated.

When doing the steps I've described for finding 'I' Chains and including reactions, if anything you notice is dense, do the Reclaiming Authority Process. Often with chronic pain, you'll encounter dense structures, indicating an Authority Chain is also related. Plus, we may have judgments about how things should be—this should or shouldn't be happening, etc.

Being the Sensation as Awareness

Once you've included: 1) any 'I's or perspectives, 2) reactions (both meta-responses and emotional connections), and 3) authorities related, you can just experience BEING the sensation (that you used to call pain) AS AWARENESS. It now is experienced as sensation. And you can breathe deeply as you are *being* the sensation as Awareness. This often becomes pleasant in itself and can make it easy to notice if anything is still holding on in a rigid way.

Here's a simple way to experience being the sensation as Awareness.

After integrating other elements, such as 'I's, reactions, and Authorities, there's likely to be a lovely experience of just being present as Awareness. Next, check, is it easy for "me as Awareness" to relax into the sensation that I used to call pain?

When you explore being the sensation as Awareness, if you encounter any reactions or judgments, you can cycle through the steps again.

A Note About Helping Someone Else with Pain

This book is intended to offer YOU a precise and systematic guide for self-exploration. Even though you will probably be excited to share your experience of Wholeness Work and to help others, this book does NOT offer the training needed to capably and safely guide others.

 The easiest way to share this with people you care about is to refer them to this book and to the free Wholeness Video introduction (using this QR code or linking to www.andreasnlp.com/resources/free-wholeness-intro-video/.)

If you want to guide others, I encourage you to start by taking a Wholeness Work training. You will learn this material in much greater depth in a training. For trainings with Connirae, visit AndreasNLP.com. For international trainings, visit TheWholenessWork.org, and WholenessWork.eu for trainings in Europe.

To explore recommendations for becoming a Coach or Trainer, please use one of the QR codes below.

To explore opportunities in Europe, use this QR code or go to www.wholenesswork.eu/certification/?lang=en.

 To explore opportunities in the United States, use this QR code or go to www.thewholenesswork.org/professional/trainer-pathway/.

Will my pain clear up if I use Wholeness Work?

In my experience so far, about 50% of the time, people using Wholeness Work with the experience of chronic pain discover that their pain either lessens significantly or may even resolve completely. Sometimes this happens when doing the first few explorations; other times this happens through using Wholeness Work over time.

There's never a guarantee that Wholeness Work will result in becoming pain-free or reducing pain. However, of all the "mind" or personal transformation methods I've used, in my experience Wholeness Work is the most likely to get beneficial results with pain. If you're interested, I encourage you to give it a try.

Of course it's also important to consult your medical professional to have your specific situation assessed and find out what information or solutions they have to offer. You can use Wholeness Work along *with* any medical solutions you choose to use and Wholeness Work will support your body's healing.

In Wholeness Work Levels II – IV, you can learn additional formats that you can use with pain—and with other challenging issues.

Physical Pain vs. Trauma

When working with trauma, we recommend starting with another deep change method called Core Transformation. Core Transformation provides extra safety in processing and healing any intense feeling responses to trauma.

(See Chapter 10 in this book for more about this topic.)

Notes: Basic Format

Beginning Feeling or Experience: _____	
Location	
Size & Shape	
Sensation Quality	

1st 'I'	
Location	
Size & Shape	
Sensation Quality	

2nd 'I'	
Location	
Size & Shape	
Sensation Quality	

3rd 'I'	
Location	
Size & Shape	
Sensation Quality	

4th 'I' (optional)	
Location	
Size & Shape	
Sensation Quality	

5th 'I' (optional)	
Location	
Size & Shape	
Sensation Quality	

Comments
Print a copy from www.thewholenesswork.org/BookResources.

Notes: Meditation Format

Beginning Feeling or Experience: _____	
Location	
Size & Shape	
Sensation Quality	

1ˢᵗ 'I'	
Location	
Size & Shape	
Sensation Quality	

2ⁿᵈ 'I' (optional)	
Location	
Size & Shape	
Sensation Quality	

3ʳᵈ 'I' (optional)	
Location	
Size & Shape	
Sensation Quality	

4ᵗʰ 'I' (optional)	
Location	
Size & Shape	
Sensation Quality	

5ᵗʰ 'I' (optional)	
Location	
Size & Shape	
Sensation Quality	

Comments	
Print a copy from www.thewholenesswork.org/BookResources.	

Notes: Reclaiming Authority

Beginning Experience: _____

Location	
Size & Shape	
Sensation Quality	

1ˢᵗ Authority (A_1)

Location	
Size & Shape	
Sensation Quality	

A_2

Location	
Size & Shape	
Sensation Quality	

A_3

Location	
Size & Shape	
Sensation Quality	

A_4 (optional)

Location	
Size & Shape	
Sensation Quality	

'I'

Location	
Size & Shape	
Sensation Quality	

Comments

Print a copy from www.thewholenesswork.org/BookResources.

Notes: What's Missing

Beginning Experience: _____	
Location	
Size & Shape	
Sensation Quality	

What's Missing (M_1)	
Location	
Size & Shape	
Sensation Quality	

M_2	
Location	
Size & Shape	
Sensation Quality	

M_3	
Location	
Size & Shape	
Sensation Quality	

M_4 (Optional)	
Location	
Size & Shape	
Sensation Quality	

'I'	
Location	
Size & Shape	
Sensation Quality	

Comments
Print a copy from www.thewholenesswork.org/BookResources.

ACKNOWLEDGEMENTS

I'm deeply grateful to Dr. Milton Erickson for awakening something in me that led to this search (as I described in the Introduction). I'm also grateful for what I've learned in the field of NLP, which gave me a background in modeling and a trust that "if one person can do something, then perhaps it's possible to find a way for all of us to do it."

I'm thankful for the spiritual teachings and teachers that were there for me when I knew my inner journey needed to go deeper. I especially appreciate the work of Ramana Maharshi which served as my inspiration for the first Wholeness Work exercise, of "finding the 'I'." [As a spiritual path to Awakening, the Maharshi advised students to continuously ask, "Who am I?" I changed that question to *"Where* is the 'I' *located?"* which I believe makes it possible to more readily fulfill the Maharshi's intention.]

All of these have been important to my development, and altogether have made this new work possible.

A big thank you to Deepa Somani, Marcela Devoto, Krisztina Havasi, Ursula Beste and Koos Wolken for volunteering to do so much of the preparatory work for this book, reviewing and correcting transcripts of seminars from which I drew the material, and to Krisztina for finding the demonstrations to use. Their efforts of the heart meant that this book is reaching your hands much faster than otherwise. Thanks to Marcela for creating the first overview flowcharts, to Andrew O'Reilly, for meticulously adding in the nonverbals to the demonstrations, and to Monica Valenti for initial proofreading.

Thanks also to … Ralph Kobler for providing the recording for the Basic Process demonstration from a training in Germany. Sonja Knecht for helping with the transcript of Germany demo. Gilad

Rubin for asking me challenging questions which helped shape the book's Introduction. Peter Van Rhoon for guiding the cover design. Ulrich Buhrle, thank you for your creative illustrations that add the human touch and enliven the book. Thanks to Stephen Josephs for advising me to make the book more personal. I thought I already had—but his encouragement led to me sharing more of my experience, in hopes it can enrich yours. Thanks to Alice Josephs for her valuable recommendations to improve the flow of the Introduction.

Thanks to Tamara Andreas and Mark Andreas. Their experience of teaching Wholeness Work and guiding clients enabled them to make insightful suggestions for how to introduce some sections, when to add a useful pointer, and where include a different perspective that might enhance the reader's understanding. And a big thank you to Susan Sanders, my editor, who has worked with me tirelessly through several stages of editing, to make the book's message more accessible to you.

A special thanks to the workshop trainees who participated in the demonstrations that made their way into this book and brought the processes to life. Thank you for providing a role model for all of us who read it.

And of course this book—and the clarity of the method in its current form—wouldn't be possible without everything I've learned from my clients and the participants in my trainings over the past years. You have helped me to understand this path more deeply, and how to make it accessible to others. Thank you.

Thank you to the team of early readers, who helped catch remaining errors and glitches.

And thanks to you, the reader, for engaging with this work. It is through you that the ripples can happen.

Thank you to that within all of us that seeks unfolding and is already beautifully perfect.

In Loving Awareness,

Connirae Andreas

ABOUT THE AUTHOR

Connirae Andreas, PhD has been an internationally-respected leader in the personal development field for over four decades. She is best known for her groundbreaking work, Core Transformation, a method through which our limitations become the doorway to a felt experience many describe "love" "peace" "presence" or "oneness." Through the steps of the process, this felt experience offers a profound healing resolving many limiting emotions and behaviors.

Connirae's new Wholeness Work begins by offering a precise way to experience "dissolving the ego," a long-time spiritual goal, in a way that releases stress and transforms many life issues. This new work then guides us in finding the universal structures of the unconscious that hold problems in place—and offers specific processes to transform each of them.

Andreas' work is strongly influenced by her personal experience with the late Dr. Milton H. Erickson.

Connirae is the author or co-author of many personal development and transformation books and manuals, including *Heart of the Mind*, and *Change Your Mind—and Keep the Change* (both co-authored with husband Steve Andreas), as well as *Core Transformation: Reaching the Wellspring Within* (co-authored with Tamara Andreas), and *Coming to Wholeness: How to Awaken and Live with Ease*. Because of her interest in making these life-changing methods available to more people, she has developed in-depth Trainer Materials for key trainings, including Core Transformation and the Wholeness Work. Her work has been translated into over 15 languages.

Prior to developing Core Transformation and the Wholeness Work, Connirae has been a key figure in the field of NLP, her work including: innovations in language patterns and conversational change and contributions to positive parenting methods, natural self-healing, and (with Steve Andreas) developing effective change protocols for resolving grief, for tapping into how we unconsciously code the experience of time, and more. The Andreases authored manuals for teaching in-depth Practitioner and Master Practitioner NLP programs oriented towards coaching and personal transformation.

Connirae enjoys teaching Wholeness Work and working with clients. She lives in Boulder, Colorado and loves visiting with her grandchildren.

Trainings & Coaching

For trainings in the Wholeness Work® visit:
AndreasNLP.com/trainings/the-wholeness-work/
TheWholenessWork.org
WholenessWork.eu

For Core Transformation® Trainings, visit:
AndreasNLP.com/trainings/core-transformation/
CoreTransformation.org

Follow us on Instagram and LinkedIn
Instagram.com/theWholenessWork

Printed in Great Britain
by Amazon

51424206R00169